THE SALVAGER

PREVIOUS BOOKS

The Host Rock
Cloud Of Arrows
Ravenswood
Blue River
O Distant Star!
Glass Mountain
Not By Bread Alone
The Doctor's Party
Chalice
Some Fell Among Thorns
Gallant Traitor
Child Of Conflict
Let's Burn Our Bridges

THE SALVAGER

The Life of Captain Tom Reid on The Great Lakes

by Mary Frances Doner

ROSS AND HAINES INC.
MINNEAPOLIS, MINN.
1958

FIRST EDITION

Printed in U. S. A.

To cover the entire range of wrecking experiences crowded into Captain Reid's life would mean a formidable undertaking. In this book I have presented some of the highlights in his career, resorting frequently to the vernacular of the sailor at points where formality might have seemed an affectation.

Inclusive excerpts are quoted from authentic logs and letters made available to me by Captain Reid and his family. I am grateful to them, and to Louis Meyers for his generous cooperation in supplying me with valuable data.

M.F.D.

Captain Thomas Reid . . . from a portrait in 1956 by the artist, Florence Avery Sanderson.

Mrs. Thomas (Anna Heumann) Reid 1871-1942

TO

Annie Laurie Williams

Isa. 25:4

CHAPTER ONE

ON that late February night in 1870, a waning moon hid behind clouds above Alpena. The little Michigan town, halfway up the eastern coast of the Lower Peninsula, emerging from a nondescript past, was now enjoying fantastic prosperity.

Lumbering was at its height. Enterprising business men had seen the possibility of great fortunes to be made in the lumber era. Saginaw Valley to the south was the focal point of eastern Michigan operations, and when the thriving cities of Saginaw and Bay City, despite an output of billions of feet of timber, could not meet the national demand, Alpena flashed into prominence and drew adventurous men to her shores in search of fortune.

Here the first steam saw-mill in Alpena County was erected. Rapidly others followed. Shingle mills. Excelsior mills. Mountains of sawdust rose around the little town. Sawdust paved the streets. Slashings helped to fight the almost unendurable cold winds sweeping in from Lake Huron. Life was hard, raw, primitive.

But there was beauty as well along the wild, rugged shore with its vast stretches of white pine, its docks lined with fishing schooners and lumber carriers with their happy-go-lucky crews, and tugmen with their rafts.

In 1870 Alpena saloons and dance halls were filled to capacity, and boarding houses were crowded with lusty lumberjacks. Bloody brawls were frequent, while the less pugnacious drunks sent chanteys echoing down the lonely streets at night. And there was the roar of the saw — the eternal roar of the saw.

On this particular night, wind and sub-zero temperatures had banked the shores of Lake Huron with icy crags and boulders. It seemed that the frigid air had discouraged any spirit that labor had not exhausted. The sawdust paved streets were still except for one twisting road near the Prentiss lumber mill. Here men worked in grim silence and with savage speed, running rollers under a newly built cottage which had been jacked up from its foundation. These hulking men worked in silence, without orders or directions; efficiently but as silently as frozen ghosts. The only sound was the occasional whinney of the horses harnessed to the treadmill which would move the house from where it stood to the road just beyond.

Jim Reid was in trouble, and the highly partisan populace had chosen sides. Two years ago Jim Reid had come to this lumbering center from Ontario to work as a carpenter. Here he had helped build houses, a hotel and a mill for the Prentiss Company. A year later he had sent for his old sweetheart, Eleanor Profit. They were married and established temporary quarters in a makeshift cabin until Jim could build a home on the lot he had managed to buy, and for which, unfamiliar with legal details, he had failed to secure a deed.

Racing with time to complete the new house so that their first child, imminently expected, might be born there, the Reids had transferred their belongings the previous week and were at once ordered to vacate by Hiram Hancock, the unscrupulous former owner of the land who claimed the place was still legally his.

Justice could wait, but not Jim Reid's family! He went about securing a lot not too far away, and with friends and strangers alike volunteering assistance, under cover of darkness they managed to jack up the little building. With final plans laid, they began to move late that dark night and had the house well off the property before the unsuspecting Hancock could secure an injunction.

Tardily discovering his defeat, Hancock came on the scene roaring furious threats. This was a language Jim Reid knew better than the tricks of the law. It was just as Jim went about settling with Hancock that an infant's first cry reached the tense, grim crowd witnessing the battle.

And so Tom Reid was born.

Tom's first memories were of the big crowded Reid boarding house — his tired, loving mother; his keen, impulsive and almost fearsome father, and the stream of workers that came and went from table, bed and parlor. His brother Will and sister Hannah, appearing in quick succession, claimed their share of the mother's time, and other brothers and sisters were to follow.

Though she might protest at the tipsy and profane, she had no chance to shield Tom and the others from the reality of that pioneer life, and from such incidents as that which happened one day when a staggering raftsman trod heavily by accident on Tom's feet with calked boots. She wept as she soothed and bandaged, aware of the pain he would not admit, though he carried the scars all his life.

Never interested in school, when he should have been studying he was piling edgings for ten cents a cord. While Will obediently attended classes, Tom stole off to haunt the barns, docks and mills; to listen to the fishermen and tugmen and woodsmen, and build a typical vocabulary. Driven by the *why* of things that motivated these men, he learned and remembered.

By now his energetic and ambitious father had an interest in the Prentiss mill. And when that company failed, Jim Reid salvaged some of the fine lumber and built a handsome house on the lake shore which he sold for fifteen thousand dollars, a fabulous price at that time. Lumber had made men rich, and these new barons were going to live it high on the hog.

The real estate profits went for booms and a tug for rafting. A lumber camp followed, and then a move to St. Ignace on the Upper Peninsula where Jim Reid set up a towing office on the docks, and where, for a while, he served as Mayor.

In the early spring of '76, the barge *Plymouth,* built at a cost of $35,000, went on the rocks in the Straits of Mackinac. Jim Reid, summoned from St. Ignace by a desperate captain, improvised a crude salvaging outfit and went to his assistance.

Placing oil barrels in the disabled craft, he laid timbers across, jacked the barrels down, braced them and succeeded in floating the barge. All equipment and material had to be brought across nine miles of ice on sleighs. Hundred-ton jacks were transported one at a time.

From such an incident began a wrecking and towing business that made history, not only on the Great Lakes but eastward to the Atlantic coast as well. And cradled in that atmosphere, Tom Reid felt the stirrings of desire toward the career to which his life later became dedicated.

At table and about the house were constant discussions of rafting, salvaging and lumbering — all encouraging a small boy of adventurous spirit to skip school whenever possible and investigate things for himself. The restrictions of the classroom became a more bitter punishment than the flat of a big man's hand or lashes from a strap. Yet in that busy life, supervision was sketchy and Tom's actions not always observed.

The Lakes were an obsession. School was a waste of time . . . anything was a waste of time . . . that did not teach of the sea. Tom Reid knew nothing of boyish games, and he made no friends or playmates as is usual with boys. Old residents claim that he never was a boy, and can only remember him as sturdy, reliant and stubborn in the view that nothing on land was worth a second look. As one old-timer put it, "Tom Reid might have been a kid, but he never let it show. He was always ready to tackle a man's job, and mostly able to make it go, too!"

One winter day, the sleigh carrying his father and Dave Becker — head of the crew — was to lead the other teams across the frozen Straits of Mackinac from St. Ignace to Mackinaw City on the Lower Peninsula.

There they would dispose of the copper cargoes to be shipped on to Lake Erie smelters. Though navigation had been closed for the season, industry must be served.

As Jim Reid guided his team across the ice, he had no idea that Tom was hidden in blankets under the front seat, and that the eager little face poked out cautiously now and then to snatch a glance at the scene as the rising sun burnished the great field of ice and the distant wooded slopes of Mackinac Island.

Impatient as he listened to Dave Becker and his father discuss problems he could not understand, he noticed Becker fingering two unsheathed knives as he talked, and wondered about it; wondered, too, about the ropes that dangled from the horses' necks.

Now and then the man-talk was punctuated with his father's orders to the horses as the whip sang briefly in the air.

"Maude's skittish today," Jim Reid complained, and struck her rump a quick blow. She reared, but soon resumed the rhythm of her partner Barney. "You can always depend on Barney," his father said. "Maude's like all women — full of notions."

Tom peeked out — nose burning with the bitter cold, hands numb in woolen mittens. It was thrilling, worth even more than the thrashing he was bound to get. There was music in the air — sleigh bells keeping time to the rhythm of hooves against ice.

A great crack now appeared in the Straits ice ahead, a break several feet wide. He had heard his father say that regardless of temperature, this was certain to happen due to the current at the meeting of the waters of Lake Michigan and Lake Huron in the narrows between Michigan's peninsulas.

He had heard, too, of the snow-surfaced timbers it

was the custom to lay across that space to facilitate the passage of freight sleighs. Today he waited excitedly as their sleigh approached the break.

At this point, Maude reared. The reins tightened, and Tom caught the note of tension in his father's voice with unease. Slowly the team was guided forward to mount the improvised bridge. Perhaps it was the splash of a wave, or objects moving beyond, for once on the runway, Maude reared again. The sleigh skidded, jerked abruptly, teetered and tipped into the icy water.

"Jump!" Tom's father shouted, though Dave Becker had already preceded him.

Tom had seen the danger from his hiding place and instantly flung himself toward the ice. He lay panting as he watched his father, speechless at the unexpected sight of his son, swiftly slash at the harness with a few well-aimed strokes, Dave Becker working beside him.

As the heavily-laden sleigh disappeared below the surface of the water, the horses struggled and whinnied in the icy bath. Then, quickly, the dangling ropes were being caught about their throats and tightened.

Appalled at the sight, Tom bit through mittens into hands as he watched the strangling animals. But — *why*? Now they would drown! He knew better than to speak, for no one was speaking. The men from the following sleighs had stopped their teams and gathered around speedily. They had brought coils of rope and another sleigh with block and tackle secured at the back.

And then Tom saw that the horses had begun to swell and were floating. And he saw, too, that by this device, their rescue had been made possible.

His father tersely directed the men, and at last Maude and Barney lay flat on the ice, ropes removed from their swollen throats. They were alive!

"Here," his father said gruffly, "use this." And gave Tom his own bandanna. Tears had begun to freeze on the boy's cheeks. "And just wait till you get home — you damned little scamp." His hand was trembling.

Maude moved now. Barney. Tom jerked convulsively toward them.

"Stand back!" shouted his father.

Maude struggled to rise, sharp shoes floundering. Then Barney.

For Tom, now, the facts began to slide into place. He had seen demonstrated the vital value of air power that could float a horse; when magnified many times — could float a ship, a principle destined to dominate his life in the work he was to follow.

Not long afterward when the Reid tug *Burnside* struck a shoal in the Straits of Mackinac while towing a raft, Tom's father improvised a salvaging outfit in the emergency. He had only a twelve inch pump, but with this, and steam provided by his tugs *Mocking Bird* and *Waldo Avery,* he saved the raft and tug *Burnside* as well as a substantial salvaging bill.

His entire assets as to general equipment at the time were the pump, rafting booms, tugs; horses, sleighs and wagons to run four camps.

Again, Tom was on hand during the incident of the *Algomah.* This was a wooden freight steamer, approximately 500 feet in length, built strong and heavy for breaking ice at a figure of around $75,000 by the Island Transportation Company of St. Ignace.

A particularly bitter season challenged her strength that year, and she broke her wheel ploughing through the Straits ice.

Encouraged by his brief success, Jim Reid boldly bid for the job of salvaging. With only faith in himself and a natural skill, around the steamer's stern he built a box big enough for a man to work in; securing it with canvas, he took off the damaged wheel and replaced it with a new one. For this he received $1,000.00.

Observing these things, Tom's dream of a future in salvaging took firm root. When still a boy, of ten he stole aboard the Reid toug *Mocking Bird* outbound on Lake Michigan to rescue the schooner *Mt. Goggin* — worth $25,000 when she was built a few years previous. Loaded with coal, the ship struck a shoal in the Straits of Mackinac.

Releasing her after difficult lightering with crude equipment of barrel, crane and chain, and with her in tow, they headed for the Wisconsin port of Manitowoc where shipyard facilities were available.

A big sea was running abreast of Squaw Island, and when they got outside the sea increased, wind now North West. Deeply loaded, the *Mt. Goggin* had very little side out. Every time she would take a dive, waves would wash over her and down the front hatch. The pump had to be going steadily or, as the saying went, they were done. The crew savagely shoveled cargo coal into buckets and dumped it overboard.

By the time they reached Point aux Barques, a danger spot on the south shore of the Upper Peninsula about twenty five miles from Manistique, the boiler was red hot. And as the water struck her aft', the steam roared and spat.

Jim Reid thundered at the Captain who had made certain miscalculations regarding wind directions and who had failed to put out a red light.

It was a fearsome experience for an adult. It was one never to be forgotten by a boy who was learning the hard way the mistakes that his father was making and rectifying.

For this terrifying experience they received $1,500.00. Pump $40.00 a day, tug *Mocking Bird* $300.00 a day, pumpers $5.00 a day each.

Tom's fearlessness suffered little discouragement despite frequent strappings. Compulsion was strong. The challenge of danger was met without hesitation, indeed with eagerness.

It was 1882 and Tom was twelve when his brother Will, two years younger, went with him on the Reid tug *Seymour* which was towing a set of booms from Detroit to the Soo. Cruising north up West Neebish channel, they came upon a bear swimming across the river. From the tug's bow, Tom shouted a warning to the Captain.

"Too bad," was the answer. "Narrow channel. Got to keep her on her course."

"But — he'll be hurt!" cried the boy, against Will's amused laughter. Seconds later there was a thud as tug and animal came together.

"Come on — get him!" called Will, and joined the raftsman who jumped into the dory. Tom followed. Will took the bow, ax ready. The helpless animal's paws had been broken. As Will swung the ax, the blow missed its mark throwing him off balance and out of the shallow boat across the bear's back.

Risking the powerful current, Tom leaped to help Will back into the boat, the raftsman chiding him for the foolhardiness that might have sent him spinning into the even stronger currents beyond.

There followed the business of looping a line around the broken paws and hoisting the moaning six foot brute aboard with the anchor davit on the tug's bow. Tom stood by until the raftsman swung the peavy high to deliver the death blow. Unnerved at the sight of suffering, he had reached the engine room before the blow struck.

At times, his father might say — as he harnessed a team to be off on some errand — "Climb aboard, Tom. You'll be a damn' nuisance, but you might come in handy." They would dash through the countryside, foam flying from the horses' bits as Jim Reid went about the business of rounding up timber. With night, those bitter sub-zero nights, they would put up wherever it was convenient; at a remote farmhouse, perhaps, where pigs and chickens shared family living quarters, and where fresh air never penetrated; where even the natural healthy appetite of a boy rebelled.

Sometimes in a blizzard the horses would flounder around in the deep snow and come to a reluctant halt, wolves howling not far behind. Jim Reid would gesture Tom toward the nearest tree and start climbing. He knew that the horses would find their way home, and help would come.

Tom learned to live with danger. It was an accepted feature of his life during teenhood, and a simple preliminary to what he was to meet in Dollarville, a town about seventy miles northwest of St. Ignace.

With a population of six hundred at the time, Dollarville boasted one mill and a vast outlying supply of untouched timber. And its location on the Tahquamenon River, with an outlet to Whitefish Bay and Lake Superior, made it most desirable for his father's plans.

By now Jim Reid's achievements were becoming known along the Lakes, and he found it less difficult to secure financial backing. Edmund Hall, a wealthy Detroit lumberman, had shown repeated confidence in him. Yet, heavy investments in booms and tugs, a big payroll to meet, a home and growing family to support, all built up a tension that aggravated his nervous nature and quick temper. And in such a day and environment, it was not surprising that he should seek unwise diversions and pay the price.

By the time Tom was fifteen he had learned to assume responsibility, and experience readied him for frequent crises. He was born to the sounds of battle, and he could meet adequately the demands of circumstance aboard the tug, in lumber camps and on rafts. But rafting was a stop-gap; salvaging was his objective. His every thought was for the day when rafting could be turned over to others. He loathed its monotony, and summoned what patience he could command. Through those early years he planned passionately and with confidence toward the time when he would make a name for himself in the field of his choice. Meanwhile he would be amenable. But the day would come . . .

At Dollarville, his aptitude and love of the Lakes made him invaluable to the father who would never have admitted it but whose acknowledgement was reflected in his unconscious attitude of a man toward a contemporaneous rival, rather than a youth.

Here Jim Reid lumbered for different concerns as well as for himself, cutting the logs of white and Norway pine by the thousand, sending them along the skidways and down the Two Hart River sixty miles above Whitefish Point, where they were herded into booms and towed by tug to designated ports.

There was the difficult routine of guiding rafts through the locks at Sault Sainte Marie and the St. Mary's River, and down to the mills in Michigan's Tawas and Bay City.

In those days, schooners would come up and 'lay over' at Sailors' Encampment, seldom running the 'Soo' River at night. Besides, there were saloons at Sailors' Encampment, and a chance to break the monotony of a long cruise.

Tugmen would fasten lights on the rafts and tow them down at night, free from the difficulty of meeting schooners in troublesome spots.

By the year 1887, due to his great physique, self-reliance and proven ability beyond his years — at seventeen Tom Reid was a vital part of the organization; 'wheeling' on his father's tugs the *Burnside, Waldo Avery* and *Mentor*, and well trained in the business of navigation by the stout Reid captain, Hugh Stephenson.

He was irritated by hearing his father's repeated complaints against the delays consequent to cutting up enormous rafts of logs in treacherous Whitefish Bay — stormiest point on the Great Lakes and known as its graveyard — in order to facilitate passage south through the Soo Locks. Eventually this inspired Tom to do an unheard of thing.

"I'm going to let this raft go over the Rapids," he declared one day as they approached Whitefish Point.

There were violent protests, arguments, threats. Such a thing had never been attempted or even considered. But Tom's authority had begun to be accepted in his father's absences, and there was a set to his jaw that said, "Obey me or fight me."

The St. Mary's River at Sault Sainte Marie is nearly a mile wide and falls twenty feet over craggy rocks in three quarters of a mile. It had been made navigable by Lock canals.

In 1797 the Northwestern Fur Company built a Lock there. A canal 5,700 feet long, navigable for vessels of about twelve foot draft, was completed by the State in 1855. Between 1870 and 1881, the Federal Government widened the canal to one hundred feet, made the draft sixteen feet, and built the Weitzel Lock — 515 feet long, eighty feet wide and sixty feet at gate openings with a lift of eighteen to twenty feet.

Intrepid tourists, eager for a thrill, entrusted themselves to Indian guides who, for a fee, manned canoes and guided them safely over the Rapids.

Now Tom Reid's orders were challenged, but sullenly carried out. The tug *Burnside* fastened a slip-line on a raft of two million feet of logs, and dropped it down stern first over the boiling waters, while tugs waited at the lower end of the Rapids to catch the booms.

Tom met Captain Stephenson's eye as the order was given.

"You're a cool one, lad," declared the officer angrily. "I'm washing my hands of this whole business — and there's witnesses!"

Along the Rapids the raft struck a great rock and the booms went over. Some local woodsmen and Indians braved the churning waves where the loosened logs had piled up, and order was restored before long without too much damage resulting. At the river below, the waiting tugs caught the rafts and dropped them down.

There followed a violent scene with his father which Tom met in smiling silence, for he realized that beyond immediate anger there was an astonished realization that the fantastic idea worked. And after that, where much had been learned and mistakes noted, Tom Reid's method was regularly followed — to the great advantage of all those involved in lumber traffic.

Notwithstanding, rafting with its long and lonely idle hours was not for Tom Reid. He lived only for his dream! He grew more restless, more impatient to join the salvage crew, but his father stubbornly assigned him to the rafts.

In the summer of 1888, monotony was somewhat relieved by his experience on the barge *Minnehaha* where he was sent in an emergency.

Towed by the wooden steamer *Hiawatha,* the *Minne-*

haha, built at a cost of $60,000, and the only four-masted barge on the Great Lakes, went ashore on Drummond Island near the Soo.

Jim Reid put in a salvage bid of $25,000, and was given the contract to raise her and deliver her to drydock. Taking Tom, a diver and crew aboard the *Mocking Bird,* he ran out a big anchor with cables. Four eighteen inch square holes were cut on each side. Ashore, logs were made square in order to pass through these openings. Spuds were fastened on the inside and outside with hundred-ton jacks.

Then began the business of lifting the boat. Each time she moved, the strain was taken up on the cables and the boat thrown several feet forward until her bow was manoeuvred into deep water.

At that time the Reid Company owned only one steam pump, a twelve inch centrifugal which had to be firmly fastened down because of the violent vibration.

A watchman was dispatched the eighteen miles to Detour Passage to telephone the Tromp office at the Soo to send a tug down to tow the *Minnehaha* in to Detour. When this was accomplished they brought the barge to the inside of the mill dock and let her sink.

She laid there for a while with only Tom and a seaman named Boney Lourie aboard. Presently Tom's father ordered the barge pumped out and brought around to the outside of the dock. Aboard the *City of London,* he would pick her up and tow her to Cleveland. The *London* put her tow line aboard, made fast to the bow of the *Minnehaha* and they started on their way.

At that time in order to move the vessel it was first necessary to prime the pumps with a foot valve and fill the pipe of the pump with water. Half way between Detour and Presque Isle, the foot-valve was found to be leaking, and water was rising in the hold. Signalling the *London* to slow down, young Tom got to his knees under water and removed the piece of line which had fouled the foot-valve, then primed the hose in the pump. It held.

The pump was started and continued to work effectively, and soon they were on their way once more with only one pump between them and lake bottom.

The ordeal had been tense and exhausting, but neither would sleep, despite great fatigue, since one must steer and one man the pump. And the *Minnehaha*, meant to carry a crew of sixteen, was manned by two.

As she reached Lake Erie and neared Cleveland, the foot-valve failed entirely. They signalled for tugs and were towed in behind the breakwater and beached.

Tom Reid and Boney Lourie slept for two days without waking.

The Reid Company cleared approximately $15,000 on the job.

CHAPTER TWO

By now, Jim Reid was rapidly augmenting his business. Hearing of a tug Company for sale at the Two Hart River on Michigan's Upper Peninsula, he investigated and made a deal at a price he hoped to be able to meet if the breaks came his way. He was learning to gamble, pyramiding his profits, with thousands still to be earned, his proven skill and knowledge serving as acceptable collateral.

Included in the property were four lumber camps. Their management fell to a great extent to Tom who at nineteen was making a solid place for himself in the Reid enterprises. His younger brothers, less venturesome and self-sufficient, would some day assume their place in the Reid affairs. Tom's self-assurance was not without the backing of earned experience.

Life up north was rough and casual. Liquor ran freely. Men took their fun where they found it. And Jim Reid's life had not been built on the 'all work, no play' policy. Truly a genius in his line, he had the faults and weaknesses to balance.

He would storm at Tom's mistakes. Tom's mother referred to his noisy rebukes as 'red-herrings', intended to divert attention from his own lapses. She knew his deep secret pride in his oldest son. Only to her did he ever admit Tom's part in the success of the Two Hart River venture.

With the purchase of the camps had been included some fine blooded ponies, and since horses had always been Tom's passion, he entered into his duties here with genuine pleasure. He enjoyed driving them along the wild wooded roads from camp to camp, a red-headed young giant swaying with the jerk and lurch of the sleighs, reins hard in his hands.

He would scout around through the country in search of beef, pork and other supplies for the camp kitchen, and return with sleigh piled high.

There were few girls in that sparsely populated area — few families, since it took the hardiest pioneer to endure those northern winters. And never afterward did he fight his way through a blizzard without remembering Killeen and the blizzard along Two Hart River that took her life.

Killeen was the daughter of John Blackhawk, head of one of the Indian families who lived in a hut not too far from camp. Killeen — the name a corruption, perhaps, of the Irish term, colleen; not unfamiliar thereabouts following the days of Irish immigration.

She was little more than sixteen when one day in passing, he saw her crouched in a snowdrift above a puppy whose back had been broken by a pawing colt. Bringing his team to a halt, he went to her and examined the puppy whose condition, obviously, was hopeless. Disposing of it gently, he comforted the Indian girl who took his kindness in imperturbable silence.

A few days later she appeared at the Reid camp looking for work, was given some menial tasks by the cook and permitted to stay. Though before others she never seemed aware of his existence, Tom had reason to know of the hard passion that enslaved her . . .

It was when the cook, a brawny Irishwoman from Dollarville, was stricken with pneumonia, that a new cook had to be found. Killeen was willing to assume the post — more willing than skilled.

After a conference, one of the lumbermen sent for his wife and children to come to camp where they could be reunited and the needs of the kitchen served.

The railroad station lay over twenty five miles away. January snow was piled high, roads unbroken. Before dawn that grim, threatening morning, Tom loaded the sleigh with feed for the ponies and the box of thick fat pork sandwiches and leathery pie that Killeen had provided, and left to meet the train.

Schedules were mere figures on paper. The train was hours late, and a blizzard had set in by the time it arrived. With roads barely passable, they started for camp with progress gradually slowing until the ponies, wandering blindly onto an old logging road, went over on their backs in the drifts.

Wolves howled near by.

Tom managed to quiet the panicky children and reassure the mother. Setting off flares, he produced Killeen's food, and afterward, covering the little group with blankets, he attended to the ponies, providing what shelter was possible.

While some miles away, staggering toward her father's cabin, Killeen went to urge him and her brothers to go in search of the overdue Tom and his passengers with the other teams.

There were no flares to scare off the wolves, no one to witness her fate . . . The men at camp were not unaware that she had found fulfillment in serving the one she loved.

Killeen — one of many. There was the little French girl he met the night his cutter almost broke through the Straits ice after a brief thaw. But the promised fun was worth the risk. She was distracting and eventually difficult. Though who, despite possible complications, would forego an occasional interlude in her tantalizing company as she veined the long bitter winter with moments of delight?

French girls, Indian girls, a Scotch lass, a British one — They came and went, incidents of color and excitement, of promise and reward — and of forgetting, his heart yet untouched .

Seasonal work varied. The rafting hauls were long and lonesome. Men must amuse themselves and each other. At night under the stars, darkness hiding their faces, they would reminisce about their experiences with women, reveal plans, boast of conquest or innocently betray rejection, while the tug went forward, weather permitting, at a mile an hour. Again, the rising wind might drive them back two for every one they made.

Hauling five or six million feet of logs, at a towing fee of $2.50 a thousand, from Spanish River on North Channel, and from French River on Georgian Bay, required skill and patience. And a healthy morale. There was little to do off watch if the weather was good. But with wind, day and night vigilance was required. And a man had to know his rafts and how to drift and handle them. There was no insurance in those early days. Loss of logs was the owner's loss — taken at his own risk. The only loss the Reid Company suffered was labor and the tow bill. Reid was not paid for the towing of lost logs, and sometimes as many as 500,000 of a raft would be lost.

Each company had its own branding mark, and when logs were sent down the river of acceptance, they came to a sorting gap and were pushed into their own space. Strict laws were enforced to punish anyone misappropriating logs.

When Tom Reid was towing rafts, he employed a thousand feet of a ten inch line. There was no way of pulling in the line except by hand. It would take the whole crew of twelve — fireman, engineers, cook, watchman, wheelsman, etc.

Early in rafting experience, Captain Hugh Stephenson improvised an outfit of his own. He ran a chain under the deck from the windless for'd, and put a spool on the shaft and a spool on the tow-post; and when he ran that, it would almost throw the men out of their bunks when it got up speed.

After that they were supplied with winches. They never used a wire line, since it was too heavy on the booms, and there were no towing machines.

In 1885, crew of a rafting tug earned as follows:

Captain	$100 a month
1st Engineer	$100 a month
Mate	$ 60 a month
Wheelsman	$ 25 a month
2nd Engineer	$ 60 a month
Cook	$ 60 a month
Watchman	$ 25 a month
Raftsman	$ 30 a month
Deckhand	$ 30 a month

The crew would number ten or twelve — with extra deck-hands, wheelsmen and watchmen.

Fuel for the tugs ran three dollars a ton.

They fed men at that time for seventy five cents a day.

Provisions required for a rafting trip might consist of—

Two sides of beef
Two sides of pork
Slabs of salt pork
Slabs of corned beef
A barrel of flour
100 pounds of sugar
A firkin of butter

The time of rafting was always indefinite because of weather. It took at the best twelve days to raft across.

Georgian Bay was a beautiful archipelago — a Mecca to admiring travelers, but for Tom the sameness of scene and routine had robbed the region of all charm. Its narrow channels represented only a hard challenge to the navigator. The beauty of the islands, some but a touch of green against the blue, some of substantial acreage, some barren — was lost in monotony.

The great Manitoulin Island, paradise of wild flowers and radiant foliage, of infrequent white farmhouses and many tiny lakes, was but another tiresomely familiar scene along the way. As were Cove Island, the 'Bustards' and the 'Ducks.'

And then suddenly the monotonous scene might change radically with a change of wind. Danger always lurked in the possibility of a broken boom. And this happened one stormy day when piloting the *Bosco Belle* with her six million foot raft in tow. The boom broke as they came opposite Michigan's Port Sanilac.

Passing beyond, the Steamer *City of Alpena* saw Tom's plight and reported it at Port Huron. But Tom had already taken matters in hand. Making his way around to the leeward side of the raft, he hauled in the tow line, returned and took the end of the boom and started to haul. Round and round he went.

The seas were tremendous, but nosing the *Bosco Belle* forward, he circled to leeward of the raft once more and managing to get the ends of the boom together, coupled them. It was a dangerous chance in bad weather. More than skill and the help of calked boots and pike pole were needed; you must be a friend of hazards. When the tug rolled, it seemed she would never right herself again. He caught the chains with a hook, shackled them together as he fought the waves, keeping his balance by the fortune that protects the foolhardy.

At last Tom succeeded in pulling the raft around until the nose piece was to the leeward. Then he coupled the tow line on, headed up, swung around and made for Port Huron. Approaching Point Edward, he saw the Reid tug *Sarnia City* steaming briskly toward them, and soon heard his father's voice from the bow.

"Lucky you didn't lose your life in that sea. Time you had a little sense!" Stunned at Tom's achievement, yet he could not bring himself to praise, or betray admiration.

Sometimes in bad weather, a rafting haul might take fifteen days. With dwindling supplies, a crew of eleven to seventeen men might find more than wind or monotony to bedevil them. Food ran out.

Faced for the first time with the hunger problem, after uneasy hours Tom sighted some fishermen's nets on a shoal spit about eighteen miles off Thunder Bay. With a mate, he lowered a dory and rowed to the scene, pulled the nets and taking a substantial number of trout and whitefish, slipped some bills and a note of explanation in a bottle which he tied to the net, replacing the lines.

Yet with all its hazards, there was money to be made in rafting, and the Reids were spread thin but wide. It was boom time in the lumbering era, and Jim Reid's enterprises by now covered considerable territory. Towing six million feet of lumber in rafts from French River in Georgian Bay to Sarnia could bring twelve thousand dollars.

Tom was mate on the tug *Mocking Bird* when his father came along to settle some business at French River where they were to pick up a raft. On the way, the Captain stopped at Bustard's Island and returned with a cub bear.

The playful animal prowled through the open-doored cabins one night, and pulling the covers off the sailors threw them on deck. Naked, the men awoke fuming and swearing, the bear cunningly out of reach. Chilled, Jim Reid stormed that the bear must go. The captain determined he would stay, for his antics kept the crew amused.

The bear stayed.

Late that season, they lost a four million foot raft — which represented approximately $8,000.00 to the Reid Company for towing. This was their greatest loss to date. And that winter they bought the log carrier *Wanipiti,* built at a cost of $75,000, from Loveland Company of Tawas. They began then to carry logs.

The *Mocking Bird* was scheduled to tow the *Wanipiti*

over to French River and Tom, as crew, joined with the others in helping load logs.

The first trip out, five men were killed while loading her. After that, Jim Reid found pressing work of another nature for Tom at Sarnia. And when the *Mocking Bird* cleared for Milwaukee soon after this, towing tow barges, Tom was aboard.

Chafing at criticism he had heard of protecting his son, Jim Reid said harshly, "You're crew on this tug, Tom. Remember that. Don't talk back to the Captain. Because I own the boat means nothing. Mind your own business."

In Milwaukee, the captain went uptown — well fortified with a few stiff drinks and accompanied by the bear. He visited numerous bars, ordering the bartenders to give the bunch a drink or he'd set the bear on them.

The Captain, sans bear, was finally taken to jail. And the Reid Wrecking and Towing Company was in trouble, without a tug master, and barges ready to clear for the lower Lakes. The loss of fifteen hundred dollars a day was no laughing matter, for they were towing a lumber carrier and her two barges from Milwaukee to Port Huron at a cost of three thousand dollars for the tow.

When old Jim roared recriminations at Tom for not advising him of the situation in time, Tom merely shrugged. "You told me to mind my own business."

Will Reid, witnessing the scene, gazed in awe at this brother of his who would dare defy the old lion. But Jim Reid turned away, though not before the amused grin betrayed him. Yet he was adamant to Tom's pleas for work with the salvage crew. Time enough for that. There were skilled men handling that end of the business. Rafting was important. There was money in it, and Tom knew all the tricks. He wanted no arguments.

Rafting — endless, tiresome hours, like dead weights

on a man's shoulders. Adverse winds, storms, and a valuable raft breaking up. Losses to follow where losses couldn't be met. Big debts growing bigger, a crushing overhead, the bank pressing, and some unexpected extravagance or recklessness of Jim Reid threatening complete defeat.

More and more Tom was forced to assume authority in his father's absences, pacifying bank and backer. Edmund Hall, wealthy Detroit lumberman, was backing Jim Reid financially and had not had reason to regret the arrangement. But there were tight moments, and every loss, though small, menaced that vital bond.

The crews began to accept Tom's responsibility and take it for granted. Because of his attitude of self-assurance, they never knew of his frequent apprehensions, but much of the time he lived in a little private hell. He might doubt the outcome of a project, but never doubted himself. He knew where he was going, and with passionate determination, knew what he had to do eventually to satisfy his existence. When the time came, he would follow the work of salvaging, if not with the Reid Company then with one of its rivals. In the meantime, he made the best of it and concentrated on rafting and its problems.

Rafts might be difficult to handle; but men were difficult, too, unless you understood them. Tom Reid made it his business to know his crews.

French River was a familiar port for the Reid tugs. Here they picked up their rafts, and oftentimes crew members as well. Tom had known early that a fellow who could play a fiddle, banjo, harmonica or jew's harp was a valuable asset aboard through the long hauls. And seldom would you find a man in that country who couldn't handle a pike pole.

Delays while waiting for rafts to be made up were never days and nights wasted. Crews would gather in some available log cabin after a general camp round-up, and dancing would begin. These up country shindigs helped pass the time away — hot nights ashore in a practical wilderness. Hotter days would follow under a broiling sun, when they crawled along with the rafts to Tawas, Bay City or Sarnia. Then back again — an eternal treadmill.

The routine itself was simple and monotonous. Long tedious days — depending, of course, on weather. Night, and the raftsman lowering a yawl and rowing back to fix the three lights on the raft, one on the stern and one on each side.

The thought of the slim copper-skinned Indian girls at French River made the return less undesirable to the handsome young red-headed Viking. Even the most stoical was not unresponsive to Tom Reid. He had a way with the girls, and laughed off the crew's ribbing, never without a secret restlessness that so far no woman had been able to satisfy.

To keep occupied during the endless hauls was important, and steady passage would have meant shorter trips. But if 'she blew,' days were added, more tedious days to while away when the wind subsided.

Crewmen would take frequent dips in the Lake to ease the discomfort of the heat, but fresh clothes were important as well, and the business of washing by hand was unpopular. As a result, soiled clothes oftentimes were resumed.

Finding that arguments were ineffectual, Tom decided on a plan.

They had great sport after that aboard the *Mocking Bird,* ridiculing the contraption that occupied Tom's spare time. Lining a barrel with staves, he fitted a rod through it, caught a piece of line around the shaft pulley on the main shaft of the engine, and threw in water and soap.

Since the *Mocking Bird* was equipped with a steam winch to hoist anchor, the shaft was placed on the side of the tow-post with a chain run from the foist under the deck. The noise was deafening, but the clothes came out clean.

Joe, the deckhand, took over the concession at a minor fee, and at least one aspect of life aboard the *Mocking Bird* was substantially improved. Cleanliness led godliness by a wider margin.

About this time occurred the incident of the wooden steamboat *Philip D. Armour.* With a cargo of 65,000 bushels of corn, she had suffered a collision, and sank in the St. Clair River. Thc *Armour* had been built by the Chicago packer at a cost of $125,000.

The salvaging of this ship was one of the first big jobs done on the Lakes. Using a flat 350 foot lumber barge, Jim Reid floated this over the *Armour,* opened the valves and let in the water; chained her to the sunken vessel, tightened the chains and started to pump her out.

Repeatedly, with success in sight, one chain would part, then another, then all — and the work had to be done over again from the beginning. Finally they were able to pump out the barge, raising her and bringing the *Armour* up with her.

Though the Reid Company received a fee of $50,000, they scarcely broke even, since the job took two years. But the magic of air-power had never been more effectively demonstrated. And certain of Tom's ideas created a more efficient technique for which he was never given verbal credit by his father, but which afterward became part of the salvaging routine.

Tom's contributions, however, were mentioned to his mother, whose pride in him was a compensating satisfaction. She had never forgotten the day in boyhood when he had brought her his first money earned while piling edgings.

A neighbor, present at the time, remarked, "That lad is older than his years — and not even twenty yet. He'll be head of this family some day."

Will had laughed but their mother had not laughed. "I am proud of Tom," she said. "He is a good boy. He will be a good man. . . . Will is a good boy, too. He will be the white-collar man. Tom will go out and meet life face to face."

She had known with the knowledge of the mother. Now the younger Will pored over ledger and vouchers, while the wind howled against protective windows.

On Tom's return from the *Armour,* she could not hide her pride. It was evident that Jim Reid had spoken kindly of their son.

"Stand by your father," she urged. "It is in you to do right — as it is in him. Only — well, you know what I mean."

He knew. She was too loyal to voice her worries. Jim Reid was a genius of sorts. But it was evident that he would burn himself out before old age. A flair for hard living and repeated and unwise financial ventures was beginning to have its effect. He made money, lost money, and was always in debt. Though invariably he had ideas ahead of his time, realizing them, yet foolishly squandering the profits in typical fashion.

Tom's mother had grown to depend on him as a balance wheel against all this. And while he and his father frequently clashed, there was warmth between them, a deep regard and devotion. This was never more evident than during the crisis aboard the tug *Mentor* when Tom was nineteen.

SEPTEMBER had come. September 1889. Benjamin Harrison occupied the White House. It was a time of labor unrest, historic strikes, rebellion of worker against capitalist. And what happened in Philadelphia, Chicago and Pittsburgh affected shipping on the Great Lakes.

September had come — the time of the equinox. With Captain Hugh Stephenson in command, the *Mentor* was bringing down a raft of over two million feet from Lake Superior. Hugging the shore, since a big sea was running with a gale from the north west, they were going before the wind.

At Whitefish Bay a roar echoed below deck, and the engineer came running up with word that a flue had burst. The water had gone out of the boiler. They let go the raft and made for land, headed toward Tahquamenon Reef — helpless, with nothing to stop them but the rocks ahead.

"Get down there — *quick,*" Captain Stephenson told the engineer. "You can see where we're heading. Get into that boiler and stop the leak."

"Not me, sir," declared Evans. "I might never come out alive. I've got a wife and four kids depending on me."

"There are eight lives on this tug, and you're responsible for the engine room," Jim Reid shouted. "Get down into that boiler, Evans!"

"Not on your life, sir." Evans was firm.

"It's your duty!"

"And it's my life. Maybe it was your duty to check with the inspector on that boiler before we cleared port."

The tug was at the mercy of wind and wave. The raft moved off by itself, undulating crazily.

A figure brushed past, and Jim Reid saw Tom leap

down the stairs. He stumbled after him and stood gray-faced as his son snatched up a soft-nosed chisel and climbed into the death-trap.

Afterward he gulped down a third of a bottle of whiskey. With Tom safe across from him—"Get into your cabin and wash up," he growled. "You look like a sewer digger."

When the *Mentor* reached Bay City with the raft, Engineer Evans quit his job, and the tug was idled until the post could be filled. Skilled men were scarce. After following several leads unsuccessfully, Jim Reid heard of a likely prospect who lived down the shore and sent Tom to investigate.

In a clearing at the edge of a woods, Tom paused at the sound of hooves along a path through the trees. Soon a girl came riding into view on a bay mare. She was autumn come to life—brown hair, gold scarf, tawny jacket and rippling skirt. Self-assured, she sat erect, reins in firm hands. Her face had warmth and beauty. Her eyes were clean and proud. She appraised him in passing and went along through the trees.

He smiled, moved toward her. She was gone. But that would not be for long. This—miraculously—was the one he had been waiting for.

His original search became an excuse to question the prospective engineer presently as to the identity of the girl on horseback.

"That sounds like Doctor Heumann's girl, Anna," the man told him. "See her often out riding through the woods."

Anna Heumann —

Where did the doctor live? The crew occasionally needed help when the tug docked.

"Oh, he ain't livin' any more. Died a couple of years

ago. She and her younger sister went to live with a married sister in town. You know —" the fellow seemed anxious to eulogize the departed physician, "Doctor Heumann was one of the finest men that ever lived. Had a big practice — the rich and the poor. Didn't make any difference to him. If an Indian down river needed him, he'd paddle off in a canoe fast as he'd call on a lumber king on Center Street. Yes, sir, even if a tramp on the street was taken bad, he'd bring him into his own nice house and use his big mahogany table in the dining room to operate on. Nope, Doctor Heumann wasn't proud. That's the kind of man he was."

"You say," Tom ventured, "that Miss Heumann is living with her sister. Where might that be?"

"Why, her sister is married to Lawyer Winslow. Nice people. Awful nice people."

The services of Lawyer Winslow were immediately sought on a matter of a slight deck accident heretofore ignored. And as one thing leads to another, before long Anna Heumann and Tom Reid met.

After his first visit to the Winslow home, "He's an absolute giant," Clara Winslow remarked. "Handsome— and a wonderful smile. But his verbs are dreadful— *dreadful.*"

Involuntarily, Anna found herself coming to Tom's defense — Anna, the purist. "Sailors have a language of their own."

"My dear, a verb is a verb in any language," Clara reminded her.

"I will take character!"

"You recognize that in a man you know only slightly?"

"I think I do. . . ."

But Anna's defense of Tom was more self-assertion before a dominating sister, than conviction. Secretly she deplored the fact that she must agree with Clara on the matter in question. Tom's verbs were bad. He was rough and awkward. And yet, after all—

Having declared herself, she defended him against Clara's disapproval, telling herself that upsetting Clara's assurance was the only reason. Then as time went on and his attentions continued, she had to admit the truth. She was falling in love.

As a frequent caller at the Winslow home, Tom was reminded of the difference in their lives, for the place contained much of what once embellished the old family home. The Heumanns had lived gently. The appointments here reflected a cultural background. Books, fine rugs, objects of art. Handsome pieces of rosewood and mahogany. Silver. Flowing brocade and velvet drapes. It was here that Anna and her younger sister had been brought to live with their older married sister at the death of their parents.

The affair progressed. It was no secret that they had arranged a signal between them so that Anna would know when Tom's tug was coming into port. Of course, all vessels had to 'blow' for the opening of the bridge so they could pass through, but Tom had a special salute for Anna. He would add an extra long blast which, where-ever she was, could not fail to reach her. If she happened to be at home she flew to her room to prepare herself for his coming. Yet when he appeared, secretly she would deplore his careless appearance, comparing his grooming with that of the handsome young bank clerk in love with her younger sister. And yet — he was Tom. Fastidiousness had no defense against his smile and kiss.

"Why wouldn't you go to school, Tom?" she wondered sadly. "Why didn't your people make you go?"

He could not expect this sheltered girl to understand

his kind of life. "Oh, Anna," he begged, "don't talk about such things now. I love you, and I'll make you happy. We love each other — and you know it!"

Pleading his cause that night, he swung back and forth across her sister's parlor, his great frame rolling as if the sea were still under him, bursting into excited declarations of love and hopes and plans.

"Tom—" She was dismayed at the intensity of her emotion, anxious for some defense against it. "Do you know what a verb is?"

Halting, he faced her with a frown. "I know what the Lakes are — from one end to the other! I've rafted since I could hold a pike pole. I've taken over the wheel of a tug in seas ready to swamp us. I've run a locomotive and handled tote teams and driven stage. How the hell does a verb stack up against *that?*"

"It isn't even in the running," she admitted, smiling through tears she ignored. "I'm afraid you win."

"And now—" he roared, snatching her to her feet, "name the day. I've waited as long as I intend to."

"It wasn't my idea," she admitted.

"What are you laughing about then? Are you serious?" he demanded.

"It's too late for you to back out now," she warned.

"Next week?" he begged, stilling the laughter.

"Next week, Tom. . . ."

"It's about time," he declared. "We've been going together for three years!"

Like a bashful child, he broke the news to his father.

"You've got a hell of a nerve—asking a girl to marry you, and not a cent to your name—nor a Master's license yet. Marriage is more than billin' and cooin'. There's bills to pay. Who's goin' to foot them? On the pay you earn you can hardly take care of yourself."

"I'll need more pay," Tom agreed bluntly.

"Humph! You will, eh? Well, you'll get none till you've got a Master's license to hang in the tug pilot house. And that's only the beginning."

Tom met the challenge, bitterly determining that he would keep his part of the bargain, and demand a raise accordingly. A fellow twenty three years old should assert himself! Hard study followed — every available moment devoted to maritime laws and rules. Then came the examination — days of suspence, and the final award.

The wedding was planned. Such, joy, it seemed, could not be his. And then a sickening blow fell!

Clara Winslow's sudden death put an end to dreams. Anna's inconsolable grief must be considered — and the period of mourning respected. Anna could not think of marriage for at least a year.

Tom went about his work trying to adjust himself to the shocking disappointment. He was not unimpressed by the significance of his next assignment, nor blind to his father's compassionate gesture when he was sent to New York for the purpose of examining and possibly buying the fire-tug *Protector* for a project that meant a profit of thousands. Such an important deal with a generous commission was the highest compliment to a youth of his age and experience.

The *Protector* was a high-pressure fire tug and a familiar sight in New York harbor; for sale principally because salt water had ruined her boilers in days when evaporators were unavailable to purify water, and loss by corrosion was heavy.

Tom Reid inspected her and saw that she was a staunch craft and would answer the desired purpose. He entered into negotiations for her purchase and went about planning her reconditioning. New boilers would have to be installed, and it seemed that could be done to meet the time requirements of his father's plan. This concerned a towing job to Chicago.

Three Spanish ships—the *Nina, Pinta* and *Santa Maria,* duplicates of Columbus' little fleet, had been leased to the United States by the Spanish Government to be exhibited as a highlight of the 1893 World's Fair which was soon to open in Chicago. And Jim Reid had contracted to tow them out from New York harbor for $25,000.

The *Protector* was brought to a near by shipyard and the work begun when a representative of the Spanish Government declared that only a United States cruiser would be permitted to tow the ships.

Part of the twenty five thousand dollar towing fee the Reids were to receive had already been expended in reconditioning the *Protector*. But a United States cruiser picked up the ships and towed them to Quebec where the Great Lakes Towing Company, the Reids' bitterest rival, took them over and brought them through the canals and Lakes to Chicago. All this — for reasons Tom could only surmise in a world of hard business rivalry and political influence.

Chagrined and humiliated, he had to acknowledge failure at the end of a period when great responsibility had rested on him and promised prestige. The Company lawyer advised him there could be no redress as *you cannot sue the Government*. Tom brought the *Protector* back from New York with the added expense of a pilot from New York to Quebec and one from Quebec to Montreal.

Anna's fond letters only served to remind him more poignantly of a greater disappointment, and humanly he tried to drown his troubles. In a world where practically only French was spoken, he was low in mind and alone, when by a pleasant coincidence he encountered an acquaintance who was an agent for the Pere Marquette Railroad, and together they made a tour of the city's gay spots. During this period, he met also a member of a Cleveland shipping firm. Disappointments were forgotten at the bar and gaming table.

The Reid Company never recovered their loss. But not long afterward, they were engaged by the Cleveland shipping firm to handle an important salvage job, with Tom given credit for the account. The job, successfully executed, brought a profit of $32,000, and a rare accolade to Tom from his father since this was 1893, the year of the World's Fair and a panic.

No sooner had Grover Cleveland taken office than the great disaster occurred, rivalling the panic of '73. It was the product of a complication of causes. Overinvestment in railways and industrial combinations, including too many of a highly speculative character, was a leading factor.

Widespread depression in Europe since 1889, involving Great Britain, Germany and France among other countries, had its influence, for it led to a withdrawal of a part of the gold which foreign capitalists had invested in American enterprises.

But most of all was the growing fear of the business classes that the rising tide of silver inflation, under the Sherman Act, would sweep the Government off a gold basis and cause a suspension of gold payments.

There began another downward trend in the price of grain and livestock. Investigation showed that under existing conditions, the cost of raising wheat and corn exceeded the prices received.

A stirring speaker of Kansas went up and down the

State exhorting the farmers to "raise less corn and more hell."

The conservative New York Evening Post declared, "We don't want any more States until we can civilize Kansas." This referred to the previous administration, that of Benjamin Harrison, when there was admission into the Union of territories that extended a thousand miles from east to west. He brought up North and South Dakota, Montana, Washington, Idaho and Wyoming — a greater number of States than were admitted in any other administration.

All this affected national business, rates, jobs, compensations. And Great Lakes shippers felt it keenly. Grain was a commodity that the big Lake freighters and the smaller wooden ones sought for those big fall loads, for winter storage. Unrest and disgruntlement in Kansas could be felt soon after from Duluth to Buffalo — and felt bitterly.

Tom's stroke of luck had its effect. In the midst of this uncertainty and business distress, a salvage job came up, and Tom was assigned.

It happened that the wooden ship *The Golden Fleece,* a schooner worth $25,000 when built a few years before, went up on the beach of Lake Erie near Dunkirk, New York, probably forty miles west of Buffalo. This is the heart of a great farming country. Here lush fields and meadows and orchards sweep down to the water. Cattle graze and dairies thrive.

But the scenery had little charm for Tom Reid. He was faced with a difficult problem. If he could manage to get the water out of *The Golden Fleece* before she broke up, she would float. Time was important.

With diver Wilfred Manion and crew aboard the *Mocking Bird,* Tom improvised a base of oil barrels —

then another row on top, and another; using available jacks. When he was about ready for the final move, with the prospects of successful salvage more than good, a violent storm came up and *The Golden Fleece* went to pieces on the beach. $5,000.00 had been bid, but already the loss stood at $7,500.00.

Tom did not relish reporting failure back home. But it happened that during the interim, a local farmer had dropped a remark about a tug having been sunk out beyond in early spring and abandoned. That meant a boiler and engine were there for the taking! But, where? The smooth surface of Lake Erie gave no hint as to the spot where the sunken tug lay.

With his diver, Tom went along the shore questioning the natives, and learned of a farmer near whose land, it was said, the accident had occurred. It was early in a torrid July, and the farmer was busy haying. Tom appealed to him for help, but the man worked as he talked, one eye on a clouding sky. No, he would not leave his haying. This kind of weather you never knew what would happen, and he had to get that hay in the barn.

"Give me that pitchfork!" demanded Tom. "I'll handle this. You show our man where you think the wreck is."

The farmer shrugged and went along the shore with the diver to approximate the location. Hours passed before they returned. Tom was hot and tired after the rugged workout, but the incident had saved him valuable time. Salvage plans were made at once and with tug and steam barge standing by, Tom made the find and brought up the valuable booty that would net the Reid Company several thousands of dollars.

Anna's pride in his achievement gave his ambition even greater impetus. The fact that she longed for the day of their marriage, understanding fully what the step would mean, proved the nature of her love. Tom had not misled her with idle promises. He had reminded her of the inevitably long separations, the difficult first years she could expect.

Her younger sister was marrying that bank clerk, and going to Chicago to live — and to a fine house, no doubt. His people had money. . . . Tom was not a man of pretense or evasion, and he faced reality. It was best to lay the cards on the table.

"Anna," he said to her one day, after listening to the glamorous plans of her younger sister, "I've found the place I can afford — to begin with. I'd like you to come and take a look." He could not bear to have her go on planning the sort of home she was used to. She must know the truth.

With happy anticipation, she went along with him down Center Street, Bay City's handsomest thoroughfare. It was a long walk to the other part of town.

"It ain't much of a place," he said heavily. "But I can get it for ten dollars a month. We'll have to take in roomers and boarders at first, and I won't be there to help out very often. I'm a hell of a fellow to expect you to walk into something like that! But I love you, Anna — and that's the only way it can be."

She dropped her cheek to his sleeve, clung to him, her tone as awed as if he had mentioned a palace. "Our home, Tom. *Our home!* —"

He took heart, but there was unease when he thought of the days and nights she would be there, meeting it alone. Would her love survive, her belief in him? He had seen other marriages fail because those involved could not withstand the pressures. How could he blame her if it proved too much? And if it did, and he lost her — what then? —

They came at last to the street near the river. Now with Anna beside him, its shabbiness seemed intensified. "There it is." He indicated a humble little two-story wooden structure. He waited for her to speak, to comment, condemn, reject. But she was silent. And the twilight deepened, and lights came on as they stood there. He had had her answer, he decided. "Well, let's go back," he sighed. "I know it isn't much — but the day will come when I can give you anything you want. By God, I'll make it come!"

She looked at him with a smile of ecstasy. "Is it really going to happen to us, Tom — at last? Our home — I just can't believe it!"

He said, "Women are the damndest—" and brushed at his eyes. "Come on — you'll catch your death of cold standing here in the wind." And folding the small gloved hand hard in his own, he threw back his head and walked on like a king.

CHAPTER THREE

Soon they were quietly married. Tom was now twenty four.

Jim Reid allowed time out for a honeymoon cruise on the new liner *Northwest,* but immediately afterward, Tom was ordered to take command of the tug *Mocking Bird* which had urgent business at Michipocoton Island north along Ontario's Lake Superior shore. Grudgingly the father agreed that Anna might go along. Anna was a good sailor. And in those glamorous days, it mattered little to either where they were as long as they were together.

Upbound, Tom took her ashore at the Soo while the tug locked through. In evidence among numerous groups of spectators watching the boats were several Indians. Anna remarked nervously at the intensity of the stare of a towering redskin.

"Can you blame him?" laughed the happy bridegroom.

But when the *Mocking Bird* locked through on her return trip, Tom was formally accosted by the same fellow who proved to be a chief of note on the neighboring reservation. And in exchange for Anna who, he declared, was the most desirable woman he had ever seen, he had brought six young squaws to give Tom. Not sharing Anna's amusement, Tom handled the situation briefly and effectively.

Then came the enforced separations, the brief but ecstatic reunions. He never returned home without a stab of jealousy toward the boarders who had the run of the place and daily contact with his wife.

On those treasured jaunts home, he marveled at her skill in creating in that simple house an atmosphere that belied the environment. Yet he suffered at the presence of strangers in his home. . . . She had found some cheap ingrain carpet for the parlor floor, but it was an unobtrusive green. She painted the dingy walls a soft beige. The furniture mostly had come from a local instalment house — inexpensive pine and cheap golden oak. Here and there a mahogany table, a Hitchcock chair, a walnut chest, a book case — from the dismantled mansion on Center Street — highlighted the scene. The bulk of Anna's share — the silver, Haviland china, the lovely linens — were put away for a happier day, laughing at the humble closets that held them.

It was in their bedroom that the contrast was sharpest. The gleaming silver toilet set, crystal perfume flacons and pearl-inlaid jewel case on the wobbly little pine dresser. The handsomely framed photographs on wall and table. The Tiffany lamp at the humble iron bedside. The little ruby satin slipper-chair. . . .

Yet Anna never voiced but one complaint. His absences. She never had reconciled herself to them, but only when loneliness drove her to it did she make any comment, gamely playing her part in their economic scheme. She had grown used to the boarders and roomers and the work, to the crockery, the red tablecloths — and to making beds with corn-husk mattresses. The men were used to such things. But not to such a hostess as Anna Reid. . .

Nor would she agree to send for him at the time of her first confinement during the second winter of their marriage. She knew that important work held him in Ludington, a coastal town on the western shore of Michigan's Lower Peninsula, where a carferry had sunk at the pier. It was an important salvage assignment, the goal he had worked toward for so long. She could see her part through alone.

But the concerned physician over-rode her protests. "She needs you, Tom," he had telephoned.

Desperate with anxiety, he was embarrassed and troubled at the thought of her in labor in the humble home he had been able to provide.

Less than an hour later, braced against the January blizzard raging in from Lake Michigan, he stalked toward the headlight of an idling switch engine bound for the distant crossing where he could catch the train from the north for Bay City. The fierce ordeal of the past forty eight hours had shaken him — hours without sleep, facing sub-zero weather and Arctic winds.

Time was a vital consideration in the salvaging of the

carferry, but he had turned her over to his men with instructions. Nearly one hundred and fifty miles lay between him and his beloved. He thought of what she meant to him — what life would mean without her.

Hers was the reasoning he was too impatient to exercise, the considered judgment of the thoughtful mind. She had helped him with criticism that might wound his vanity and stir his anger — and reveal the truth. To merit her praise and approval was a challenge that made the impossible seem simple.

Tufts of red hair poked out from under ear muffs and the peak of his sealskin cap, above eyes that stung — and not with the cold. He had learned early to sublimate emotion. Experience was deepening the grim lines already suggested in the long thin face, and the cryptic young sailor's bearing scarcely suggested a man in love as he fought against terror. Women died in childbirth, and the doctor had seemed worried. Suppose something should happen to Anna giving birth to their child? *Their child!* A feeling of profound strangeness came over him at the thought of seeing his son for the first time.

But a daughter was born that night, and the son did not arrive until two years later. And that night . . . .

In the early hours of morning he reached home. The house was brightly lighted. A thick cloud of tobacco smoke billowed out as he opened the door. Then from upstairs, he heard a baby's cry. Dazed with exhaustion and excitement, he glared at the parlor table where a group of tipsy, noisy boarders, coats off and shirts loosened, were playing poker.

"By God!" he roared, wrenching the nearest lodger out of his chair. He flung the startled man back against the wall. "You God damned son of a bitch — where in hell do you think you are — *tonight*?"

It made no difference that money was scarce, that bills would be greater now. Nothing made any difference but that Anna should have privacy and quiet and a decent home.

But he was not dealing with tender spirits. These hard-muscled, brawny woodsmen had bargained for room and board and a place to enjoy their leisure. Whiskey had its slowing effect, but stepped up their belligerence. With the strength of the enraged, Tom managed to eject them, to lock the door after them; then stand half-conscious, bruised and bloody, until he could focus his swelling eyes and go to his wife.

The timid little neighbor who had been attending Anna peered over the stair rail in horror. He stumbled past her.

"Oh, Tom — what have you done?" Anna begged. "We can't afford it — not yet, Tom." She smoothed the tumbled red hair. It was a faint smile, but proud.

"Wait and see," he said grimly. "Now — *where's that baby?*"

As weeks passed, Jim Reid found that he had a different individual to deal with in Tom's new estate as father. Two years had done something to Tom — two years of hard tempering.

Corrigan, McKinney Company of Cleveland had offered him a job. Considering it, he gave his father an ultimatum. Unless a salary demand was met, Jim Reid could find himself another assistant. Jim Reid cursed mildly and met the terms. He had anticipated this, but held out as long as possible. That was his way of doing business, and his way usually worked. But not always —

It was about this time that his salvaging work on the sunken steamer *Cayuga* was attracting attention all over the country. A package freighter built at a cost of $200,-

000 and belonging to the Lehigh Railroad Company, she had come to grief off Waugoshance Point in the Straits of Mackinac. Here in the island-divided channel, a long spit of dead-white shingle outcrops above the water. Lights on Ile-aux-Galets (or Skilligalee, as the sailors call it), Beaver and Fox Islands, flash a warning. But fog and snow and treacherous currents will have their way. And weather — which is the sailor's Nemesis.

The *Cayuga* lay in one hundred feet of water, practically undamaged and as good as new. Her machinery, it was said, was unharmed. She was a new ship. Backed financially in the project by Edmund Hall, Jim Reid bought expensive equipment and a special tug, the *Whalen;* pumped out the grain cargo, which was swelling and threatening to buckle the plates, and employed extra skilled labor.

Using six steel pontoons, costing around $15,000, thirty six feet long and thirteen feet in diameter, bought from Roebling Company in Chicago, Jim Reid employed cables with two eyes in them and encircled the pontoons. Slipping cables underneath the boat, the pontoons were lowered, shackled and filled with air and kept off the bottom until the diver could adjust the cables on them and let them fill entirely. When this was done, results were expected. But one pontoon parted an eight inch cable — and another, and another. The operation proved useless.

This was the only time the Reid Company ever lost a diver. As the two divers started down, Jim Reid cautioned them to go down gradually to that intense depth, and wait for air; submerge twenty feet and wait. Then another twenty feet, and so on. But the men disregarded these warnings and one paid with his life. His head became so full of blood that they had difficulty in removing the helmet.

The pontoons are still there. The loss of the job to the Reid Company was $150,000. And two suspenseful, expensive nerve-wracking years were lost as well. The *Cayuga* refused to respond. Hall's confidence in Jim Reid had been high, and the future had looked bright for the Reid Company, for it was said that if Jim's efforts to raise the *Cayuga* were successful, it would be one of the greatest achievements ever recorded in connection with fresh water wrecking. But his efforts failed. It was a bad guess on Jim Reid's part and the loss was hard to face. His morale affected after wide adulatory newspaper publicity, failure left him chagrined and embarrassed and fearful that his backer would risk nothing further financially. As was usual after severe reverses, he disappeared for a while to meet failure in his own way.

In that interlude, in the year 1898, Tom's son Thom was born, and the incident of the *Sharpless* occurred. At Anna's side, overcome with gratitude at her safe delivery and the birth of little Thom, Tom gave small thought to the Reid Company and its problems. But he had been home only a few hours when the office called insisting on his immediate return.

Still smarting from the *Cayuga* debacle — with Jim Reid unavailable — the Reid Company had stumbled on a piece of luck. The *Sharpless,* a bulk freighter of 4,500 tons, canal size, built at a cost of $150,000 and owned by the Quebec Steamship Company, had run on Duck Island, along the eastern shore of Lake Huron with a full load of grain, and foundered. The owners seeking bids contracted the Reids. This was a welcome and badly needed opportunity.

Desperate with anxiety for his wife, longing to stay with her yet goaded by the urgency of the matter that called him back, Tom knelt beside Anna's bed trying to explain his plight.

"Get there as fast as you can." She smiled feebly. "And bid wisely, Tom. You're in a tight place . . . Can you handle the job alone — with your father away, and—"

"I could raise it alone — *now*!" He picked up his son with awkward gentleness, studied him with awe. "Anna, you ain't got any idea what you mean to me."

"Oh, *ain't* I?" The pain-shadowed eyes twinkled. "Now hurry up and get back there — before the Great Lakes Towing Company sneak the job away from you."

On reaching the distressed ship and inspecting her, Tom found that the expense of raising and repairing her for the Company's use would run into at least $25,000. She was built high in the bow, no cabins aft', 260 feet in length, tonnage 2,000.

His bid was lowest. Later conferring with the owners, he saw their disinclination to follow through on a project that insurance did not cover substantially. Tom feared complete rejection and loss of a badly needed job, so he made a proposition on his own — out of the blue. He had seen that with certain expenditures the *Sharpless* could be reconditioned, taken over and made available for the Reid use. The freight rates for moving ore, coal and grain were high, and the venture was sure to prove lucrative. She would pay for herself and the salvaging several times over — and repay a financial backer in the enterprise with generous interest.

He asked the *Sharpless* owners if they would consider selling her where she lay — at a price he dared mention. $8,500. After some discussion, the owners agreed.

Emboldened by this, Tom now braced himself to approach Edmund Hall, and managed to blurt out the salient points of his argument before Hall gestured him aside contemptuously. Hall had suffered a big loss in the matter of the *Cayuga*.

"Your father showed poor judgment in sending you here with such a proposition as this," he told Tom coldly. "I thought he had more sense — after what's happened."

"My father has nothing to do with it!" roared Tom, feeling now there was nothing to lose. "He doesn't even know I'm here."

"That's likely!" scoffed Hall. "Who's running that business anyway — a young renegade like you?"

"He runs it," flamed Tom, "but it's a helluva a big business. One man can't be everywhere."

"And just where is he — that's more important?" The Hall gaze was stony.

"He's — he's in Montreal," Tom blurted out. "On a bigger proposition. He's tied up. I'm handling this on my own." He'd never know how he though up that wild one.

"Well, you young puppy — " Hall got to his feet. "And you think for one minute I'd sink another cent in a Reid deal — after the *Cayuga*? Money's too hard to come by to throw it away like that."

Tom walked over to him looking down from his great height, white with anger. "You can sit at your desk and gamble, sir. Out on the boats, we gamble with our lives and you take the profits. There are other men I can go to. They have money — and vision. Good day, sir!"

Edmund Hall's scorn was hard to take. Things looked bad. Jim Reid was still absent, business too quiet, and no profitable prospects in sight.

And then Edmund Hall sent for Tom. He had investigated the *Sharpless* situation, and a hot-headed Tom, modern edition of his keen, fighting father, had sold him on an idea. Hall liked fearlessness and frankness and initiative, and he knew ability when he saw it. The *Sharpless* was bought from the underwriters.

Jim Reid returned to the scene, stunned at Tom's successful move and at finding his Company again under the financial sponsorship of Edmund Hall — something he hadn't hoped for ever again.

The *Sharpless* was salvaged, the debt paid, and a new source of revenue acquired for the Reid Company. The prestige and assets of the firm had increased, but such assets meant new expenses of maintenance, demanded more jobs in the salvage field. And there were other debts. There was, too, a Reid mill at Bay City and one at Alpena, units to maintain and keep busy. The Trenton mill, south of Detroit and owned by Edmund Hall, processed the logs from Hall's vast Canadian timber interests. This was a source of steady income for the Reids who had secured a good contract.

Then unexpectedly, the Canadian Government passed a law forbidding the rafting of logs to the United States for processing. This was a blow to the very heart of the Reid Company which was running many millions of feet of Canadian logs a year. Jim Reid wrestled with the problem and decided to move to Sarnia, Ontario, and to carry on his business from that base under the name of The Reid Wrecking and Towing Company of Sarnia.

At this time, for $25,000, he bought the Dunford-Alverson drydock across the river in Port Huron, Michigan, from a lumber dealer named Haynes who had taken over the mortgage for that amount. This had never proven a paying investment because of what seemed to be the dock's irremediable faults. Sand working out from under the gates made it impossible to empty the dock satisfactorily.

James Reid studied the situation and ordered an excavation on the side of the gate. He pumped out all the sand. After diver Dave Seagrave sank a pipe, the space was filled with concrete and the fault rectified. There was no further leakage, and the Reid Company from then on used the drydock to repair ships.

Now Reid's Detroit mill at Bay City was dismantled and the equipment shipped to his shore property at Sarnia on the St. Clair River. On his barge MacDougal were loaded the two big gang saws, two great circular saws, engines and such. And with this tow, the tug *Protector,* with Tom Reid in command, set out on the morning of a day that was to go down in history. The day of the Galveston 'blow.'

Saginaw Bay in the best of weather is never calm, but the sea was bad that day. And the valuable cargo, though well secured, threatened to break loose. The *Protector* made her way out into Lake Huron in the worst storm ever to strike the Lakes up to that time. The Galveston 'blow' played no favorites. From Lake Michigan where the steamers were stormbound, where the great Traverse Bay Orchards were shattered, where thousands of dollars worth of fruit waiting shipment on the docks was destroyed; to Lake Superior, where angry waves battered the shores and menaced unfortunate ships enroute — to Lake Huron, where hurricane winds tossed the *Protector* and barge *MacDougal* about like toys.

"We're in a bad way, sir," muttered the wheelsman, looking back over his shoulder at the frothing sea as it piled over the stern and hid the plunging tow with its vital cargo aboard.

"Kincardin harbor's over there." Tom gestured east toward Ontario's shore and gave a steering order.

The man repeated it dutifully, his voice doubtful —

almost mutinous. He added, "She's the shallowest harbor on this coast, and we're deep draught."

"We're a good fifty miles from Goderich." Captain Tom filled his pipe. "Sure, there's a wind. It's blowin' hard, but wind raises the water. Where's your guts, man?"

They made Kincardin, and the wind raised the water and their draught was accommodated. Behind them not far off, another ship kept to her course, headed for Goderich. She went down with all aboard.

But Tom was inclined to count too much on his luck. That December of 1899, his father entrusted to him the piloting of their tug *Aldrich* which had been contracted for by the Pere Marquette Railroad to break ice in the St. Clair River and to facilitate cross-river ferry passage between Sarnia and Port Huron. Through no fault of Tom's, the *Aldrich* 'got pinched' in the yard-deep ice and sank despite all efforts to release her. Tom and the crew walked ashore.

There was a violent scene with his father. "How about Spring — and navigation?" roared the old man. "How about river traffic? Penalties?"

"When the ice goes out," Tom said grimly, "I'll raise her.

"And you think I'd let you handle our equipment — you — you bungling —"

Tom walked away, white-lipped. The accident had not been his fault. The humiliation stung.

When the ice went out in the Spring, his father happened to be in Montreal. With air-power, Tom raised the *Aldrich.* He stripped her of machinery, bought another old hull on his own, one growing moss in the shipyard, and after that investment of a few hundred dollars, went about reconditioning the ship which was eventually called the *J. M. Diver,* a tug to be proud of. Named after the president of the Cleveland Saw Mill Company, that gentleman's pleasure reinstated Tom in his father's good graces.

"He's almost got me believing it was his own idea," Tom told Will.

"He didn't get where he is today by letting the other fellow take the glory," chuckled Will.

The *Diver* — originally built at a cost of $15,000 was eventually sold for $28,000 to a Company in Quebec. And there was a thousand dollar bonus for Tom which he promptly endorsed over to Anna for a sealskin coat.

The check went into the bank instead, in a separate account, planned for the children's education. Her brown cloth coat, she insisted, would do for another year.

Always fond of jewels, Tom had longed to give her a diamond at the time of their engagement. Whenever he mentioned it, she laughed at his regret. One day he brought her a piece of amethyst quartz he found along the shore of Lake Superior. And when she exclaimed at its beauty, "Some day," he promised, "I'll give you an emerald as big as a hen's egg. Wait and see!" She only smiled. She was thinking of college for Thom — music for Helen. Emeralds, indeed!

Their son Thom was a boy of two and another daughter, Clara, had arrived when Tom — now thirty — moved his family from Bay City to Port Huron. Port Huron, too, had its handsome thoroughfare skirting the St. Clair River — broad, tree-lined Military Street.

But Anna had no social ambitions. She wanted the good life for her family — a sound house in a wholesome if less important section. And that was found, bought and sacrificed for. Luxuries could wait. The foundation of an educational fund must be laid, and no nonsense about it. To Anna, the basic values came first.

Though it was necessary to live aboard the tugs much of the time, there were brief periods of inactivity which permitted a few hours at home with Anna and the children — just across the river. Inspection was managed then, boilers washed, lifeboats checked — perhaps a timber required to replace a fender streak, painting or repairs accomplished. And brief jaunts into the Lake to 'shoot ashes.'

The monotonous rafting cruises were a hard discipline for a man of Tom's vitality and drive. There was too much time to worry over problems, too little opportunity to release energy. He was building up toward a mental and physical crisis. Responsible for vast acres of logs, he was helpless against weather and sea. There was always the possibility of break-up and loss, when debts already hounded the company. The dangers of salvaging seemed minor by comparison. But there was money in rafting, and the Reid Company needed every penny to be made before the day would come when they were not only solvent but rich.

The Reids were early in towing traffic across Lake Huron. Most of the logs came from Spanish River in Georgian Bay. The logs were cut during the winter and with spring floods dropped into the river and floated down. A boom stretched across the river at its mouth, and behind this the logs were guided into a chute which led to the bagging booms. When a boom was filled, a tug would haul it away and replace it with another.

Two types of booms were used. Round booms were contrived by taking large cork pine logs and drilling a four-inch augur hole near each end. A piece of hard maple was let into the log, between the bole and the end, obliquely, to take the wear of the chain that held the logs together. The chain allowed the logs to ride about a foot apart, the open end of the chain being closed with a cold-shut link.

For bagging booms or rafting in calm weather, especially when towing, the enclosed logs tended to jump over or slip under the boom. To meet this difficulty, James Reid devised the Patent Towing Boom. This consisted of four logs bolted together with a separating block at each end and the middle. It floated with the lightest log at top, well out of water, and the lower log well below the draft of the loose logs inside the boom.

From the bagging booms, a raft of some three or four million feet of logs would be assembled, surrounded by a round boom, and outside this a patent boom. The tug would make fast and start out of Mississauga Passage, choosing her weather if possible. Once clear of the Passage, she took the weather as it came.

A sound tug with power could handle such rafts alone. Later, for greater safety, two tugs were used. The *Winslow* was famous for her good lines and exceptional speed. The *James Reid,* the *Sarnia City,* the *J. M. Diver* and the *S. M. Fisher* were capable of meeting any requirement.

Pilot rules demanded that the tug warn navigation that it had a raft in tow. And the warning consisted of a blast from three to five seconds on a Modoc whistle. The sound of a Modoc whistle approximated the eerie screech of an air raid siren. As it swung up and down the scale across the water it seemed to echo to the ends of the earth.

A log raft drubbed along at perhaps a mile an hour. At night, stakes set in the patent boom carried warning lights — one on either beam and a third astern. The tug carried two extra white lights for'd, besides ordinary running lights. In good weather, the raft-lights could be lit without difficulty as a crew member made the rounds in a yawl. But in bad weather, they had to trust to chance.

One night, the *Bosco Belle,* with Tom Reid at the wheel, was downbound with a raft when an upbound steamer was detected not far off — the *Jewett* of the Western Line. A big steamer of the day, built at a cost of more than $200,000, she loomed formidably against the spangled sky.

The weather was bad. The *Bosco Belle* sounded her siren, but the *Jewett* came on. The tug slowed, veered off her course so her stack would not hide the raft from the steamer's searchlight. The captain of the *Jewett* either did not see the raft or decided it was getting out of his way. The inevitable happened. He hit the raft, the stem of his ship went over the boom, and probably before he realized it his steamer was corralled inside the far-reaching boom and within a sea of logs.

An exchange of diatribes followed that ran the gamut of marine profanity. The *Jewett* captain demanded that the boom be opened. Tom laughed at him. The *Jewett* captain threatened to smash his way out. Tom dared him to face the bill for such an act.

The boom was not opened, and the *Jewett* remained a humiliated captive through the night, moving at a snail's pace with the raft. With daylight, Tom unshackled the boom and released him. There was a brief and pungent exchange of farewells.

In heavy weather, even a double boom was not enough to hold the logs. If the boom broke, the tugs would cast off and take hold of the open ends and try to round up strays, and unshackle. Logs that escaped would eventually drift ashore, to be salvaged by fishermen and beachcombers.

When a raft was sighted off the lightship at the mouth

of the St. Clair River, extra tugs would steam out to assist, bringing along a cutting boom. The patent boom would be unshackled and the inner boom opened. Each tug would take an end of the round boom and an end of the cutting boom and move in to the bobbing logs. Here they would meet with a wide sweep about the middle, and enclose half the logs in the cutting boom.

The cutting boom ran slack, and as the raft moved along, two tugs would manouever it into an approximate rectangle. Then stay lines, consisting of steel hawsers with chain ends, would be carried across the raft at each third of its length and made fast. This made for successful passage through the rapids and adjusted its width so other ships could pass the raft in the narrow channel.

With the rapid current at this point, the raft might make four miles an hour, and it was then necessary to beach it. Here an open shore boom waited to close on it. Then the tugs would return for the remaining section, repeat the process and after a brief lay over, start north again, towing their empty booms back to Spanish River.

A typical season in the beginning of the century is recorded fragmentarily in the following log of the tug *James T. Reid:*

May 10—Departed Sarnia for Byng Inlet 1 AM. Lightship 1:40 AM. Deckhand had bad accident in fire hole. 6:30 AM. Hauled in for Harbor Beach 7:45 AM. Put deckhand James Francis ashore and had doctor attend him. Departed Harbor Beach 10:45 AM. Cove Island 9:45 PM. Byng Inlet gas buoy 3 AM. Mouth of river 3:30 AM. Went up to dock at 5 AM. Lay for rest of day. Wind NW to N blowing hard.

May 11—Lying in Byng Inlet awaiting weather to start raft. Wind NW blowing hard.

May 12—5:30 AM. Left Byng Inlet dock for mouth of river. Arrived mouth 6 AM. Wind NW blowing hard. Went back to dock to lay for rest of day.

May 13—Lying in Byng Inlet awaiting weather to start raft. Wind NW to W blowing hard.

May 14—4:10 AM. Left dock for mouth of river. Lay until 5:10 AM awaiting tug *Magnetawan* to come down and let go snubs. Wind NE light. *Magnetawan* went back and got tug *McNaughton* to come and help tail raft out. 9:30 AM. Put tow-line on and started for Midland with raft.

May 15—Pulled all day. Variable winds shifting to NE and blowing fresh.

May 16—Pulled all day. Moderate NE wind.

May 17—Pulled all day. Moderate variable winds.

May 18—Pulled all day. Western Island 1:20 AM S to W winds. Going astern from 1 PM. Started ahead again 5 PM.

May 19—Pulled all day. Hope Island 1 AM. Giant's Tomb 10 AM. West NW wind blowing hard. Let go tow line and left for Penetang. 5:45 PM. When tug *Wanipiti* came out and took charge of raft. Arrived Penetang 6:10 PM. Departed Penetang for Sarnia 8 PM.

May 20—Cabot's Head 3:15 AM. Flower Pot 5:05 AM. Cove Island 5:35 AM. Harbor Beach 3:50 PM. Sanilac 6:35 PM. Lightship 9:05 PM. Sarnia 9:30 PM.

May 21—Left dock to pull patent booms out of pond

9 AM. Finished work on booms 11:45 AM. Left for Miller's coal dock 12:30 PM. Started coaling. Put on 25 tons fuel. Finished coaling 1:30 PM. Arrived drydock 1:50 PM.

Intervening days at drydock.

May 26—Finished coaling 6:20 PM and left for Sarnia. Put ice and supplies aboard and lay for rest of night.

May 27—Lay at dock all day awaiting weather to start with booms for Byng Inlet. Fresh northerly winds and NE storm signals up. Came back to dock 5 PM and lay for rest of night.

May 28—Lay at dock awaiting weather to start with booms for Byng Inlet. Left dock for booms. Weather bad. Went out and shoved tail of booms in and made them fast. Arrived back at dock 5:10 PM. Strong NE wind.

May 29—Lying at dock awaiting weather to start with booms for Byng Inlet. Fresh NE wind. Left dock for booms 3:15 PM when wind moderated. 3:40 PM. Put tow-line on and departed with booms for Byng Inlet. Lightship 5:45 PM. Light northerly winds.

Much of the same to June 17th—

3:45 AM. Left dock to tow cutting booms out to raft. Arrived raft 8 AM. Coupled cutting booms on raft, waited un *Fisher* pulled it in closer. 12:30 PM. Started guying up. Piston in reverse broke. 1:40 PM. Left raft for Port Huron drydock to have repairs made. Had new piston rod made at drydock. Arrived back at Sarnia midnight.

And on June 22nd—

7 AM. Left for Byng Inlet dock to send message to Sarnia. Blowing too hard from NW to spill raft into patent-booms. Lay at dock until 1:30 PM, taking coal out of stern, then went back to raft. Lay by raft until 5:20 PM. Until wind moderated and tug *McNaughton* arrived with another bag to put in raft. Started spilling 5:20 PM. Finished spilling 11 PM.

Days of waiting for weather. Then on July 10th—

Pulled all day. Strong NE wind. Tug Sarnia City arrived 12 midnight. Cove Island 2:30 AM. Bear's Rump 2:55 AM. Byng Inlet gas buoy 3 PM. Byng Inlet 4 PM. Made booms fast and went back to look for 65 booms which broke adrift on way over. Lay at Bear's Rump until daylight.

July 11—6 AM. Weather foggy. Went over to Flower Pot Island and then down to Dunk's Bay to try to locate booms. Located booms in Tobermory at 9 AM. Left for Inlet with booms at 9:30 AM. Arrived Inlet 9 PM. Lay by raft rest of night.

This sketched an average period of Tom Reid's life. An hour or two occasionally with Anna and the children, then back to the tug; fueling, supplies, and north again for the rafts. The dread monotony, the anxieties, the crises when a boom broke, logs scattered, storms came up and drove them back for miles that must be traversed again.

The four years of financial panic that preceded McKinley's election to presidential office had worked hardships on the Reid Company. With his accession to office, business began to grow better and prosperity was slowly resumed.

But in the meantime, Jim Reid's health had suffered. Loss of sleep, financial crises, anxiety — these were not without effect. Yet his amazing vitality, which was reflected and intensified in his son Tom, seemed fairly resilient. He denied sickness, and called upon his reserve strength with fierce determination. And now in the bitter November weather of 1900, suffering from fever and lung congestion, he prepared to leave for Montreal on a business trip with the slim hope of recouping some losses.

As he came into the office, color high, eyes glazed with fever, Tom and the others were deep in discussion of national affairs. The United States had annexed Hawaii. It had also fought Spain for the liberation of Cuba, and in the war had conquered and annexed the Spanish colonies of Puerto Rico and the Philippines.

Busy at the safe, rounding up his papers, over his shoulder Jim Reid observed, "You may live to see trouble over this thing. McKinley's a great man, but he's flung the American flag across the path of Japanese imperialism. Some day those little yellow men may sink their fangs into us."

There were cynical guffaws in answer. But Tom stood looking thoughtfully out at the river.

His father, without revealing his own plans, regarded him briefly. "You there, Tom—" He was sharp, but deep in his tone was the always betraying pride in the son who thought things through. "Get off to Marquette on the *Bosco Belle*. Pick up those booms before winter closes in."

Tom's favorite tug was the *Bosco Belle*. She had begun life in 1888 as a little passenger steamer, and had had negligible success in the field for which she was intended. Her initial cost was $50,000. Her next role was action across Lake Michigan, towing scows loaded with freight cars. But when this failed to pay, she was offered for sale at which time James Reid bought her for his rafting business for approximately $15,000. At last she had found the field for which she was best fitted. Many a long lonely night Tom piloted her through the darkness, his hand hard and sure on a wheel he could trust.

The day was to come when James Reid had her completely overhauled, changed the machinery, scrapped the passenger structure and renamed her the *Ottawa.* But Tom felt her own name suited her best. And when some years later she burned at the dock in Bayfield, Wisconsin, he blustered and swore as if at the bad turn of luck, but grieved as he would at the passing of a friend.

But in that November of 1900, following his father's orders, he boarded the *Bosco Belle* and left for Marquette. Reaching Lake Superior, the tug ran into a severe northwest gale and he made Marquette with difficulty around midnight.

Michigan's Marquette harbor is encircled with timber-crowned hills that overlook the endless blue of Lake Superior—shielding the city within the curve of Iron Bay. The wooded arm of Presque Isle is studded with black rock formations and red sandstone bluffs. And the long iron ore dock serves the freighters with the rich mine yield from Ishpeming and Negaunee a few miles inland.

This is bleak country in early winter. And that night after the *Bosco Belle* had berthed at Spear's dock, a watchman came down with a message from Mr. Harvey, the managing director of The Pittsburg Steamship Company, who was waiting to contact Tom Reid by telephone from Duluth.

Tom called and learned that a Steel Trust barge towed by the freighter *James H. Court*—a whaleback built at a cost of $200,000 a few years before—was adrift near Grand Island about forty miles east.

"I'm sending our shore officer, Captain Kidd, down tonight," Harvey told him. "He gets into Marquette at two. Take him with you, and go out and pick up the barge."

Tom agreed, and followed through. With daylight, he left in search of the 'pig' barge. A tremendous sea was running and visibility was bad. But at last the derelict was sighted. She was dangerous to work around, and in the trough of the sea was rolling badly. A sailor could not stand on her rounded deck.

Tying an inch and a quarter line to a 1200 foot, ten inch hawser, Tom made the other end of the line fast to the tug and approached her as close as possible against the heavy sea — ship wobbling, wind blowing savagely. Then with a bolt in the end to weight it, he threw the heaving line and managed to get a tow line on. This he did with the windlass end. The boat drifted badly, but when Tom 'fetched up' on the line, they had it fast. He towed the barge in to Marquette and there news of further trouble awaited him. Manager Harvey had wired Captain Kidd. Their barge *Smeaton,* worth $100,000 to her owners, was 'on' at Au Train Island, about twenty five miles away. Reid was to go to her aid.

Nature lovers will tell you that Au Train Island is a little paradise just beyond Laughing Fish Point where it hugs Shelter Bay — its forests a dream world, its terrain a fragrant stretch of wild flowers. But sailors will tell you that its beckoning shores offer a rocky trap in stormy weather.

The *Bosco Belle* set out again and reaching the *John Smeaton* found the rival tug *Favorite* of the Great Lakes Towing Company (in which the Pittsburg Steamship Company had an interest) pulling on the barge.

For seven days the *Bosco Belle* pulled until the intensity of the storm forced her to leave for Marquette. Tom had obeyed Manager Harvey's orders. He had gone to the *Smeaton's* assistance and followed the procedure indicated. But he knew that was not the answer. He contacted the Captain of the *Favorite* and the Company's insurance agent aboard her; told them it was not a matter of pulling her off. That had been proven. Air-power would handle it.

The shore captain presently admitted he was about to turn the salvaging job over to the *Favorite* alone, since the *Favorite's* captain was an older man, familiar with salvaging for years, and should know more about it than a fellow of Tom's age. However, he agreed that Tom might go aboard the *Smeaton* and outline his ideas—length of time, extra equipment necessary and estimated price, since Tom was so emphatically confident the job could be done his way. Calculating rapidly, Tom gave a price of $50,000 to raise the *Smeaton,* and declared he could release her with air-power in two days.

Manager Harvey was contacted by the insurance agent. The bid was accepted, and Tom left at once with the *Bosco Belle* for Sarnia. Harvey had confidence in the Reid name.

When Tom reached Detour, he found the $50,000 steam barge *Harvey Kendall* lying at anchor. The distressed Captain tried to make a deal to tow his ship to Detroit because there was engine trouble, and navigation about to close.

Tom considered briefly. It would mean a fat towing fee in addition to the Steel Trust commission.

The deal was made.

Taking the booms to Detour, he laid them up for the winter and, rehearsing an argument to give his father in a crisis, telephoned the tug office at Sarnia. He found that James Reid was hospitalized in Montreal with pleurisy. With the complication of interference from that quarter dismissed, Tom made his plans.

Towing the *Kendall* to Port Huron south across Lake Huron was managed with utmost — almost dangerous — speed, but without incident despite the lateness of the season and bad weather. As he neared Port Huron, the tug *Sarnia City* came out as arranged, took over the lines and towed the *Kendall* to Detroit.

The *Bosco Belle's* return trip to Marquette was not so simple. The two air compressors, each weighing a ton, were secured, and they started off on one of the roughest voyages Tom ever made. But they reached the Lake Superior port safely.

Securing the air compressors, the crew placed timbers across two lifeboats, raised the *Smeaton* on her davits and set up the compressors. The hose was attached to the tanks and the air compressors started.

The compressors had been running several hours when it occurred to Tom that the 'pig' *James H. Court,* was loaded with coal and lying at the dock. He decided while the compressors were running to go up and telephone Harvey for permission to use the *Court*. Her added power would supply the extra help needed.

Harvey agreed, under the condition that the tug *Schenck* would go with the *Court* — the Reid Company paying one hundred dollars an hour for the tug. If the *Smeaton* was not released — no pay.

Tom took the chance, and with the *Bosco Belle,* went back to lie near the *Smeaton* until morning when the *Court* and *Schenck* would come out to help.

But with daylight, he saw the *Smeaton*—responding to his earlier efforts—afloat, and tugging at her anchors against the strong waves. Securing the lines, he towed her in to Marquette. As they rounded the breakwater, the *Court* and *Schenck* loomed up, and the clamor of whistles seemed thunderous in the quiet northern morning. Admiring crews lined up on tug and 'pig.' And Tom, grinning with pride, saluted them. His faith in air-power vindicated, he had won a fifty thousand dollar contract for the Reid Company. He had earned $5,000.00 for the *Kendall* towing, $3,000.00 for the 'pig' — and the whole trip up and back, all told, had not cost them over $5,000.00, at a time when they were deeply in debt. It was a most profitable trip. And Manager Harvey's good will and admiration were an added gain.

James Reid arrived home just before Christmas without notifying the office of his plans. He happened in at a moment when Tom was parading up and down with a silk hat at an angle over one eye, 'galluses' loose over the shoulders of his red-plaid wool shirt.

"Now Anna will have to have a satin dress and velvet opera cloak to go with this top hat," he declared.

"What kind of shenanigans is this?" demanded the father, still white and drawn from his recent illness.

Tom plucked a note from the hat box and handed it to him — a note signed by the Captain of the *Kendall*—

> "For towing the *Kendall* down Lake Huron faster than a horse can run. Was the devil after you, Tom?"

Old Jim grinned and tossed the note aside. "I guess he never had the scent of $50,000 in his nostrils," he said, by way of accolade, having been kept informed of Tom's activities. "Anyone seen my pipe?"

"I don't know about your pipe," Tom spoke up briskly. "But I hereby announce none of you will see me for the next week or two. I'm spending the holidays home, and you don't need to call me. I won't be around. Why, I ain't had a good look at my new baby yet, and her nine months old!"

With release, he fled to his home, ever amazed at his Anna. The days of catering to boarders were over. Now she could devote her entire time to her family. She could scent out a bargain better than he could scent out a deal; a touch here, a touch there — and charm resulted. Fiercely she protected their income, making the most of household supply sales, making the children's clothes, concocting economical dishes and achieving miracles for the table.

But Tom was unhappy. This wasn't good enough for Anna. Some day — she'd see. Maybe the time wasn't far off. She wouldn't have to work the whole day through — cleaning, cooking, polishing, washing and ironing. He could not forget the way he had found her, and longed to restore her to that estate.

But she laughed off his occasional declarations. "What's the matter with you, Tom Reid? Why, I'm the luckiest woman on earth. Who could want more?"

"You're going to get it — and soon!" he promised.

And the day he came home with the silk hat, he handed her some bank notes. "Go down and get yourself a new outfit. The day after Christmas we're going to Detroit and have a little outing at The Russell House."

"But — the children?" she gasped.

"We'll get Mrs. Sterling to look after them. I said— *"we're going!"*

They went, and in style. Her poise and manner at table, her knowledge of food, her graciousness made him proud. He felt that his dignity was restored in providing her with that interlude — while she bemoaned the extravagance. But he knew that she found a taste of the old life sweet. And his resolve grew. Some day — and soon — he'd buy her a house on Military Street, the kind she belonged in, the kind their children belonged in, and there wasn't enough danger in the world to scare him off from realizing that ambition!

He went back to the nerve-wracking routine, grateful for that brief time with his wife and family. The Christmas season remained glamorous in memory. Christmas was the best time of the year. He would always spend it with his family — no matter what happened. He had promised Anna, and he would keep that promise, so help him God!

But the next year found him helpless again. . . .

CHAPTER FOUR

Late in the fall of 1901 the Steamer *Newago,* loaded with grain, went ashore on Cove Island in Georgian Bay on the inside channel. She was owned by Henry McMorran, Port Huron industrialist. Built a few years earlier at a cost of $75,000 in the Marine City shipyard, she was intended as a lumber carrier — a ship 260 feet in length. The insurance company awarded the Reids the contract at a price of $25,000.

Now almost December, Tom realized that if salvage work were begun, Christmas must be sacrificed since it would take some time. But plans were immediately effected, and his father dispatched him to the scene on the tug *Protector* with the barge *Mary Battle* in tow, and which they planned to use as a lighter. The *Bosco Belle* went along.

The ship *Newago* was badly exposed to the lake shore winds where she lay, almost defying rescue. Followed the eternal wait for weather and no contact immediately with the outside world, while Christmas grew closer. Snow by now was ten feet high. Trails had to be broken through from Big Tobermory to Little Tobermory across the peninsula, as there was no other method of communication. A paradise in summer, this was a wintry hell.

Tom muttered to himself that he should give up the whole thing and find a way to a better life. And grumbling, knew in his heart that this always was and always would be the thing he had to do.

Now James Reid came north on another tug. There was a scene—Tom rebellious and angry, his father grim and determined. The tugs and lighter would stay there until the *Newago* was released.

"You've got the contract, and no time limit," Tom argued. "It's impossible to go to work on the wreck in this weather. It will last for days—maybe all winter."

"I'll make the decisions," his father told him. "If the weather broke tomorrow, we'd have her off in no time." But he knew that was not true and Tom knew that he knew it.

When James Reid sailed off, he left stern orders. Tom was silent.

One evening not long afterward, with Christmas just around the corner, most of the men were having a game on the *Bosco Belle*. Toward two in the morning, with a skeleton crew only too delighted to cooperate, Tom cast off the *Protector's* lines and started for home.

The wind was north west and a heavy snow was falling. He made Cove Island, set a course for the Ducks, with the wind like the devil on the loose. At the Ducks, he had to cross mid-lake for Port Huron, but brought up at Port Clark. There were no lights, buoys or ranges, for the season of navigation had closed. But he could just discern the lighthouse.

At that point he was a hundred miles away from Port Huron. The ice was jamming bad by then, but the iron-nosed *Protector* was staunch, and the man at the wheel knew his business.

At last Point Edward came into view, and the tug fought through the ice to the rapids and finally reached a channel opening. And to the rage of the men who operated the International ferry between Port Huron and Sarnia, Tom boldly appropriated the open channel and brought the *Protector* to the dock.

Tom tied her up and went stomping into the tug office—ready for anything. If his father didn't fire him, he'd quit. He was through with the whole damned business.

As it happened, his father was there at the time. He gave Tom a long, thoughtful look, turned to the clerk who was standing by. "Like I was saying, Dick— a man's got to make his own decisions and take the consequences. He's got to have judgment — got to know when he's right or wrong; act, and abide by it. . . . Now get that message out to the *Bosco Belle*. She'll have to be there a month at least. And it looks like the *Mary Battle* is doomed for the winter there. The *Newago* will have to wait till Spring."

"Merry Christmas!" Tom shouted after him as he turned away. The answer was a shrug and a hint of a smile.

The loss on that job was about $25,000. With the *Bosco Belle* there a month, the *Mary Battle* all winter—double crews on each boat, divers, pumps, the overhead was heavy. They never got the *Newago* off. She went to pieces where she lay.

CHAPTER FIVE

He was lucky that year. He made his own luck. But it wasn't always possible. With fall came the storms — late navigation and the attendant hazards. That November of 1902 was bad from the beginning — worse than usual, and he knew he was gambling with chance for Christmas at home. For such weather would breed a bitter December.

It came to pass as he feared. And it was in a violent December storm that the Steamer *Nippewa* — a fast little ship of canal size — met with trouble. Built in England at a cost of $150,000, she had originally been employed in carrying grain. Now her duty was to serve the lighthouses along the upper Lakes and, while following her usual routine, she 'went on' at Otter Head, some miles up Lake Superior toward Port Arthur.

It was a strange accident. The force of the waves sent her in between two high-walled rocks and flung her back so that she was not visible from the open sea.

With diver and crew aboard the tug *Sarnia City,* Tom cleared for Lake Superior. There was considerable difficulty in locating the *Nippewa,* but she was found protected in a small natural harbor beyond the rocks, though in a spot not to be reached by the tug. His bid of $28,000 was offered and accepted.

With pumps aboard, Tom found the bilges all ripped for'd and aft'. A catwalk was constructed to facilitate passage back and forth. Tents were improvised from blankets and little poplar poles, and the *Nippewa* crew lived ashore.

At such times, their resourcefulness saved them from the pressure of isolation and merciless weather. A jew's harp, mouth-organ or fiddle could prove a life-saver; and a merry natured sailor was a godsend. The two crews exhausted their repertoires of stories to sustain morale. Sven Johnson's dialect and bewildered interpretation of the American and Canadian scenes provided hilarity.

There was the instance of his losses in the Ice Pool in Manitoba, and other experiences in a new country where native games puzzled him then, and still puzzled him in the telling. He would look vague and confused, yielding to slyly persuasive questions. And he would gaze almost piteously from one to the other as they roared and slapped their thighs at his sober account of his brush with the game of Bingo.

"— and ever'body, he sit still. And the man call out—like—'ten,' and some people put penny on number. Maybe he say 'fifteen'—and more people put penny on that number. Ever'body ver' still. And then maybe he say 'four' —and someone shout 'Bingo!' And then lot of people they shout 'Aw sit!' And that the big game. Bingo — Aw Sit. What you think of that? Humph!"

Blankly he regarded their boisterous amusement. But because of Sven and his kind, the long job seemed less grim.

Work went on. The diver and his assistant were patching the full length of the ship with cement, since gravel was available. They planned to let the cement set for four or five days. But twenty four hours after it had been placed, an ominously brewing storm forced Tom to take a chance and pump her out. He then refloated her and manoeuvred her out and to a near by harbor where he put her on a sandy bottom. There the diver affixed a permanent patch after which the *Sarnia City* set off for the lower Lakes with the *Nippewa* in tow.

With a $28,000 bid for the job, and expense running to only $3,000 with the breaks all their way, the Reid Company made a handsome profit that was sorely needed after their recent losses.

Tom and his men were on their way home, with Christmas in the offing. But bad news awaited them at Sarnia. Several freighters, loaded with grain, had been about to clear from Port Arthur for Lake Erie when the first big freeze set in. Freighters and tugs alike were imprisoned in that northern Lake Superior port. And as yet, with navigation about to close, the lighthouse keepers along the upper Lakes had not been picked up.

Lacking an ice-breaker at Port Arthur, the Canadian Department of Marine commissioned the Reid Company to go to the scene at once.

The prospects were not too happy as Tom and his

crew set out. The trip north was a steady battle against wind, sub-zero temperature and ice. But the tug *Reid,* the only boat out on Lake Superior at the time, fought through and reached Port Arthur safely. She 'broke out' the freighters, then went on her way to pick up the lighthouse keepers at Michipocoton, Passage Island, Otter Head and Caribou Island.

Along the way, Tom uneasily recognized the bad physical condition of the Captain. Not a young man, Captain LaFlamboise was apparently suffering from a bad cold, though never deserting his post regardless of storm and the wild pitching and jerk of the ship. Repeatedly urged to go to his cabin, he denied an inability to carry on.

Leaving Port Arthur, the *Reid* picked up the lighthouse keepers at Passage Island, Michopocoton and Otter Head, then went on to Caribou. When the Caribou lighthouse came into view, snow had piled on the ice fields to a depth of probably six feet, and visibility was waning. The *Reid* gave the blasts which meant rescue, but received no response. The wind was in the wrong direction, but it seemed if the men were there they should be on watch.

Deciding that another tug had preceded him to the scene, Tom advised the Captain to head for the Soo where he put off his passengers. Then he went down river to coal up, but checking with the authorities, he found that the men had not been taken from Caribou Island. Their families and the authorities were anxious.

A telegram from Ottawa to the local representative of the Canadian Department of Marine, commissioned Tom Reid to proceed to Lonely Island in Georgian Bay and pick up the lighthouse keepers there.

He was unaware that while he had been coaling, the tug *Boynton* had been sent there by the local government, fearing that further delay might be serious.

Making his way to the scene, Tom was waylaid by a message stating the *Boynton* reported that men at Lonely Island had chanced it by foot across the ice to shore, fearful of some slip-up in plans to relieve them.

Again Tom headed north for the dread Whitefish Bay and Caribou Island. Reaching Pointe Aux Pins, he spent the night, after a stormy day, and left at daylight. A gale was blowing hard from the north west, and a big sea running. If the men were still at Caribou, why hadn't they answered his signals? If the *Boynton* had not taken them off, they still must be there.

Under his orders, the *Reid* pushed forward through extremely rough weather. Tom knew the *Boynton* had been sent on also, to stand by, but she was nowhere in evidence on that bleak horizon.

When they passed Bay Mills, north of the Soo, the *Boynton* came out and followed them as far as Point Iroquois, seas washing over her. Then abruptly she turned around and went back, obviously finding conditions too risky.

The *Reid* went on, Tom deciding they would be in the lee of the Island, simplifying rescue. Approaching, he laid there waiting for the moment to attempt launching his one life boat but was driven away by wind, sea and ice-floes. By now the *Reid* was badly iced up, and it was necessary to head for Whitefish Point for shelter. There they were forced to remain for three days.

Then back to the Soo for fuel, their bunker almost empty. At the Soo they picked up a fishing boat and crew, planning to send the men ashore at Caribou Island since, if their own boat was lost, they would be without a dory at the mercy of Whitefish Bay.

This time fortunately the sea subsided, though the snow was thick.

Christmas Eve . . . . The men tried to keep it gay, and the cook struggled with a meal as festive as supplies permitted. The battered old Victrola wheezed out some popular songs. Tom opened a bottle of Scotch and the cook produced brandy from a kitchen shelf.

Christmas day found Tom aboard the fishing craft with the fishermen he had hired, and heading for shore when he saw the lighthouse keepers approaching in their own boat. Scantily dressed, they were taking no chances on another confusion of signals. Rescue could easily have come too late.

Their Christmas dinner had been a limited ration of dried fish and stale biscuits. But there were no complaints — rather, Pierre the French-Canadian winked as he said the *Reid* might have waited another hour. For after losing at pinochle for several days, his luck was coming up. Now Tony was ahead.

And Tony said he kind of hated to leave the old place alone out there for the winter. After all, a fellow's home is his castle. He managed to keep a straight face as he said it, but the pinched features, the darkly shadowed eyes told their own story.

There was laughter—and clean jokes and ribald ones. Men at last rescued from danger. And not one would have exchanged places with a business tycoon safe on land.

The *Reid* made for Michopocoton Harbor where the whole crew had their Christmas dinner and were warm and safe again. All except the Captain of the *Reid*. Tom had haunted that room where the man lay in his bunk, desperately sick in those hours when the tug had been laying over for weather. Though once again at sea, Captain LaFlamboise had made his way to the pilot house to command his ship, despite the fact that he could hardly stand.

Throughout the ordeal, Tom had seen the man, suffering from a previous lung infection, vomiting frequently day after day in a room with temperature below zero, door opening and closing constantly — so cold that the excretion would freeze in the pail. Yet feverish, the Captain would throw off the blankets, suffering further exposure.

When the rescue was finally managed and the *Reid* had reached the dock, a Marine Service doctor was called and gave a diagnosis of spinal meningitis, urging hospitalization as soon as possible.

Tom took a long chance. Once before he had seen these symptoms during a winter over at French River. His own private convictions were that the veins were frozen, and decided to follow the advice of the old adage —'like cures like'. He laid ice packs around the man's body.

Before long Captain LaFlamboise began to improve. By the time they reached the Soo—where piers were lined with joyously welcoming crowds — he was conscious. There a doctor examined him and declared that Tom's treatment had saved the Captain's life.

Taking command of the tug, Tom went to fuel, then started down St. Mary's River and struggled through six-foot ice all the way to Sailors' Encampment.

The authorities contracted with him to keep the channel open at the fee of $25.00 an hour until weather forbade further activities. And it was on a day near the end of January when he wired Anna and facetiously announced his imminent arrival to celebrate Christmas.

Her vigil began at that moment, but it was two o'clock in the morning when he came up the snowy steps balancing two suitcases jammed with Christmas gifts. Hands still in the cold wet gloves, he fumbled for the key as Anna opened the door. Anna was always waiting for him.

She had a way with words, but there were times when her silent understanding was the healing restfulness his heart needed. Now she drew off his coat, settled him in the big chair before the fire and went to prepare a hot toddy.

Exhausted, he slept. When he awoke, she was huddled on the little footstool at his knee.

She stirred. "Better go to bed, Tom. It's almost five."

"Why didn't you wake me? The fire is out. You're cold."

"I'm all right."

"I'm sorry about Christmas, Anna. It couldn't be helped."

"What do you mean? We never had such a wonderful Christmas."

He frowned. Sarcasm was not Anna's way. "Then—you didn't miss me?"

"To tell the truth," she laughed softly, "I didn't know if it was Christmas or the Fourth of July."

"What are you talking about?"

"Well, don't forget — I read the papers. There's a fellow named Reid who's been getting a lot of space lately about some rescues on Lake Superior. Show off, I calls him! Took all my time to keep track of his shenanigans. Personally, I think the paper was making it up. They were running out of news. He'd have to be two men to do half they said he did."

"See what I mean?" he grinned. "I always said you can't believe half the stuff you read in the papers."

"I know. And this time, they put in on so thick—*honestly!*—"

He drew her close hungrily, gratefully.

"Oh, Tom, Tom — if anything had happened to you—you crazy, wonderful fool!"

"All in a day's work."

They went up the stairs together.

CHAPTER SIX

The national political and financial picture at this time was not good. President Theodore Roosevelt was wielding 'The Big Stick,' but organized wealth was active in state and national governments. Laws to restrain railroads and trusts were openly flouted.

The panic of 1903 was indicated far in advance by financial developments which were in reality warning signals, but which at the time were not recognized for what they were. The depression was not very long or very serious and the upturn came in August 1904. Stock prices and security listings advanced vigorously.

It was at this time that Louis Meyers came into the Reid employ and remained a valuable asset for the rest of his working years. Born in Germany in 1875 where he learned the carpentry trade, he migrated to America in his twenties, and was working as ship's carpenter at the Reid's Port Huron drydock when, one spring day, busy on a steamer that lay on the stocks with the bottom out, he discovered that the dock had developed a leak. He summoned a diver to correct the trouble.

Occasionally after payday, it was this fellow's custom to disappear for an interval. If available, he was invariably tipsy. But in this instance, his absence was prolonged; and the dock, having been inefficiently repaired, developed further difficulty. Time was important, divers scarce, and the ship on the stocks in danger of suffering serious damage.

When all efforts to locate the diver failed, Louis Meyers considered the situation and the difference between a diver's pay and that of a ship's carpenter: from $2.50 and $3.00 a day for the latter, as against $5.00 a day for a diver — and $15.00 for each submersion.

"Why the hell can't I go down?" Meyers demanded of Tom Reid. "I know as much about it as that fellow you had."

There was little choice at the moment. Tom assigned him to the job. His repair work was a success, and he was taken on as diver for The Reid Company.

At that time diving equipment consisted of suit, helmet, weights, a five pound hammer, leather shoes with lead soles and an air hose one inch and a half in diameter. A pruning knife—built up inside, and caught to him by a chain with a snap. A four-foot rule. A carpenter's flat pencil shellacked and wrapped in electric tape — then shellacked again, with a brass knob at the end so as to stand perpendicular if dropped. A pine board six by twelve — diagram hole at the top, and a heaving line on one end tied to a cedar buoy to make survey. These were the essential tools of the diver's trade.

Modern air hose is now reduced to half the former size with the same strength. When size can be diminished, the strain is released, as the diver is pushing against the current and it is an ordeal to drag a fifty to seventy foot hose along the bottom.

A five pound hammer when striking under water becomes twenty pounds. Today an air hammer is used. And shoes are now of cast iron on the outside with rubber inner shoes and straps.

There were numerous hazards. For instance — vapor would form on the inside of the diving helmet. Sloshing vinegar against the glass would eliminate it, but for a short time only. To overcome that, a lumberjack's knitted cap was used which projected far enough to give room to rub the nose against the window and clear it.

Insured from boyhood, Meyers was now refused as a risk. But he had found the work for which he was intended and enjoyed the complete cooperation of his company. Tom Reid was frequently heard to declare that Louis Meyers could work with tools under water better than many can ashore.

Louis Meyers could build a bulkhead or coffer-dam to meet the most exacting requirements. A bulkhead is an upright partition designed to separate ship compartments or shut off water.

A coffer-dam is a superstructure built to bring a ship to the surface. It is the only practical way of raising a submerged ship where there is not more than approximately twenty feet depth. If in deeper water, pontoons are used. A superstructure cannot be built beyond twenty two feet and enjoy success.

The size of the coffer-dam depends on the depth of the water. One of these, conceived by Louis Meyers, which took forty two men four weeks to construct, had to be built on land — launched and towed out; all this with the exception of the protecting canvas, or apron.

The depth of the water indicates the required depth of the coffer-dam which has to withstand pressure on account of material found necessary to use.

To workers, Louis Meyers would indicate desirable trees in available timber tracts, trees wide enough in diameter and tall enough to reach from the tank-top of the vessel in question to the top of the hatch; to be spaced four feet apart all the way across. These would be supported with braces on opposite sides to take care of pressure. Then planking — since nothing was uniform. This affixed crosswise required fillers. There were no smooth surfaces, and equal pressure was impossible.

One coffer-dam Meyers constructed was used on two occasions afterward; taken apart and put together again, proof of his skill. He was a careful worker, but unexpected dangers were always around the corner. The curious public offered a particular menace.

On one occasion when he was submerging through a hole in the St. Clair River ice in search of a body, insistent crowds surged out and jammed close to the opening. Had the surface given away, diving equipment and assistant would have broken through as well, and Meyers would have suffocated. The police dispersed the mob just in time.

His closest brush with danger involved work on a swing-bridge in Duluth, Minnesota, which The Reid Company had contracted to restore after it had been jolted off its central pier by a ship, one end lodging deep in the river-bed mud.

As he stepped into an opening to investigate the situation, his helmet with attached goose-neck became fouled, and instantly he was swung around and inverted, with the air-hose functioning too well, and the legs of his suit over-inflated. As long as the air-pump continued, he could not right himself. Hanging upside down, he tried to signal his tender to shut off the airhose so he could right himself and surface. The tender misunderstood the signal and kept the pump going. Finally he was able to draw up his knees and get the air out of his suit-legs, soon disentangling himself. Rising rapidly to the surface, he lost consciousness. It was the closest he ever came to death.

He was completely dependable, and his loyal cooperation eased the heavy load Tom Reid was gradually being forced to assume.

Tom's time away from home was lengthening, responsibilities increasing. He was fighting for success, advantages for his family and for his relatives as well, and his nerves were wearing thin. Still only thirty five, the years of strain had begun to tell. Anna urged a more temperate approach to his work, but Tom knew that the years of his father's life were limited now as strength and judgment waned and the famous temper increased. Tom was the buffer between 'the old man' and business contacts.

Anna was expecting their fourth child, and she was not well. The doctor had been frank as to the possible outcome of her confinement. This, added to worries about debt and business problems, built up a nervous tension, and sparks flew between him and his father. A crisis came with the *Edenborn* incident.

This five hundred foot, 8,000 ton $300,000 bulk freighter of the Pittsburg Steamship Line, with its $75,000 barge *Manila,* bound for Two Harbors 'light' in early spring, went ashore in a severe storm on Split Rock between the cities of Duluth and Two Harbors. The impact drove the barge broadside to the cliff, and the steamer went up against the projecting rock and broke in two.

Contacted by Harry Colby, manager of the Pittsburg line, Tom and his father with diver Louis Meyers boarded the tug *Fisher* and went north to examine the wreck. They figured ways and means to salvage, made a bid of $35,000 for the *Edenborn* and $15,000 for the *Manila,* and the contract was signed.

Using five hundred-ton jacks, they forced the *Edenborn* up and went to work. Soon Colby and a Company associate came up from Cleveland. Impatient with what seemed to them a slow process, they ordered Jim Reid to put more men to work on the job.

At that point the famous temper broke. Reid reminded them of the signed contract and agreement, and suggested that they go about their own business and he would attend to his. The scene promised to end all future business relations between the two companies, and with the Pittsburg Steamship Company's fleet the largest on the Great Lakes, a fine source of revenue seemed lost permanently to the Reid Company.

This was a matter of small consequence to Jim Reid at the moment. He brushed off Tom's reasoning and remained adamant.

With the work finally done, they made $25,000 on the contract, but Tom regarded the check sadly. He felt that was the last contract his Company would ever have with the important Steel Trust. His own health was not too good. Anna was approaching her time. The doctor was in daily attendance and fearful of complications due to a heart condition. If anything should happen to Anna — —

Then, incredibly, the Pittsburg Steamship Company

again turned to the Reids for help. Harry Colby had had no feud with Tom who by now was considered practically the head of the firm, with James Reid's health slowly breaking. And one day the call came through from Colby. It seemed that their $250,000 freighter *William B. Schiller* — 587 foot, 8,000 tonner — had run into trouble at Point Iroquois. They had sent their own wrecker and equipment to work at releasing her. Several weeks had elapsed without results. Would Tom Reid board one of their northbound freighters at Port Huron, confer with their man at the Soo and learn if possible what the trouble was?

It was a delicate project for a rival wrecker, but Tom managed it diplomatically, though amazed at the request. He followed through, telephoned Colby stating his findings and suggestions given The Great Lakes Towing Company, one in which the Pittsburg people had an interest.

Colby was warmly appreciative and named a fee to be given. Tom refused it. He was wise enough to see that the reestablishment of good relations was of far greater value. As a result, business was resumed with the largest steamship company on the Great Lakes.

He had been afraid to hint of such a thing to Anna for fear of disappointment. And at this time, Tom felt she could not stand any let down for he was constantly apprehensive as to her condition. Now he could go to her with the bracing news! Hurrying home, he realized that the best part of it all was her pride in him, her confidence that he would always win no matter how difficult the problem.

A grave situation awaited him. Anna was very ill. Opiates had been necessary to deaden the pain, and the outcome of imminent confinement was not too promising. He sat beside her, waiting for the smile of recognition, the hand that would grope for his, the reassurance that she was all right, that it would soon be over.

"You look tuckered out," the doctor told him. "Do you ever get any sleep?"

"I've had a few hours this past week," shrugged Tom.

"Go to bed, man. There's nothing to be done at the moment. I'm going along home now, but I'll be on call. And the nurse will stand by. Don't worry. I believe Anna will come through all right, but it's a bad complication, we can't deny that," he added quietly.

Tom had reached the door with the doctor when the telephone rang. And answering, the words he heard were deadly blows against his tired brain.

"It's the *Annie Moiles*. She's gone down in the Rapids — "

"The men? — " cried Tom.

"She went down with all aboard."

The big Reid tug *Annie Moiles*. Towing her barge to Sarnia from Bay City and turning around in the Rapids to dock, she had tipped over in the whirlpool that lies in wait at that key spot where Lake Huron empties into the St. Clair River. The barge had broken away and was caught on a sand bar farther down the river.

Tom fumbled to return the receiver, his eyes wild.

"Trouble?" The doctor closed the half-opened door.

"I've got to go — " Tom told him the story. "But — how can I go now?"

"It's your job, Tom. You're needed."

"But — Anna — "

"She'd want you to go. You know that."

"It's always been like this when she's needed me." He spoke like a man in his sleep, vaguely, gaze wantering, aimless fingers plucking at hair. Always the hard decision to make, the conflicting pressure. As he got his things together and stumbled out, the doctor looked after him anxiously and shook his head. Tom Reid was pushing himself too hard. There was a look in his eyes that warned of trouble to come.

Tom stumbled along blindly. *She went down with all aboard.*

Diver Louis Meyers on that day had been sent to a job near Detroit. Now in the grim pre-dawn, Tom Reid donned a diver's outfit and went down to investigate the position and condition of the sunken tug. This was a horrible mistake, for when the seven trapped bodies, driven by the current, moved toward him — his crew— his friends — Tom's mind snapped.

The tender and assistant hauled him up when repeated signals were ignored. They took him, in a state of collapse, to the hospital and as soon as he could be moved, his brother Will — obeying Doctor's orders — accompanied him to Hot Springs, Arkansas, where he remained until his health improved. But for Tom, waiting was worse than any illness. Tom Reid despised weaklings and scorned the nursing that he called pampering. Anna was on his mind — Anna and his new daughter, Virginia. He had been assured of Anna's complete recovery, but he would be content only when he could judge for himself. Tom demanded release, and when Tom Reid voiced demands, it was best to be agreeable.

CHAPTER SEVEN

In the best of times, contracts were not always easy to come by. Competition was heavy and rival companies alert.

The Reid's main competition was the Great Lakes Towing Company of Cleveland, a sort of subsidiary of The Pittsburg Steamship Company. They had a fleet of tugs with the tug *Favorite* the flagship, their wrecker stationed at St. Ignace, and their lighters stationed at Sault Sainte Marie, St. Ignace, Detroit, Port Huron and Cleveland. While the *Favorite* was an excellent tug, she was not a wrecker and needed the assistance of a lighter to achieve salvage.

A lighter, resembling a barge in appearance, is used to remove sufficient cargo from a distressed ship in order to facilitate salvage. She has cabin and boilers astern, and one big central hatch along each side of which is built a track. On both rails, built up for foundation, rests a hoisting apparatus called a "Mickmiler.' Movable, it runs back and forth. There is a boom attached, and on cables there is a clam-shell with which to remove cargo.

The Reid Wrecking and Towing Company owned and operated what was probably the finest and most complete wrecker on the Great Lakes — the *Manistique*. As a super-tug she had that advantage over the *Favorite*. With a roomy hatch and clam-shell, she was able to carry substantial displacement. And the tug *Protector* (a close second to her in the Reid fleet) took no back talk from the Great Lakes Towing Company.

There were the MacQueen tugs of Amherstburg, Ontario (near Detroit), the Ruhl Line at Detroit, the John Roehn Line of Sturgeon Bay, Wisconsin (near Green Bay) and others. But the one rival Tom Reid recognized was the *Favorite* with her skilled skipper, Captain Alex Cummings. Between them there was a good-natured yet hard rivalry, two experts with admiration for each other, but always the determination to get there first — to pick up the jobs after the divers had gone down, reviewed the damage to the ship's bottom, estimated the number of plates to be removed and renewed — and presented findings to the insurance company which let out the bids.

Tugmen, even in the days of limited communication had sources of information. Tom Reid cultivated a girl in a local telegraph office, and the dividends on an investment of a five pound box of Lowney's chocolates sometimes brought a valuable tip.

He was at home one day when the girl telephoned. It happened that Anna answered the call. An unfamiliar voice asked for Tom. *Tom* —

The moment he took the instrument and realized who was calling, his tone became eager. One would not imagine that a matter of vital concern to the Reid Company was being discussed. Soon he terminated the conversation with a warm — " — and goodbye for now, my dear."

Eyes flashing, "Who was the woman?" demanded Anna.

He snatched up hat and coat, kissed her in passing and raced out to his car. The girl had told him of the disaster to the Steamer *Faye* — a wooden freighter worth $100,000 which had gone ashore at Point aux Barques, a tiny hamlet situated along the finger of land that juts down into Lake Michigan from Michigan's Upper Peninsula to create Big Bay de Noquet. She had given him a tip that could mean $50,000 to The Reid Company — and there wasn't a minute to lose, for a rival was being officially notified. The ship's owners in Cleveland, the girl had relayed, was ordering the tug *Favorite* to the scene.

A Reid tug could race her there and possibly pick up the job. There had been no time to go into details with Anna, involving an explanaton of certain ruses to which she would undoubtedly object. He would call her later from Sarnia.

A gale was blowing from the north west, wind offshore. The late fall 'blow.' But the Reid tug *Protector* had weathered the worst storms the Lakes had to offer, and plunged sturdily through the heavy seas at twelve miles an hour. Before long Tom sighted the *Favorite* making with all speed for the Straits of Mackinac and Lake Michigan. But her speed could not match that of the *Protector*.

After passing her, Tom kept pulling down his lights in order to confuse his rival, until they went out. Then went on to the ship *Faye* in command of Captain 'Windy' Young.

When the Reid tug pulled up, he called out, "I knew you'd be here, Reid, before anyone else. You can smell these things out. But the *Favorite* was ordered. They've got the job."

"You won't see her," shouted Tom. "She couldn't face this weather. She's an old tug."

But to Captain Young, orders were orders. Though there lay the *Protector* with its big swing crane and equipment ready to lighter and pump out, and seas were pounding hard against the *Faye* — pounding she couldn't take for long.

After an hour or two, the uneasy captain yielded and the *Protector* went to work. There were no clam-shells aboard her, but booms with a hoist which could swing over, load in and dump.

Wind and wave increased, and the *Protector* was forced to seek temporary shelter at the little port of Naubinway. But soon Tom was contacted by the owners of the *Faye* and asked to return to Point aux Barques as quickly as possible to help save the distressed ship.

When he reached there, he saw that the *Faye*'s smokestack was down, her rudder gone, and she was at the mercy of the waves. The *Favorite* had arrived . . .

Working day and night for over a week — at $50.00 an hour — the Reid crew released her and, with the *Favorite* steering, began towing her to Sheboygan at the tip of Michigan's Lower Peninsula.

Winter was closing in rapidly, and as they approached the Straits of Mackinac, they sighted a package freighter trapped in the ice off Waugoshance Point. The captain of the unfortunate ship signalled Tom for help, and he answered with an assuring message.

Delivering the *Faye,* he turned back and through the slow, deadly Arctic freeze, went to the assistance of the distressed ship. The tough-nosed tug with its mighty engine freed her, then started down Lake Huron for Sarnia and home.

James Reid called his son a black-hearted pirate, but smiled with satisfaction as he fingered the two fat salvaging checks.

Tom left at once for home, impatient to tell Anna the story, but he was unprepared for the reception that awaited him.

Anna rejected his kiss. "And how is your — *dear*?"

Amused, he told her the facts.

"Tom Reid, I call that downright dishonest!" she declared, but her tone was gay as a spring morning, and the frown faded.

"You fraud!" he chuckled. "That's not what's bothering you."

She buried her face against him.

"You ain't got anything to worry about, Anna. You know what you mean to me."

She looked up and followed his gaze to the river beyond. And as their eyes met, she knew, as she had always known, that her only rival was and ever would be the sea.

CHAPTER EIGHT

Baby Virginia's first birthday was to be celebrated on Thanksgiving in 1906, and festive plans were made for the occasion.

Anna and Tom considered their numerous blessings. Anna's health had been restored, and Tom's. Virginia was a strong, healthy child. Little Clara, sturdy and happy, gave them no worries. The boy Thom was showing splendid promise, and delicate Helen was slowly outgrowing the physical difficulties of early childhood.

The Reids had taken a fine house on Military Street in

Port Huron. The garden was impressive, and the view of the river from the broad windows enabled Anna to see the Reid tugs and barges come and go.

Tom was proud to herd that little family to church on the rare occasions that circumstance permitted. The minister's words always sent him away feeling good and mulling over constructive resolutions.

This year he was looking forward particularly to Thanksgiving day. The minister and his wife and a few close friends had been invited to dinner. Anna was radiant with anticipation. And Tom had planned that on Thanksgiving morning he would give her the solitaire she should have had on their engagement day.

But again, the blow fell. A big Steel Trust freighter ran into trouble, and Manager Harry Colby contacted the Reid Company.

As Tom gave Anna her ring and turned away from the tears she tried to hide, he thought such a moment took more out of a man than all the dangers of salvaging. He stormed off to resume his work — this time truly a rugged assignment.

The 4,500 ton *Mataafa,* worth $200,000 and with barge *Naysmith* in tow, had crashed into a pier in a violent storm when trying to enter the harbor at Duluth, Minnesota.

Here is one of the finest natural harbors in the country. Duluth is situated at the west end of Lake Superior at the mouth of the St. Louis River and on the side and along the base of a bluff rising hundreds of feet above Lake level. The city lies at the west end of Duluth Harbor directly opposite the city of Superior, Wisconsin. Minnesota Point, a narrow strip of land seven miles in length, projects from the Wisconsin shore, separates the bay from the Lake and, with St. Louis Bay, forms a natural harbor. The entrance is the narrow channel between the two points but there is also a ship canal across Minnesota Point, spanned by an aerial bridge four hundred feet long and one hundred and eighty six feet above the water. The ore dock, within this harbor, was the ship's destination.

The *Mataafa* had no deck cabins aft' — galley, mess room and crew quarters were below. The nine men who had taken refuge aft', froze in ventilators and on the shelf piece or were swept overboard. The tow *Naysmith* rode out the storm.

Tom's salvage bid of $40,000 was accepted. He ordered the wrecker *Manistique* (with Louis Meyers aboard) and the tug *Sarnia City* into action. They steamed north, and as they went, the weather grew progressively worse.

After several tries, they managed to get salvaging equipment aboard the *Mataafa*. Pumps were put down on the cylinder head and intensive work begun. Louis Meyers submerged and went over the bottom of the ship. He found her rudder gone, her wheel bent, and damage between the stern and the collision bulkhead. But this was not the answer, he knew. The leak was somewhere else.

He examined the tank top, the compartments, then retraced his steps in the heavy diver's outfit in sub-zero weather, covering the entire ship. He found nothing significant.

Impatient with the passing of time, Tom then got into a diving outfit to try his luck. He jumped instead of descending the ladder and almost lost his life when the hoses tangled on a stanchion.

Deciding at length that the tiny break in the section of tank top between stern and collision bulkhead was the cause, he sent a watchman ashore in a yawl with a number of gunny sacks to hunt up the nearest livery stable and secure as much horse manure as possible. Salvagers found that in case of a small break or loosened rivets, the fibres of such offal cling through suction to the opening and provide a block. This method had been known to halt trouble until the ship could be drydocked. But in this instance, it failed.

On the following day, the men knelt together on deck peering down into the flooded engine room, hoping to detect some enlightening hint. It was at this point that Louis Meyers caught sight of a string wavering on the surface of the water. Obviously the string had snagged, and was moved by a current. And a current meant a leak. But — where? They had examined every inch of the ship; had plugged the outlet of the exhaust pipe leading from the big Westinghouse stationary pump in the engine room — since the current seemed to come from that direction.

Meyers submerged again and at last discovered where the trouble lay. Perhaps a foot from the opening of the exhaust pipe, and out of sight, he found the break.

Soon the ship was able to be released, and they took her into the harbor to the entrance of the drydock. But the contract called for delivery *in* drydock. It was the only time they ever made that mistake — and, according to Tom Reid, they 'got stung.' Sizing up the situation, Tom told the dock superintendent he would have to crib the dock because the *Mataafa*'s bottom was in such bad shape. The man agreed.

They were working at night unloading the boat when she broke in two and cracked some plates. When she broke, she 'went off' like a cannon. Thirty laborers working in the hold shoveling ore, tried wildly to get out through the booby hatch but got stuck in it. There was no danger, had they known, as the ship filled slowly.

They shoved her into the drydock at night and placed her on the blocks, and she filled with water at the dock. If left outside, she would have sunk.

The dock superintendent was furious. They pumped the dock out and when it was done, all the blocks went down — squashed, according to Tom Reid. They had to close up the break and pump out the boat — pump out the dock as well, and fix the blocks. But they cribbed under the boat this time and she was successfully repaired. During these operations they had taken the ore out of each end but left fifty ton in the middle to hold her down.

The Reid Company lost about $5,000.00 on the deal. The bid would have netted them a nice profit had Tom not agreed to put the *Mataafa* in the drydock rather than at it. It was the first and last contract of that kind.

The Pittsburg Steamship Company agreed to give Tom the ore if he removed it. Tom sold the ore, but it cost $3.00 a ton to get it out.

The *Mataafa* returned to circulation, but nine of her gallant crew had lost their lives. That was her one accident. Her career has been without major trouble all the years since. She continued to ply the Lakes as an ore carrier for The Pittsburg Steamship Company until 1948 when she was sold to The Nicholson Transportation Company and brought to Detroit and converted into an automobile carrier. A flight deck was added to accomodate more cars. Since that time she has run steadily between Detroit and Cleveland and Buffalo, carrying automobiles — perhaps five hundred to the load. A tough, sturdy ship, out early and late. The *Mataafa* proved with the years that she could take it.

But that Thanksgiving day back in 1906, Anna Reid

opened the newspaper to see the story of the wrecked *Mataafa;* the pictures of the lost sailors, their wives and children. And when with the next Thanksgiving Tom was called to Lake Michigan to salvage the ship *Argo* which had gone aground at the city of Holland, she took it in stride with a prayer.

CHAPTER NINE

Holland lies midway up the western shore of Michigan's Lower Peninsula. Here once was the camping ground of the Pottawatomie Indian tribes, and today it is the center of the Dutch population of America. And here the *Argo, a* Booth Transportation Company passenger ship, 200 feet long and worth $150,000, ran ashore in a fog.

Contacted by her owners, Tom ordered out the tugs *Salvor* and *Aldrich.* With ice in the Straits of Mackinac, the passage was difficult. He found the *Argo* lying broadside on the beach, up on the sand — a treacherous bed since sand will lift and drop a boat with the wash of the sea. A bad storm breaking had found her there and buried her in the sand, decks-to. Before that she had been out probably ten feet.

Tom's bid of $9,000 to raise and deliver her across the Lake to the Manitowoc shipyard was accepted. Though she was not leaking, Tom put pumps aboard from shore. When she floated, she slipped into this bed she had made, with only four feet of water beyond.

They raised steam on her by then. The *Aldrich* and *Salvor* stood by. With the *Aldrich* working her wheel, she dredged her way alongside the *Argo* until she could be released through her own and the tugs' power. With her rudder stock bent and rudder unshipped, Tom towed her into the harbor at Holland where it was necessary to lift her rudder out and place it on the dock. A fire was built, the stock straightened and replaced in order that she could propel herself to the drydock at Manitowoc with milder weather.

The *Aldrich* and *Salvor* were laid up at the dock in Holland for the winter. During this time the sea-cock on the *Salvor* froze and burst, and the tug sank. In the Spring it was necessary to coffer-dam and pump out the tug with the assistance of the *Aldrich's* steam. She was what Tom Reid termed 'an awful mess,' with cabins below decks loaded and water-soaked.

With Spring, he salvaged the ship and was about to clear for Manitowoc when a new complication arose. Tom Reid had American papers. But the Government refused him permission to use Canadian tugs and man-power to deliver the ship to Manitowoc — since the ports involved did not touch Canadian waters.

Furious, "To hell with it!" roared Tom. "I'll sail

her myself!" And taking the wheel, he brought the *Argo* to Manitowoc under her own power and without incident.

But it cost The Reid Company $8,700 to raise and salvage the *Salvor* . . .

Unflinching, Tom met the challenges and dangers of his profession — but the tight economic crises were things he could not control. With the panic of 1907, he knew some frightening moments — moments that he tried to hide from Anna. But she knew. A word here, a gesture there betrayed it. Tenderness, and patience with the gruff word, the dark mood, the harsh complaint — all told that she shared his anxiety in her own way.

The panic of 1907 was severe. Industrial production turned downward in July. It was at its worst in October and November. The volume of industrial production fell from nearly eight percent above the computed normal level to more than 17% below it. This bitterly affected freight activity on the Lakes. The Reid Company felt the pinch, but their shipyard at Port Huron proved a rewarding asset at a time when ship owners found it possible to handle overdue repairs to their idling vessels. It was during this time — and such times as these — that tugmen met the hard days of spasmodic employment with tightened belts.

CHAPTER TEN

With the years and more experience, greater prestige and broadening contacts, the Reids had achieved a standard of living expensive to maintain. A large mansion, a domestic staff, several cars and the attendant expenses of certain social obligations required a sound exchequer. But the pressure of business permitted Tom less time at home. Family discipline and home management fell heavily on Anna.

By now, however, her health had improved. But she had never quite adjusted to her husband's long absences from home. Yielding one day to an overwhelming impulse, she boarded the ferry to Sarnia, bound for The Reid Company's headquarters.

The buzz at desks ended abruptly as she entered and stormed on toward Will Reid's office. An absurd little flowered hat trembled on heavy brown hair, and her eyes flashed with purpose as she faced him.

"Things have got to change," she declared. "Tom is a stranger to his children — and to me. It's no way of life. He simply can't be away so much. There must be someone who can serve in his place once in a while."

"What brought this about?" Will idly lit a cigar. "You should be used to the routine by this time."

"I'll never be used to it!"

"You make out pretty well, Anna," he reminded. "Clothes, cars — everything you and your family want."

"I want my husband. Don't you understand?" she flamed. "And somehow we're going to see more of him and have him at home."

Will gestured toward a heavily pinned map on the wall. "There's the layout. If you can figure a way to keep Tom here — and manage that, okay!"

"He isn't the whole Reid Company, is he? Why can't the responsibility be shared? There are others, or — are there?" she added slowly, perhaps with sudden realization that numbers had no bearing on the matter. Tom Reid was the dominant force.

Will flushed at her tone, and perhaps the truth of the implication. "Sure there are. Tom's got the public fooled, that's all. Makes 'em think he's the only one in the outfit that knows the answers. Why — I could show him up any day out on the jobs. Nothin' to it." He struck another match, watched her with a smile through the flame.

"It amuses you — and it breaks my heart. It's worse as time goes on, Will. Because he's away more and more. I need him, and I miss him. The children need him. I always felt self-sufficient until I had Tom. Now I'm only half alive. I wait and watch and plan. And he comes and goes like the wind — and I'm waiting again."

Will said, "I'd like to tell you things will change, Anna. But you know as well as I do that they won't. Business is growing, and so is his reputation. He's run the show ever since I can remember. It's in his blood. You know the story. You've played along, and you'll go on doing it. He knew it when he married you. You are a team, and a solid one."

"I'm a lonesome, practically deserted wife! I don't want compliments. I want Tom!" She brushed at impatient tears.

"And you've got him — to the finish. You're the kind of a mate a fellow like Tom would pick. He always knows what he's doing. A woman has to be brave to see it through alone, the way you have."

"Brave?" she sniffed. "What have I done, except stay at home and look after my family?"

Never conscious of her courage, that night she was less than ever aware of it when a disgruntled dock-walloper whom Tom had discharged, broke into the house. In a matter of minutes, on hearing footsteps downstairs, she herded the children into her room and locked the door. Not unaware of the crisis, they were quieted by her apparent lack of fear, the security of her reassurance.

At last, when all was still again, she dared emerge, lock the children in and search the house. Then closing the back door through which the marauder had escaped, she returned — made light of the incident, tucked the children in bed and fell to her limp knees with a prayer of thanksgiving.

Sometimes on Tom's return his pockets would bulge with jeweled stones from the shores of Lake Superior — gifts for the children. And as he regaled them with stories of his experiences, Anna realized the power of her rival — the sea. She must share him wholeheartedly, or not possess him at all.

In the long lonely stretches, she learned to find compensation in his unspoken need of her and in their children's need. She read extensively and gathered materials for stories with which to amuse them, but she saw that Tom's stories genuinely held them. Where other fathers dwelt on the doings of bears and wolves, fairies and elves, Tom's tales were of the Lakes, wrecks — ships that were as people to him; lonely, crippled, gallant people. His children looked on him as a hero, dedicated to rescue; and, as Anna often reminded them, a figure making history on the Great Lakes.

She impressed them with the lasting significance of events on the day they were taken to the shipyard down river at St. Clair, when Tom Reid began to tow the first of the six 200 foot sections for the Detroit-Windsor motor tunnel, a milestone in international traffic relations. And she told them the story behind the big rock in the Reid's front garden — a rock that had spelled disaster for the ship *Matoa*. As a souvenir of memorable experience, Tom had brought it home on a tug and placed it in the yard.

The M*atoa* — a 325 foot, 7,500 ton steel freighter of the Minnesota Line (later taken over by the Pittsburg Steamship Lines to augment their own Company) had foundered on that rock at Port Hope near the tip of Michigan's 'Thumb' in a summer fog the year before.

Worth at that time $150,000, today she is worth half a million.

Another wrecking company had attempted salvage for months without success and then given it up as hopeless. The *Matoa* was declared a total loss, and the insurance underwriters offered her for sale.

While the gravely damaged hull seemed an impossible salvage risk, Tom was willing to take the chance. He made an offer of $2,500 for the wreck where she lay. His offer was accepted. No one believed the job could be done.

Riding the rocks, time, wind and weather had shattered and weakened a fine ship. The *Matoa* had no tank top in the engine room; rather, false tanks. The rock had been plunged up into her hull, and Tom decided to leave it where it was, utilizing it as a plug, with the addition of a cement patch. It was a gamble, but it worked.

Rebuilt in the Reid drydock, Tom sold her later to the Warren Coal Company of Boston. But another problem then arose as, contingent on the sale for $75,000, was the delivery of the *Matoa* to the east coast and her new owner. This meant passage through the Welland Canal. Her length for such a journey was prohibitive, because the Locks could not accommodate her. His bid of $8,000 for the job was accepted.

Tom Reid then superintended the bisecting and bulkheading of the ship at the drydock where she had been repaired. Again confronted with an obstacle in the matter of motive power, he solved this by having the after end tow the forward end. And the *Matoa,* in two sections, sailed off 'hindside foremost' to her new home. She was the first ship to be cut in two and taken down the canal. With the years, she was to return to the Lakes and become one of the Nicholson Transportation Company's fleet as an automobile carrier.

Before the Reid fire one night, he sat alone with Anna — one of those rare quiet hours together. For her scrapbook, she had clipped the write-up of his achievements, the volume growing steadily thicker.

"They gave just the rough outline in the paper, Tom," she recalled. "Tell me how you went about cutting a boat in two to get it through the canal — how you thought of such a thing!"

"There was nothing else to do," he shrugged. Her admiration was sweet.

"But, Tom — who but you would ever *dream* it could be done?"

"Nonsense. Anybody with half a brain."

He made light of it to no one, however, when the Steamer *Parks Foster* went ashore 'light' on the rocks at the port of Black River along Lake Huron between the coastal towns of Alpena and Harrisburg. The 262 foot ship, worth about $80,000 at the time of launching, was a freighter of 1729 tons. She was built in Cleveland in 1889, and owned by John Prindiville and Sons of Chicago.

This was a particularly difficult problem for salvagers to attempt because of the narrows in which the accident happened. Advent of Winter compounded the hazards. The ship was without cargo, so only her water ballast could be discharged. She was caught at an angle that almost defied rescue.

In a matter of days, Tom Reid and his men managed to get her off, patched her up so she was able to limp into Alpena, then later to Sarnia. But beaten destructively by the elements during the time of exposure, she was termed a total loss by the insurance underwriters.

Tom Reid, however, could see possibilities in the craft. With his own shipyard at Port Huron in mind, he decided to make the underwriters an offer. They had been put to a great expense, and were ready to salvage even a negligible amount, so his offer of $5,000 was accepted.

The *Parks Foster* was taken to the Reid shipyard and put in drydock, made seaworthy and sold for $35,000 to James Playfair of Montreal who renamed her the *Superior* — not losing by the transaction, for she has been a gold mine for her owner ever since, carrying package freight and automobiles.

There had been a heavy expense in reconditioning her, but the Reid Company made $10,000 on the operation. Tom's share had been planned from the moment it went through. One of his passions was fine cars, and as his exchequer improved, he chose Packards which were then probably the finest cars available.

This time he had Anna in mind, and one blustery, wintry day, about to return home, he telephoned suggesting that she watch for him. He had a surprise!

The streets were icy and snow banked high along the curbs. The Reid children were making snowmen in the front garden. When he appeared, little Virginia screamed excitedly as the handsome new Packard drove up, and went racing out toward it. Tom shouted a warning, but she came on regardless — slipped, and went under the wheels. Later examination proved she was not seriously hurt, but Tom Reid aged in those hours.

"You drive too fast," Anna accused. "You've got to do everything faster than anyone else." She was right. Nervous tension had to have an outlet. His car would race along the road to Detroit, to Cleveland, up the shore. Never at a moderate speed. Time was important. He had to make time.

He grieved over the incident, considered ways to please the child and Anna. Late that next spring a plan suggested itself. This had to do with the Steamer *Monarch,* a Canadian passenger ship which was to enjoy her last trip in that capacity in early July, after which she would be converted into a package freighter. Her history was legend. Built at Sarnia in 1888, she was the pride of her Canadian owners. The detail in her construction was minute. For instance, the doors to the cabins were so fitted that a coin could enter between frame and door all around — with an eye to any sagging or change while the ship was at sea. Her passenger list had carried famous names on her maiden voyage, and her menus made news; her decor, orchestras and salons were noted in the social columns. Built at a cost of $150,000, much of her early grandeur was to be revived this last trip; this trip with which Tom planned to surprise Anna and Virginia.

The child's devotion to her father stirred his tenderness. She was a lovable little girl, warm, intelligent and full of illusions. Aboard the *Monarch* she attracted much attention. People would turn to glance again as she danced along, holding her father's hand.

Then one day at lunch, she demanded one of the little silver pots on a tea-tray served her mother.

"I can't give it to you," Tom explained quietly. "It belongs to the ship."

She argued tearfully. It was the first time he had ever failed to grant her wish. "Mother always said you could do anything!" Disillusioned, she was still. But after that when he caught her studying him with that strange expression, it troubled him. She knew now — as he knew — there was much he couldn't do . . .

After that trip, the *Monarch* went to the shipyard for an overhauling, and soon began running package freight. In that year's bitter mid-November, she was caught in a sub-zero spell and froze in the ice at Sailors' Encampment at the Soo. Her Company notified The Reid Wrecking Company, and Tom left Sarnia on the tug *Reid* to go to her assistance, ordering the tug *Sarnian* to follow. Through seven long days they broke their way through the ice across Mud Lake to reach the *Monarch,* with the channel closing slowly behind them.

Arriving, they found the coal supply practically exhausted. Tom went immediately to Detour and took on fuel to be transferred; returned, and was forced to buy cordwood for the *Monarch* and tug *Sarnian.* The temperature kept falling, and it was impossible to make over two or three miles a day, breaking ice all the way from Detour to Encampment.

Sending for the Reid tug *Protector,* and forming a chain, with a wild gale blowing and waves washing over the pilot house, they pushed their way through at last to the open punishment of Lake Huron; past great ice boulders that lined the Rapids, some thundering down.

For that service with three tugs at $25.00 an hour for twelve days the Reid Company received more than twenty thousand dollars, a profit of $10,000. And the *Monarch* had freight contracts and a winter's schedule to meet in order for her owners to break even. Despite weather, she was sent out again, and managed the trips without incident.

In mid-December another year, carrying a cargo of grain from Port Arthur, the *Monarch* departed for Sarnia on her last trip of the season — with a grateful and sorely tried crew. Her next crisis proved to be her last. The crew remarked at the excellent time she was making, despite the fact that a blizzard raged and a northeast gale was blowing. A wheelsman said he had just seen Passage Light abreast of them, faintly through the storm. Another uneasily got to his feet. They were not due abreast of

Passage Light for another half hour. He was suddenly jerked off his feet as the ship crashed against a cliff on the northeast end of Isle Royale.

Isle Royale — that paradise for summer tourists and vacations — seems, as one approaches in fair weather, as if it might be floating in the bright blue water of Lake Superior. And it has been called the moving island, or lost island. Indian lore repeats some beautiful legends about this northernmost point of the State of Michigan. The rocky shoreline is a series of coves and bays. The Rock of Ages lighthouse looms high on the rocks at the Washington Bay. And on Harlem Reef, at the entrance to Siskowit Bay, is superb trout fishing.

But the *Monarch* approached Isle Royale in foul weather, and reached the end of her course. The engine room was flooded at once, and soundings registered a depth of ninety feet and no bottom. The engineer coaxed the engines to keep turning, the better to anchor the ship on any ledge that might hold, rather than let her slip back into water and sink.

Lifeboats were lowered and lost. Water reached the dynamo. The lights went out, and then the fires. The line was put ashore and all made their precarious way to safety, except for one who lost his hold and was never seen again.

The men improvised shelters, salvaged some bags of flour that were washed ashore, and built signal fires. Help came before they froze, but there was no help for the *Monarch*. Tilted at a forty-five degree angle, she was locked now on the rocks where, after futile efforts to salvage her, she was abandoned — slowly being beaten to pieces by wind and sea. And until the wrecking of the Steamer *Savona* later on, and incidents relative to the *Savona*'s salvaging, the *Monarch* was ignored.

The *Savona* — a 300 foot, 5,000 ton freighter of the Tomlinson Line, went ashore on Sand Island off Bayfield, Wisconsin, one bitter December night. She represented an investment of $200,000 when built. In view of the weather and time of year, it was decided to leave her where she was for the winter as it was obvious that any attempts at salvaging immediately would be futile.

Bids were considered, and the contract finally let to the Reid Company for $50,000. With Spring, Tom Reid and Louis Meyers went to the scene and made further examination and plans for salvage.

A coffer dam 426 feet long and sixteen feet high was built ashore and towed out as you would a ship. Bolts, brackets and angles were purchased in Port Huron and brought north where the great logs for coffer-damming were available.

The *Savona* was refloated, only to suffer further disaster. And this time, it was agreed her plight was hopeless. Besides, she was a menace to navigation. A derrick was brought with one hundred ton lifting power. Dynamite was used, and salvaging her boilers and engines, they put them aboard the barge *Kilderhouse* after taking out the latter's decks so as to load the machinery in the hold. There was no help for the *Savona*. She was finally blown to pieces and sold for scrap.

As the tugs *George H. Parker, Salvor* and *Ottawa,* with barge *Kilderhouse* and a derrick scow were about to leave, a storm was brewing. But they had been advised to go to the *Monarch* wreck, still on the rock of Isle Royale — her stern in over ninety feet of water, bow ashore. It was probably the last opportunity to salvage anything available still aboard her.

When the convoy reached the scene, Louis Meyers went down into the doomed ship and with helpers removed the boilers and engine and transferred them to the barge. Working with him, Tom saw a shining little object in a pile of debris. He investigated, and found it to be an individual silver tea-pot bearing the ship's crest. Tom put it in his pocket, smiling gently at a sudden thought. . . .

Soon then, their work accomplished, they started across the Lake for home port. The weather worsened, and they put in at Jackfish Bay for shelter — a tiny harbor on Lake Superior's north shore near the New York Times' pulp outlet of Terrace Bay. They rounded up some food and returned by tug to the *Kilderhouse,* signalled the seaman in charge of the derrick-scow in tow to come and get provisions — a fellow named Jack Hamlin. He testily demanded why they had stopped for weather. Better get on home, he declared. The food he and his companion had would do, and he denied that the weather was bad enough to force the convoy to take shelter.

With daylight, they took passage inside Michipocoton Island. Tom and Captain Hill of the *Salvor* were uneasy over the plunging barometer, and decided to 'lay over.' The men on the derrick-scow again shouted complaints to Captain Cooper of the *Ottawa.* Why did they have to go in for shelter and the sea dead calm? Better go on, they insisted. They could make time through the night.

Against his better judgment, Tom gave orders to proceed. The gale came up as feared. From the pilot house, Tom and the Captain gravely watched the mountainous waves that washed out of Whitefish Bay. The launches towed by the derrick-scow might have been corks in the distance.

There was nothing to do but go on. Tom had feared the significance of the calm before the storm that had received the scow's officer. And his fears were realized. The scow capsized. At once they let go the ilne, fought the sea to circle her but could not find her. And the men who had insisted on braving a dipping barometer perished. There was a brief time when it looked as if they might lose the *Kilderhouse* as well.

The entire loss was approximately $50,000. The derrick-scow with its 100 ton derrick, and the launches as well as valuable machinery on the scow.

The *Savona* and the *Monarch* were two heartbreaking failures in the long list of Reid salvaging triumphs.

CHAPTER ELEVEN

Certain ships passing along the river and once raised from the grave by her husband, represented milestones in Anna's life. She saw them as ghosts, enemies of her happiness — even while she knew that their existence meant the comfort and luxury in which she lived.

But a normal life was her dream. Time was passing. Their children were growing up. She needed the comfort of Tom coming home in the evening like other husbands after a day's work was done. Tom at her side in church, the theater, on the trips to Detroit, the visits to her sister in Chicago. Tom being part of her life. As it was, he seemed only an occasional caller — sometimes almost a stranger. More and more he was preoccupied, nervous, troubled with problems and growing responsibilities as his father slowly withdrew from active business.

Tom's bag was always packed, ready if he should rush into the house, embrace her, snatch up the children for a quick kiss and hurry off, calling back over his shoulder that he was leaving for Lake Superior, Georgian Bay or up the St. Lawrence.

Her checking account was always ample. She and the children were showered with gifts. But more and more the time away from her increased. She brooded about the possibility of other women. He was attractive, virile, generous. And he was human. Sometimes she pictured him unfaithful to her. She told herself he deliberately prolonged these stays, perhaps invented some salvaging excuse.

Perhaps some contact, jealous of her happiness, might drop a provocative remark — Captain Reid was away a lot, wasn't he? . . . And when he had salvaging work aboard some of those passenger boats — well, you couldn't tell *her* that some bold hussy wouldn't make eyes at him. And after all, men were weak —

About the time of the sinking of the *Moreland* in 1911, she worked herself into a frenzy of doubt. It happened that her sister's daughter was to be married in their Chicago home. For days there had been plans and preparations. Tom had promised to be available, and she had confidently assumed it would be so. This time, the entire Reid family would appear together. Helen and Clara were to serve as wedding attendants.

Three days before the event, the *Moreland* ran into trouble. Tom could not face Anna's disappointment, and telephoned home.

"Very well," she told him. "Go ahead. And I don't care if I never see you again." She threw herself on the bed and wept without restraint. Suddenly stillness penetrated — stillness in a house unused to stillness. Stirring, she saw her children's faces tense with fear and shock. They huddled together near the door.

She held out her arms and, troubled, they fled to her. She was reminded that her role in life was of her own choosing. Blessings and joys must be paid for with patience, understanding and self-control. She represented security to these children; an anchor to Tom. She had let them all down in a crisis. Evasions wouldn't do. Children were direct. She managed the situation with dignity and intelligent frankness. There was no use trying to reach Tom now. That would have to wait. . . .

She did not know that she had sent him away to meet even more tragedy than the sinking of the *Moreland*. She did not know that on that very day, Jim Reid had been stricken with paralysis, and the entire responsibility of the Company had fallen on Tom's shoulders.

The morning paper carried the story of the Steamer *W. C. Moreland* wreck. On her fifth trip, the new boat, a 15,000 ton bulk freighter of the Jones, Laughlin fleet, built at a cost of $400,000, had run onto Sawtooth Reef off Eagle Harbor in Lake Superior.

This tiny village is situated on the northern rocky tip of Michigan's Upper Peninsula. In Civil War days, it was an active lake port and center of a thriving mining community. The busy docks had served a great fleet and the rocks along its shores had taken their toll. Now it was the *Moreland's* turn.

Tom and his diver and crew boarded the wrecking tug *Manistique* and accompanied by the tug *Sarnia City,* set out for Lake Superior to check damage and estimate the cost of salvaging. His accepted bid was $75,000 or 75% of the ship on a 'no cure, no pay' basis.

Tom had little heart for the scene he found at Eagle Harbor. The ship had been practically stripped by looters, a not uncommon occurrence in such instances. And the giant freighter had broken in two at number 12 hatch, a tragic casualty of the sea.

Through brutal weather, Tom and his men worked to release her. With equipment aboard, they began to pump out the *Moreland,* but the weather became so extreme they had to desert her frequently and seek shelter.

They had pumped the ship part way down when a most violent gale and blizzard set in. Tom considered the advisability of further attempts under such adverse conditions and then ordered his men to prepare to abandon the wreck until Spring — wrecking crew to take the tug *Sarnia City* to protection at the Portage (a canal and Lake bisecting the Keweenaw Peninsula). With Louis Meyers and tug crew, he would follow on the *Manistique.*

Time was required to condition ship and equipment for departure. The barometer was down, with a wind from sixty to seventy miles an hour. Visibility zero.

The *Sarnia City,* reaching Portage, waited with concern for word or sight of the *Manistique.* She should have appeared long since. The land was scourged by the late November storm. Not ten miles away in Mandan, a mailman on his rounds was found frozen in the snow. Schools were closed, and the Keweenaw Peninsula seemed isolated in the Arctic.

Days passed. The *Sarnia City* made her way to Houghton, and waited. There was no word, no sight of the *Manistique.* Ten days — and then the *Manistique* was reported safe in Copper Harbor after almost foundering in the giant seas.

Soon she arrived in Houghton where the two ships laid up side by side for the rest of the winter. When asked on reaching shore about his reaction to that experience, Tom shrugged, "Quite a wash. . . ."

Anna, too, had waited. Newspapers carried headlines. Graphic accounts played up the importance of Tom Reid in the local scene — family, residence, career. They outlined as well the life of Louis Meyers. To Anna the accounts seemed obituaries. She hid the papers from the children. But they knew.

There was no satisfaction from the office in Sarnia. Their kindness savored of pity. She could not hint of her terror to the children. She had to talk to someone who understood, and she made her way through the blinding snow to the Meyers' home where Mabel Meyers and her little daughter Naomi waited for word.

Two women, holding fast to faith, quietly chatting over a cup of tea on subjects in which neither had an interest, finding in mutual restraint and dignity the strength to believe what they wanted to believe, each a source of reassurance to the other. The courage of their men was the hard, battling courage of self-preservation; theirs, the courage of hard hope and of faith in God without which such hours of suspense would have been unbearable.

At last the call came through. Their men were safe.

She was waiting in the night for him, the telegram crushed innumerable times in her restless hands. Alone at the window. Tom coming home again — safe, thank God!

She was at the door as he came up the steps — in his arms while the wind whistled against the sheer challis robe, pressing him close gratefully.

"It's all right now," he said, his voice unsteady. "It's all right now, Anna. . . ."

He could not tell her that night that he would have to return to Houghton tomorrow if possible to check on another wreck, the Steamer *Vulcan;* that the wire had reached him enroute. But he had come home, close to exhaustion, fighting for a few hours with her and their children.

By nine in the morning he was on the telephone with Perry Jones in Cleveland, assembling the details on the *Vulcan* wreck. The 350 foot, 6,000 ton bulk freighter, loaded with coal, had sunk mysteriously at the Houghton dock. He left within the hour for the wild, frigid Upper Peninsula.

December weather prohibited an immediate salvage attempt, but he gave a bid of $40,000 to be followed through in the Spring. At that time, with bid accepted, he brought the tug *Whalen* and barge *Empire* from Port Arthur, coffer-dammed and pumped out the *Vulcan* successfully, raised her — the Reid Company earning $20,000 on the contract.

With Spring, too, the *Moreland* was still a prisoner, but for two years the struggle to salvage her continued. Finally she was afloat again and ready to resume her run to the lower Lakes, due to the patient genuis of Tom Reid, Louis Meyers and their crews.

Then by an incredible circumstance, on her first trip out — and no one cares to settle the blame definitely— the *Moreland* went on the rocks a second time, broke in two at number 24 hatch and sank in two hundred feet of water. This time only the stern section was saved.

They placed a bulkhead in the salvaged section and started to tow her down the Lake. But this was not without incident, for a north east 'blow' came up. Water roared into her open hatches almost as fast as the two eighteen-inch pumps could handle it.

The tug *Reid,* with only Tom and Louis Meyers aboard, finally manoeuvred the *Moreland's* stern section behind North Point at Alpena, and safety. When the weather cleared, they started down the Lake again, and this time they succeeded in delivering what was left of the once beautiful ship to the Great Lakes drydock at Detroit.

The underwriters now advertised her for sale, and were made an offer of only $15,000. One boiler alone was worth $30,000. The Reid Company towed her to Windsor, Ontario, and let her lie there for the winter. Then with harbor facilities crowded, they towed her to Port Huron and eased her onto the bank of the St. Clair River. She was left there until World War I, when the underwriters settled with the Company, which gave the Reid Company the ship by way of compensation. But the Reid Company's loss already approximated $40,000.

Roy Wolvin, a northern steamship Company's owner, bought her for $25,000 and ordered her towed to Port Arthur where they built a new forward section of greater length, at which time she became a Canadian ship. When she was again ready to resume navigation, she sailed for a while under the name *Sir Trevor Dawson.* Later she was sold to the Hutchinson Steamship Company of Cleveland, Ohio, and renamed the *Charles L. Hutchinson.*

CHAPTER TWELVE

1913. Tom was now forty-three.

About this time the Reids' oldest daughter, Helen, was to graduate from high school. Always a small, delicate child, she seemed steadily to grow more frail.

Clara was the dreamer, Virginia full of play and moods. Thom already had ideas for the future. He was interested in machines, industrial production and distribution rather than ships and the Lakes. His hobbies were not without some return. At this point, fascinated by pyrography, he was decorating little plaques and objects, and selling them locally at a profit. He was a born merchandiser.

Uneasy over this, his father would frequently bluster in, demanding, "Where's Thom? Get him into his bib and tucker. I'm taking him along this time. Let him see what's going on around the Lakes. When I was his age, I was earning wages."

Determined that some day Thom would head the Reid Company, Tom took him along as often as circumstance, and his mother, would permit. On this particular occasion he was anxious for Thom to see an unusual wreck. The *Saxona,* a 416 foot freighter of the Tomlinson fleet, (built at a cost of $300,000) carrying 8,000 tons of coal, had suffered a head-on collision with the *Pentecost Mitchell,* of the Pittsburg Steamship Company. It happened below Pipe Island, near Detour, at the entrance to the St. Mary's River near the Soo. Wedged together, the ships had sunk in 60 feet of water.

Anna's argument about Thom's absence from school was brushed aside. Tom's plans for the future were crystalizing. His own father would not be with them much longer. The generations must take their place. Young Thom must be prepared, and there was more than school work to be learned. There was the business of ships, and it was an involved business. Men had to learn it young.

Anna might plan college for Thom and his sisters. College was fine. But what you learned on the deck of a ship or in the hold or pilot house was what counted in the long run.

And so he took Thom off to the Soo to view the tragic scene — two fine ships locked together and lying on the bottom with only their stacks showing.

Reid's was the only bid entered this time. He promised to raise the *Saxona* for a price of $75,000. This meant a session in Chicago to order the timber to be used in coffer-damming which the steam barge *Mary Battle* would pick up. But first he would drop Thom off at home.

He had no hint of the situation that awaited him in Port Huron. The delicate Helen, with graduation imminent, had overtaxed her strength. A heart never too strong had rebelled. The attack was serious.

Tom faced increasing burdens. Helen was now an invalid if her life continued. His father was fading away. The weight of the Company's business rested heavily on him. There was his home to consider, his children's future. And Anna — — —

At Chicago, Perry Jones wired him that the contract would have to be cancelled. Their wrecking advisors had declared the *Saxona* and *Pentecost Mitchell* would have to be raised together, since they were interlocked. And there would be a ten per cent charge above the cost of raising the *Saxona* alone.

Tom and Louis Meyers had made a thorough examination of the disabled ships, and were convinced they would not have to be raised together; convinced as well that the underwriters' deduction was not the basic influence in the matter. They had apparently decided that they could raise both ships together more cheaply than as units.

Tom left at once for Cleveland to see Perry Jones; advised him that he had ordered all the timber, canvas and boats to be used in the salvaging, and had purchased other miscellaneous equipment.

Jones assured him that they would be fair in the matter. Then added, "By the way, why don't you buy the boat and cargo right where she is?"

Tom considered it, figured briefly on the back of an envelope. "Okay. I'll give you $75,000 for the boat and cargo."

Perry Jones recommended this to Lloyd's head office in London. The offer was accepted, and work begun at once. The bow of the *Saxona* was badly smashed, and the preliminary work of cleaning out the coal cargo from the damaged area was slow and delaying.

Meyers, working steadily, built two coffer-dams — each one hundred and fifty feet long and the width of the boat, twenty five feet high inside the gunwhale bars. While they were being constructed, boxes also were built and launched while Meyers and his helper had the additional work of bulkheading number one hatch — since the after-end of the ship was not pumped out from bulkhead to stern. If the bulkheads had let go, that would have finished the *Saxona.*

The coffer-dams were then launched, towed out, lifted by crane and floated over the boat deck. Ten-ton blocks were placed on each corner while bolting coffer dam to deck. Canvas was secured around the boxes, and with a pump on the coffer dam and a pump on deck, they emptied the hold.

The *Pentecost Mitchell* in the meantime was in the hands of other wreckers who had built steel boxes over the individual hatches and were preparing to raise her. But they failed to take into consideration the pressure of water on the deck between the hatches. The entire ship should have been coffer-dammed. When the pumps went into action, the pressure caused the decks to collapse. The *Pentecost Mitchell* was then in worse condition than when they had begun salvaging.

By this time the *Saxona* was refloated and on her way to Detour where, at the bank, they pumped out her boiler room, engine room and coal bunker, because her decks were above water. This brought her into balance.

Forty days had elapsed since the job was begun.

They now started on their way, passing the *Pentecost Mitchell,* which was still on the bottom and was to remain there for weeks to come. Enroute to the shipyard at Collingwood on Georgian Bay, a bad storm closed in as they reached Mississauga Passage, and the tugs were forced to leave her. From the pilot house on top of the coffer dam, Tom ran her into Meldrum Bay under her own steam.

The *Saxona* was rebuilt at Collingwood and sold later to shipowners Roy Wolvin, J. W. Norcross and Harold Smith; later again to Matthews of the Colonial Steamship Company when she became the *Laketon.*

For his part in the successful salvaging, Louis Meyers received a bonus of $5,000. The Reid Company made $45,000 on a contract that had originally been called impossible by the owners. And for Tom Reid it was fortunate that things turned out well, for he was facing a major crisis in his life.

Tom frequently visited the sanitarium outside Detroit, where, it was evident, such visits were almost over. Captain Jim Reid was nearing the end. He had made big money, lost it — made more, and was always in debt. He had made many men rich. Even now, with death near, after a vastly successful career, he owed the bank over $100,000, an obligation which Tom determined to assume personally. There were Company debts, too, that must somehow, be wiped out. Some one must put more hours in the day!

Each time Tom visited the sanitarium, he reassured his father, wondering as he did where he would turn, how he would meet the problems to come. It still seemed strange to see the old lion lying there helpless, the once booming voice lowered to a quaver as he talked with Tom of ships and deals, of times as they had been and now were; counseling, arguing, advising, yet adding, "You'll get along. It ain't as if you haven't been trying to run the business since you could reach a wheel."

At the last, for each of Tom's brothers and sisters, there was some admonition to keep along the years to come. And there was the final blustering, "Now get out, all of you, and let a man sleep without your chitter-chatter. A business don't run by itself. You, Will — keep an eye on the books, and don't let any of them pirates cheat you. And you, Boldt — no bossin' the men out of turn, remember!" And so along the line.

He turned then to his wife and in that silent gaze between them was supplication for forgiveness for sins committed and pardon granted.

That was his farewell. James Reid — come to America nearly fifty years before; and by guts, hard work and keen judgment, had built up the finest rafting, towing and salvage business on the Great Lakes.

At that time, the old family home was in Sarnia. With his death, relatives and friends gathered there. Arrangements were made locally to send to Detroit for the body. But Tom had his own plans. Summoning the crew of the tug *Constitution,* he cast off lines and set out for Detroit.

At dawn next day, with James Reid's casket aboard, his burgee at half-mast, the *Constitution* headed north for Sarnia with Tom at the wheel. It was mid-September. The haze of autumn lay over the water. Waves lapped idly against the tug's bow. There was quiet aboard. The men respected Tom's thoughts . . . .

Death had a way of changing things. Yet nothing was changed — nothing but you. Much that was good had happened — much that had slipped your mind. And much that had seemed bad went out of focus.

The giant of your childhood — he was the best, the biggest, the greatest . . . He could compute the price of a job in a few minutes. Tug six hundred dollars a day. His men and their expenses. Other help, and theirs. Then double the price, in case of trouble . . .

Tom smiled — then sobered, recalling an old secret hurt. His father had always been partial to Will. And now he wondered? Was that why he had denied Will the trip? because at the end he wanted James Reid to himself? They had clashed often through the years, exchanged hard words. But in the crises —

Childhood again — That day in Alpena. The fire engine. Will ahead — blindly reckless as always. Will disappearing under the wheels, and miraculously escaping death only because the streets were paved with sawdust and had a deep resilience. The wheels had not passed over a vital spot . . . He had stumbled over sickly to help his brother and was whirled aside by a mighty fist as their gray-faced father lifted his injured son. Yet, as he walked away with the crumpled child in his arms, he turned to give Tom a glance of compassion.

Who had such skill in handling a ship? James Reid sailed by the barometer, sensitive to wind and cloud as if he enjoyed a secret understanding with them. Who else had ever sailed a tug towing four barges in a storm through the piers at Harbor Beach — and made it without incident?

Boutell used to handle the Reid logs at Bay City. Jim Reid made it possible for the man to amass a fortune. Boutell died a millionaire. Jim Reid always lost money. He towed millions of feet of logs, and there was money in it. But he preferred wrecking. He loved the hazards, the challenge.

And those first Reid wreckers — those pitiful little tugs with their half-size derricks! No clam-shells with which to lighter, but improvised half-barrels with ropes to send a bucket down into the hold to clam. And yet out of such things had grown an important business.

And — there had been sins. But Jim Reid's mistakes had been big ones, with a kind of negative grandeur. He was contemptuous of the little, the mean and sly. And Tom had learned with time that the sins he found hard to forgive in his father were easy to commit . . .

A giant Steel Trust freighter slipped by now and saluted, for all the Lakes knew Jim Reid had gone. His burgee flew at half-mast. A Cleveland Cliffs ore carrier passed, a Reiss Steamship leviathan — another tug. All saluted. And with each one, Tom caught the whistle pull and gave his father's salute in answer.

Aboard the *Constitution* no one spoke. They had admired and loved 'the old man.'

At Sarnia, mourners waited in the Reid home; the daughters of the Reid brothers in white organdie with black velvet sashes, the women in severe black. There were floral replicas of anchors, lighthouses, ships representing the great names of the Lakes.

Only the men followed the hearse to the cemetery. It was not the local custom for the women to accompany them there.

Eleanor Profit Reid quietly watched Jim leave home for the last time. Forty five years of living as his wife had taught her poise and control. There had been hard years, years of poverty, suspense and heartbreak; then success and riches. More heartbreak. There had been the sins of a man to bear; pain, sickness, disillusionment. But to the end there had been devotion, loyalty in the fullest measure his nature permitted him to give.

CHAPTER THIRTEEN

Tom Reid now faced the ordeal of straightening out his father's complicated affairs. It was necessary to sell many valuable assets — among them the *Inland,* the *Matoa,* the *John B. Ketchum* — sales amounting to $300,000.

Then the Government sued the Reid Company for back income taxes amounting to practically that figure. There was an audition in Detroit — protest and anxiety. The Government had evaluated the shipyard as of the current time — assessing the Company on a basis of a

$600,000 valuation rather than the original $25,000. It was a tense, desperate time. If things had not been fairly resolved, the Reid Company would have been no more.

But the situation was settled in the Reid favor, and Tom resumed his work with hope and confidence. There were legal details to be settled, mother and sisters and brothers to be considered. And there was the inevitable family conflict.

Tom sold the drydock property to The Foundation Company of New York for $600,000 — $200,000 in cash, $200,000 in bonds, and the balance in common stock. But there were fabulous debts to meet. And before that matter was settled, business must proceed as usual.

In the meantime, on November 9, 1913, the most violent storm ever to strike the Great Lakes broke at midnight with gale winds, a blinding blizzard and dropping barometer. Over two hundred and fifty men and eleven freighters were lost, with many other ships damaged.

Tom was keeping vigil at the tug office when the Coast Guard called. Their boats had been smashed and wrecked at the Station just north along the Lake, and it seemed there was a big freighter in distress just opposite.

With dawn, Tom was nosing out into the wildly churning Lake aboard the tug *Sarnia City,* trying to negotiate the short distance from the mouth of the river. He passed the lightship on Corsica Shoal which had been torn from its moorings and was lying at anchor. Some distance ahead he saw the 600 foot freighter *Matthew Andrews* — worth $250,000 — struggling to 'make the river.' He was watching through the glasses when she struck the bar that had caught and held the floundering lightship. He had never before actually seen a ship strike.

The *Sarnia City* fought her way along and now they sighted the distressed ship they had been summoned to assist. Upside down, only her bow was visible above water. There was no way of identifying her at the time. But when the sea was calm again, Louis Meyers submerged and chiseled the letters off the stern of the mysterious ship. She proved to be the *Charles S. Price,* a 600 foot bulk freighter.

The bodies of her captain and numerous crew members were washed ashore before long, and a further mystery developed. Men identified as sailors from the *Price* were wearing life-jackets carrying the name of the ship *Regina* which also was lost in that same area. There was much conjecture, but authorities felt that the two ships possibly collided, and some crewmen either jumped or were thrown by the impact from one ship to another. The real facts were never learned.

On two occasions, Tom tried to salvage the *Price,* but found it hopeless. He thought her capsizing was understandable in view of certain structural considerations. In the fore and after-peak, the *Price* had a five foot water tank which was pumped out and kept so. She also had side tanks. In the fury of the storm, when she tried to turn around and return to the river, she was caught in the trough of the sea. Patent hatches, it is said, fall off when a ship turns over. Hatches thus were admitting water, with air in the bottom of the ship. Consequently the result was inevitable.

His family saw little of Tom the rest of that year, and he was grateful for a crowded schedule that kept his troubled mind off more trying business matters.

Anna understood. Her heart was heavy with the shadow that hung over Helen, and she was disturbed about young Thom. Now fifteen, and tall as his father, he had no interest in the Lakes but definite ideas about the future. The day was not far off when he and his father would clash on that issue.

Industry interested Thom. A brilliant student, he criticized his father's English with the superior arrogance of the young and shrugged off his mother's reasoning and advice. He knew what he wanted, which seemed to make him a true male Reid.

Anna wanted to spare Tom every possible worry, for he was carrying a tremendous load. The wholesale loss of life and ships in the November storm had frightened her and increased her concern for her husband. She was reminded of the precariousness of his life, since the sailor-husbands of some of her friends had been taken.

The day he stormed in announcing that he was off for Thunder Bay to aid the disabled steamer *I. W. Nichols* of the Steinbrenner fleet, she made no protest though he was gaunt with fatigue. Argument was futile. But there was prayer —

Winter was advancing. With luck, sometimes they observed Thanksgiving and Christmas on the proper days. Birthday festivities were important to her, but Tom was seldom able to be present.

Thanksgiving in 1913 had been just another day in the Reid home. And Christmas. It was 'the black fall,' when shipping had suffered as never before, and Tom became almost a stranger to his family. A telephone call, brief greetings — these had to suffice. Tom Reid's course was mapped, and it held little room for enjoyment of the home comforts his life of danger had purchased for his family.

One evening Anna sat at her fireside considering it, then summoned the children to discuss plans for Tom's return, resolving to be more tolerant. February 27th was not far off. Tom's birthday. She began to make preparations.

At this time Tom had gone to the assistance of the Steamer *I. W. Nichols,* bulk freighter built at a cost of $100,000 some years previous. The ship was loaded with flax and had gone ashore on a reef off Thunder Bay Island on the east shore of Lake Michigan. With his diver, Tom went down into the hold of the ship — up to their arm-pits in flax — to investigate damage. His bid was $30,000.

The business of lightering presented a big problem as the saturated flax began to congeal. But finally this was managed. A patch was affixed to the damaged plates, and she was towed in to Alpena where the owners and underwriters could inspect her and plan for further action.

Now Perry Jones of Lloyd's advised Tom that they had $100,000 insurance for total loss only, which meant that the *Nichols*' wrecking and repairing bill must be above three quarters of the insurance. Then the underwriters would have to pay total loss or repair ship. Jones advised Tom to put a watchman aboard and leave her for the winter, as he figured she was a total loss, and the underwriters would take her down in the Spring for repair.

Tom complied and hurried back to Port Huron ready for the birthday celebration when Perry Jones again contacted him. It seemed the underwriters must repair the *Nichols* at once or deliver her to drydock. Did Tom think he could get her as far as Port Huron and the drydock there? If so, and the procedure was without incident, there would be a fee of $27,000.

Tom agreed, fitted out the tugs *Fisher* and *Reid* and started up Lake Huron, breaking the way through deep ice. He knew he was taking a long chance on delivering the *Nichols* to the Port Huron shipyard, but danger was his business. From the Lake shore in, they fought ice all the way back from Black River to Alpena, the tug *Fisher* in the lead. Barges were pulled out from the dock and cables were strung across the river to hold the barges away from the dock so they could freeze out there and permit the men to work.

The *Fisher* was high. Cables hit her bow. They would have taken the pilot house off the tug *Reid*.

With difficulty, they raised steam on the *Nichols*. A wind rose when they were ready to leave — a north east gale swinging hard across Lake Huron, and a blizzard cut visibility. The *Nichols* rode on her tank top, rolling perilously. By the time she came abreast of Harbor Beach, the situation had become desperate. Approaching the harbor entrance with only a hope and a prayer to guide him, Tom sent the tug *Reid* ahead to blow her whistle and warn of their approach. He cleared the pier by some miracle, since there were no lights, buoys or ranges; signalled hard and long, and managed to enter and tie up at the dock.

When the storm subsided, they went on the sixty miles to Port Huron where the drydock received the *Nichols*. There the tank top was examined by Perry Jones and George Steinbrenner, and it was reluctantly agreed that the *Nichols* was a total loss.

Tom saw possibilities in the craft, however, and made a deal with Lloyds' agent for the wrecked 'junk' for a price of $5,000. He had plans for her at Montreal. Tom ordered her cut in two at the drydock, eliminated the bad spot, and reduced her length to 265 feet, which would permit passage through the canal.

Renamed the *Inland,* she proved a worthy investment as well as a small gold mine along the Quebec waterways where she made a new life for herself and a small fortune for her owners. And the Reid Company had profited by Tom's shrewd foresight to the amount of $25,000. . . .

With Spring, Anna refused to accept defeat to her earlier birthday plans, and when Tom came home toward the middle of March, he was greeted with a celebration.

Young Thom's gift was a burnt wood plaque which carried a rather lengthy composition entitled HOW TO MAKE A COFFER DAM. The father read it aloud thoughtfully —

> "A coffer dam has to be watertight. You put it around a space where you want to pump the water out and work without anything getting wet. You take a couple of rows of piles and pound clay in between them. You put them close together, and make grooves in them. If the water is not very deep you can set them farther apart and fit the boards in the grooves. You have to watch out about water coming in, and leaks, and the thing has got to be strong. If you are working on rock, you cannot drive in piles, of course. You have got to use stone and clay then."

Tom looked up as he finished reading. "That's good, Thom. Thank you." He would have enjoyed going into the matter thoroughly; enjoyed giving an expert's definition from practical experience rather than have the boy accept an objective version available, probably, in an encyclopaedia.

Thom glowed under the brief but sincere praise. "Boy, you've got to have brains to make one of them, sir. Your heart's got to be in your work. I could never make one in a thousand years."

Tom regarded his son gravely over his glasses. "Why do you say you could never be a sailor?"

"I didn't say that," protested Thom, flushing.

"That's what you meant."

Thom avoided his father's eyes.

"It's in the Reid blood, son. Make up your mind to it — the Lakes are waiting for you, like they were with your grandfather and me. Don't go fighting against the thing you should do, just because some crazy idea gets hold of you. Be true to yourself."

"You tell me that," Thom argued, "and yet — you try to make me into something I'm not. Just because you like the Lakes, that's no reason I've got to. Why, I'll bet if you had to take your choice between your work and your family, we'd come in second."

"Thom, don't be rude!" Anna was stern.

"You said so yourself, Mother."

Unhappy, the father left the room.

"Why did you have to hurt him?" asked Anna.

"You hurt him often." Thom was defiant now because he was ashamed.

"I don't set out to hurt him, though . . . Some times I hate the Lakes. They own him. Oh, he has to go — I know. His work is his life. It's what he has to do."

"Then why can't I do what I have to do? Why must I do what he wants?"

"He wants you to be prepared to take over, Thom, when he's through. He's struggled to make a success of the business, to give you a future — "

"A future I don't want!" stormed Thom. And yet — as she did, he wanted to please his father; particularly at this time, for he realized he was adding to heavy burdens that Tom Reid was carrying in these troubled days. And there was a deep anxiety Thom did not suspect.

World War I was raging across the sea, and no doubt the United States would get into it — and if it lasted, young Thom would have to go —

The birthday celebration failed, and when Tom left to salvage the Steamer *Howard M. Hanna, Junior,* the parting was not without constraint. In the sharp March wind, he boarded the tug *Sarnia City* and headed for the tip of Michigan's Thumb where the *Hanna* lay helpless — as she had all winter after almost sinking in the November storm.

Built by the Hanna Transit Company of Cleveland, Ohio, at a cost of $350,000 and carrying 10,000 tons of coal, the 500 foot freighter had gone ashore at Port Austin.

Lake Huron washes no more picturesque shoreline than here, where rock formations tower above the water. Near by stands the fine old mansion of the late Professor William Lyon Phelps, with the brightly painted blackamoors at the drive, and the little weathered church — where he preached frequently in summer — sunning itself near the ancient elms.

Just down the shore a bit lies the ghost town, Grindstone City, which was dealt a death blow at the invention of carborundum, its formidable coast still challenging the mariner.

Here rocks lie in fantastic confusion among the sumac, locust and willow — a storybook scene when the weather is fair, but a deadly menace to navigation in wind or fog. And among these rocks, the *Hanna* went ashore.

With weather consistently treacherous, and the ship at a particularly bad spot, salvaging at the time of the accident had been out of the question. Lloyds' agent now conferred with Tom Reid, offering him 75% of the ship for raising her. The percentage of a ship, it seems, is as her value when she is 'taken off.'

Tom considered this. "You know the deal I got in the *Moreland* case," he reminded Perry Jones. "I invested $40,000 in salvaging equipment and labor, and got $15,000 for my trouble. And I'm going to get the same deal here. What will you take for her where she is right now — boat and cargo?"

Jones recognized the negative possibilities of the deal — yet also, the Company's responsibility, in view of Admiralty Law.

Tom made an outright offer of $13,000. It was accepted. By the time negotiations were closed, the *Hanna* was practically raised. The Reid Company finished the job, the *Hanna* was patched and afloat again, ready for the shipyard and eventual service. Bids were immediately offered the Reid Company for her, and she was sold to Playfair of the Canadian Steamship Company in Sarnia for $100,000 — $25,000 when landed, $75,000 when bonded, Playfair to assume all costs of repair.

Renamed the *Glenshe* — on her first trip down the St. Clair River, she 'went on' above the Cut, and once again the Reid Company was called, and once again released her.

"You had a hell of a nerve to send me a bill on her first trip out!" Playfair stormed at Tom.

But they laughed about it many times afterward over a good cigar when the *Glenshe* could be seen cruising north and south, making fat dividends for her Company and stockholders.

That was a grim period in Great Lakes navigation. For months to come it was to face repercussions of that November storm. The matter of *The Golden Rule,* Government lightship No. 82 — worth $60,000 with vital equipment — that sank in 7 minutes in Lake Erie just outside of Buffalo, was an example. And she had taken seven men to their death.

The Government sent divers out to reclaim the bodies thought to be trapped in the boat, but none were there. And nothing further was done until Spring when the Government summoned the Reid Company to salvage her where she lay in 65 feet of water.

It was mid-June when Tom Reid and his diver went to make an examination of the submerged boat, and found her covered with silt. Yet it was seen that she could still propel herself. She had been at anchor, possibly with only steam enough to operate deck winches and such. The storm had broken the anchor-chain and the anchor was never found.

Tom decided to employ two wooden pontoons, each capable of lifting 200 tons, to get anchor chains under the ship. Four chains were needed. A pump was installed in the boat's side with flexible hose to pump silt at keel. It was hard work in intensely hot weather. The success of the procedure could be ascertained by the appearance of the water at the surface. If clear, the pump was not working.

One day, with the temperature at 99 degrees, Louis Meyers surfaced for the noon meal, divested himself of his trappings and, there being no decompression chamber, walked briskly down the deck. Passing the galley, he saw a tray of freshly fried doughnuts on the sill, and helped himself to some that were still hot.

The dinner bell rang a few minutes later. He went in and had a solid meal. That day, he suffered the 'bends.' It was the only time in all his experience that such a thing happened. They immediately immersed him in hot water, briskly massaged him while the tug pulled at full speed for shore. Blood blisters appeared all over his body; arms and legs were paralyzed with cramps.

For a time it was feared Meyers would be crippled.

But soon he began to improve, and it was not long before he resumed his work, undaunted by the experience. He had learned a valuable lesson.

The bodies of the men lost on the Government Lightship were never found. But the craft was restored to service after a short period of salvaging. The salvage bid was $15,000 and the profit came to $5,000.

Anna's plans were always, of necessity, tentative. She was learning to meet disappointment without tears — as a general thing. But Tom could see that the fresh, inspiring optimism was being tempered and that the spirit was less ebullient than in those first days. Anna was tasting the life he had warned her would follow their marriage. She was trying hard to adjust to continued disappointments.

A little club to which they belonged — and well used to Tom's absences — was to meet at the Reid home the day Tom was called to Detroit to the Steamer *John W. Moore,* a 300 foot, 6,000 ton bulk freighter, built at a cost of $150,000. She had suffered a collision with another freighter in the Detroit River. Abreast of Wyandotte, she was between Grosse Isle and Mamajudy when another freighter — loaded, ran into her and knocked the whole bow off and drove her keel down into the mud.

With the tug *Salvor* standing by, Louis Meyers put in a bulkhead, braced it with big timbers and steel beams. They pumped her out and got up steam, but her bow stayed down and wouldn't let go. The tug kept swinging, trying to loosen her, and finally the bulkhead let go with the pressure. Thus they were forced to do the work all over again. The entire job required several months, though eventually they were successful in raising her. The accepted bid was $25,000, but the profit inevitably small.

After Tom's inspection and bid, he took time out to hurry up to Traub's where he chose a little pearl pin as a peace offering. It was designed as a lover's knot.

Anna accepted it with a sly smile — the edge of disappointment by then wearing away. "It should be in the shape of an anchor or life-preserver—"

"Or skull and crossbones, why don't you say?" he put in. They laughed together. . . . And he went back to Detroit and the hard problem before him.

Despite his busy, harried life, always in the undercurrent of his thoughts was concern over Thom. He finally realized that no pressure could persuade a true acceptance of something undesired. Thom had his own ideas. He wanted to go into industry. And eventually that would happen.

At home when the conversation turned to the future, and Thom's imminent enrollment at the University of Michigan, Tom made no comment. One night in early September when he dropped in to pick up a bag and see his family briefly before leaving for Montreal, Anna said, "Can't you stay for an hour at least? There's something I want to discuss with you."

"I'm off to figure on a job up at Newfoundland. If you need money — " he shrugged. There was tension in his home these days. Helen's frailty to face. Thom's decision. In Clara and Virginia he found his only normal outlet, because he felt that Anna was against him in this business of Thom. Her son was her idol. What the boy wanted would suit her, regardless.

"I don't need money," she denied. "You provide well. You spoil us all that way. I need to see more of you. There are problems about the children. I need your help, Tom."

"That's the last thing you need," he said grimly. "Our children seem to be handling things pretty well for themselves. Especially Thom. What is there to discuss about him? He's made his plans. He wants no advice from me."

"On the contrary, Tom. You see, he's planning to take up marine engineering at college. He intends to make that his life's work."

"When did this come about?" Tom was incredulous.

"Thom has thought it out," Anna replied, without admitting her part in persuading such a decision.

Tom went off to Montreal lighter hearted than he had been in some time. Anna had managed it. If she agitated for the continuance of the plan and Thom became seriously interested, perhaps he would follow through!

With late Spring, a matter came up that persuaded Tom to take his son out of class temporarily to accompany him to Sydney, Nova Scotia. He felt it might prove the turning point in the boy's thinking if he witnessed the preliminary stages of salvaging *The African Prince.*

Built in England at a cost of $300,000, in the Spring of 1915 and during World War I, the big bulk freighter — 500 feet long — had run on the rocks outside Sydney. She carried a cargo of 20,000 casks of alcohol, loaded in Norfolk, Virginia. Alcohol being a wartime commodity, the cargo was vital. Bound for Halifax, she had been hugging the coast to avoid submarines, and ran into trouble.

The Canadian Minister of Marine had contacted The Reid Company and, lining up his wrecker the *Maggie Marshall,* Tom went to the scene. Here young Thom glimpsed a kind of life he had never seen before, but a kind his father took in daily stride. In a dirty, foul-smelling tug, commanded by a chronically drunk captain, father and son daily went out to the wreck.

The bow of *The African Prince* lay on the beach, her stern in the ocean, while soldiers patrolled the area to prevent highjacking and since submarines might be skulking off the coast, waiting until the steamer was salvaged and off to sea again. More than one boatload of French and British seamen had come ashore in dories, their ships victims of submarine attack.

The crew of negroes from Norfolk, singing as they worked, unloaded casks of alcohol onto the decks of the wrecker *Maggie Marshall.* Young Thom's uneasy comments at the sound of wild, hilarious laughter was shrugged off by his father. But Captain Tom's expression was grim rather than indifferent, for the air reeked with pungent fumes. A certain amount of breakage was inevitable in the disposition of any cargo, and several casks had been broken, the fate of their contents obvious.

It was disturbing to watch the great, brawny negroes handle the heavy casks with such casual ease. Discipline was difficult, and the few young armed soldiers stationed on the ship were a humble match for them even under peaceful conditions.

However the salvage work continued without incident until *The African Prince* yielded to the pulling and lightering and slipped into the sea. And not too soon. A bad storm was making up in the west.

Tom gave orders to the ship's captain to get up steam, and as the captain relayed orders to the crew, the drunken negroes struck. Emboldened by liquor and with shores receding, they made ridiculous demands and refused to obey. Wresting guns from the young soldiers, and threatening violence, they took over the pilot-house.

The ship, without control, drifted aimlessly, a danger to other craft as well as itself, and the storm bore down upon them.

Only a foolhardy youth would have made that next move. Young Thom, a giant in stature and completely fearless, snatched up a crowbar and struck out indiscriminately at the leaders of the riot, felling the two most belligerent.

It was one of those things that happen in the odd percentage of luck, but the incident cowed the others and order was restored after a brief battle while the safety of lives and the ship hung in the balance.

Perhaps the breaking storm, with almost hurricane force, helped the situation, for the frightened negroes were beset by superstition. When they were subdued and the ship secured again, the officers and Reids left her at anchor as they went ashore in the little harbor tug with her never-quite-sober master; Tom taking the wheel and young Thom at the engine through a storm designed in hell. Thom's choice of industry as a career had suffered no set-back whatever.

CHAPTER FOURTEEN

But Captain Tom still secretly hoped, counting on the Reid blood to effect his son's final decision. Necessary methods of persuasion annoyed him. He realized he was facing the result of over-indulgence. He had yielded without question to his children's whims. In days when few of the younger set were given cars, the young Reids drove their own. Helen had now been entered at National Park Seminary. He had glanced indifferently at the bills for her clothes. Expense was unimportant if her health improved and she had what she wanted.

Anna's goal from the beginning had been education and privilege for her children. She had built a library at home — read to them, encouraged their interest in cultural pursuits.

He guessed Anna was right. Education was important. Maybe if he'd been more interested, he would have learned in youth the word-forms that meant so much to Anna. The rightness of her speech was like music. She used words as he used cables and torches and chains . . .

Clara was now in high school. When she coaxed for a new fur coat, more spending money, a different car, he yielded. He could not deny his children anything. And Virginia, now entering her teens — and his idol — had her wishes granted almost before they were expressed. The worries and demands of his work were little enough to pay for providing luxury for those he loved.

Sometimes, laboring on a job, he would pause and consider the danger to which he was exposing them through indulgence. Only because he had been conditioned from childhood had he been able to follow through the demands of circumstance. A foundation was important — rejection, occasional frustration. A person needed such things to build him up, toughen him for what lay ahead.

His children had known none of these, and Anna was as indulgent as he. They discussed it, but never arrived at a plan of correction; aware, though not acknowledging the fact, that they lacked the moral strength to meet such a demand on their emotions.

Events began to crowd so rapidly during the war years that Tom was seldom home, and the entire problem lay in Anna's hands. It was a period in his life when he was almost a stranger to his family.

In 1917, with submarine warfare growing steadily

worse, the need for ships increased. Every possible craft, whatever her condition, was considered for use. Old ships long abandoned, were reconditioned and brought into service. Wrecked ships, once left to be beaten to pieces by the elements and dissolve with time, were patched, refloated, and brought limping to the shipyards by the Reid Company. Some derelicts rebelled at over-long neglect and gave up the struggle in the middle of the Lake.

The main problem that arose was to deliver the prospects to the Atlantic coast. The Welland Canal provided the only passage, as the Chicago Drainage Canal was not suited to such purposes at the time. The Welland Canal Locks were thirty-six feet wide and 267 feet long in those days. Many vessels proved too large for passage, but the problem had to be solved.

It was decided to experiment with the Steamer *Van Heyse*. Stripping her of machinery and cabins down to the bare hull, they cut her in two. In the center they placed a bulkhead, loaded one side with water and the boat rolled up on the edge. In that position she could negotiate the Canal.

There were 24 Locks in the Canal. Somehow in the construction, the walls were not truly perpendicular. When on edge, the ship was drawing 14 foot limit. When they attempted to lower her, the irregular wall was in the way — caught and held her. They replaced the water, but she would not float. Louis Meyers adjusted hydraulic jacks on the bottom and side, and eventually she was released. But it was an expensive experiment. Tom Reid's crew worked by the day, with the *Manistique* standing by. The Reid Company cleared about $10,000 after expenses.

While the experiment proved discouraging, ships are not built in a day, and further chances were imperative.

Sometimes these met with success, though not always without incident. As in the case of the Steamer *Northwest,* once the glamorous queen of the Lakes and built at a cost of over $1,000,000.

In 1888, James J. Hill, head of the Great Northern Railroad, had organized a subsidiary enterprise, the Northern Steamship Company. In 1894, that fleet was augmented by two luxury liners, the *Northwest* and the *Northland.* Their top speed was 22 miles an hour, with cruising speed that could cover the thousand miles from Buffalo to Duluth in sixty-seven hours.

Jim Hill, a perfectionist, demanded that his trains run on exact schedule, and exacted the same performance from his ships. This eventually proved unfortunate. Indifferent to cost, the railroad tycoon determined that his liners should have no rivals on the Lakes. The woodwork was of mahogany, embellished with exquisite carving. The soft cream panels were edged with gold. The great mahogany staircase, branching half way up in two, extended from the spar deck to the dining room. Table linen, especially woven damask imported from Ireland at a fabulous cost, depicted nautical scenes, including replicas of the ships themselves.

President McKinley's name headed the imposing passenger list on the *Northwest's* maiden voyage. Famous orchestras entertained in her salon, famous chefs presided in her galley. And as she sailed along the waterways, people who could never hope to enjoy such expensive pleasures, experienced a vicarious thrill in possessing her as part of a familiar scene.

On her maiden trip up the St. Clair River, the *Northwest* set out to make a record. The vessel caused a tremendous wash. As she steamed on, the water dropped several feet and a small tidal wave resulted. Boat houses were loosened by the suction and floated on the river. Small craft were tossed ashore. After that passage, many boat-houses had to be rebuilt — at the expense of The Northern Steamship Company. But the publicity lasted and had its effect. And no Great Lakes Captain cared to meet her in the narrow channels of the St. Clair River where the powerful suction would inevitably throw a freighter off her course.

However, the handsome liners never made money, while The Northern Steamship Company's freighters — the *North Wind, North Star, Northern Queen, Northern King, Northern Wave* and *Northern Light* always showed a good profit. Deficits proved too much for the Great Northern, and the big passenger liners were taken out of service.

The *Northland* caught fire at her dock and was badly damaged. Now, with the World War situation demanding ever more transports, the *Northwest* was bought by Canadian shipping interests, and the Reid Company was approached. Could they cut her in two and get her through the Welland Canal to the sea?

Tom Reid made a bid of $600 a day and the contract was signed. It was on the Steamer *Northwest* that he and Anna had spent their honeymoon. And the day he made his decision to salvage her, he paused in one of the palatial staterooms to write her a note on the dusty, crested stationery. While its syntax and spelling might have been faulty, its rugged beauty recaptured for Anna a memorable interlude. . . .

Captain Tom turned the *Northwest* over to a Buffalo shipyard where she was bisected, and while the after-end of the ship gave them no trouble, the for'd end seemed resistant to their efforts to remake her. She did not easily relinquish her glory.

Finally the work was accomplished, and with both sections declared seaworthy, The Reid Company accepted her for delivery in Montreal. Ordering his tugs *Sarnia City* and *Smith* from Sarnia to Buffalo, Tom left at once to make plans for the operation. And with the halves of the *Northwest* soundly canvassed and bulkheaded, they went on their way.

A violent storm came up when they reached Lake Ontario, and despite all efforts to bring her safely to harbor, the for'd end foundered and sank, though without loss of life. Captain Tom went on with the after end, and headed up the St. Lawrence River, still facing some major problems. There were the Locks to negotiate at the town of Iroquois — at Rapid Plat, Morrisburg, the Long Sault. Things progressed satisfactorily until they reached Lock 18, when she settled down in the water and stuck fast. Efforts to raise her failed.

In the meantime, vital traffic to the coast was halted. Tom sent for his wrecker *Manistique*. But Canadian officials were not inclined to view the situation with tolerance while the submarine pack howled at coastal harbors, and lost time only added to the opportunities of the enemy.

Using hundred-ton jacks, Tom ordered fender rails cut, and bolted angle irons removed. The ship section was taken from the Lock within three days, and she was on her way. Tom then drove on to Montreal on further salvage business where he received word that the stern end of the *Northwest* was in Cornwall Canal where dock authorities denied further passage for fear of blocking.

Once more, he managed the problem for the authorities. But half a sound ship was of little value to the Canadian Government now. It was then decided to dock her at a Quebec shipyard, secure the original blueprints and build a new for'd end. There a time record was made by employing a large working crew for 24 hours a day.

Again the *Northwest* was launched and contributed her bit to the war effort, carrying troops and supplies across the ocean through the world conflict and, luckily, with convoy, evading submarines. In 1920 she was bought by The Canada Steamship Company and again cut in two at a Montreal shipyard. And again the Reid Company was commissioned to tow both parts up the Lakes. But in a career never without incident, the *Northwest* was to encounter further trouble.

They reached the Cornwall Lock with her after-end, and all was well. By now she was running on her own engines, with four tugs to assist on account of the current at that particular spot. Just as she left the Lock in early morning and started out through the Canal past the piers, the tow-line parted at the eye on the tug *Smith.* And immediately she began to float, stern first, down the Rapids.

Aboard, Tom directed the men and managed to swing her against the bank — three tugs working desperately to hold her there. Now the barge *Brighton* was summoned. She carried 1,500 feet of two inch cable, and a pulling machine.

The pier which was their objective was some distance up the river. Tom ran lines down to her port side, took lumberheads and drew her abreast of the pier. Tugs pulled her out finally, and over to the American side of the river. The for'd end of the *Northwest* was ahead with her own tugs, making the port of Kingston, so they took the stern end on, and at Kingston assembled the ship. Again she ran the Lakes for some time as a grain carrier.

One bitter day early in December, bound up 'light,' she 'went on' in a heavy snowstorm at Magnetic Shoals off Mississauga Passage at the entrance to Georgian Bay. She laid there all winter, exposed to wind and sea.

With Spring, Tom negotiated with her owners, bought her for $2,500 and towed her over to the shipyards at Collingwood where she was converted into a wrecker which he called the *Maplecourt.* It cost him close to $20,000 to recondition her. They put new plates on, welded some, and practically reconstructed the frame. They made her seaworthy, but did not have to submit to Lloyd's inspection because she was to carry no cargo.

Once she almost cost her owners more than she was worth, through no fault of her own. This had to do with a shoal south of Slate Island off Jackfish Bay in Lake Superior. Eight or ten miles out from shore, and almost in the channel, a reef with a vicious tooth-pronged rock— and 100 feet of water on either side — menaced navigation, and had caused much trouble. Action was finally taken when in a storm, a small craft with two men aboard ran afoul of it and were lost.

The Government awarded the Reid Company the contract to blow up the rock — price $600 a day for wrecker, and additional expenses for crew, utilities, etc. Tom called his diver, and taking 25 tons of dynamite aboard, started for Lake Superior.

The usual guards were on duty when the *Maplecourt* passed through the Soo Locks, but no mention was made of the contraband in clearance, though the mission of the *Maplecourt* was not unknown. Approaching the designated spot, Tom woefully studied the horizon. Weather - weather - They stood by, four days, six days — eight days! Each time they manoeuvred into position, the weather intervened. After twenty days, they finally managed to set off the charges. Trout and whitefish were scattered all over, and enormous waves increased the effect of the storm then raging. But the project was successful, and the *Maplecourt* headed back to Sarnia.

This time when they reached the Soo, the officials on duty demanded to know if dynamite was aboard. Tom admitted there was. An official accused him then not only of deliberately breaking the law, but of having previously passed through the vital Locks secretly carrying explosives. Such an offense, he was reminded, was punishable by twenty years' imprisonment.

Tom was not unaware of this, but quoted a Government official at Ottawa with whom he had made the agreement to blast the rock — reminding the Soo officer that his Government was paying $600 a day for the Reid wrecker *Maplecourt,* and every hour's delay must be accounted for since it involved Government expense. He added that to unload above the Locks and reload below would be a long, expensive process, as well as dangerous.

Ottawa was contacted. There were grim warnings but permission was given and Tom and the *Maplecourt* went through without further incident. The tension and stillness at the almost deserted scene was never forgotten.

In 1941 the Government again took over the *Maplecourt* for a price of $100,000, and Tom was again commissioned to deliver her to Kingston, Ontario, where once more she was cut in two, towed through the canal to Montreal where she was again reassembled and sent into ocean service.

On her first trip out she cleared for Boston. And leaving there, started across the sea only to be pursued and wrecked by the submarine wolfpack. The colorful career of a gallant lady had come to an end.

CHAPTER FIFTEEN

But back in the year 1917, war affected many lives—and the Reids did not escape. Events were happening that would deprive the family of Tom for many months to come — perhaps years.

On December sixth, the city of Halifax, Nova Scotia, suffered incredible devastation when the Swedish ship *Imo* — a 400 foot package freighter — was leaving the harbor and the big French freighter *Mt. Blanc* was entering. They collided. Having cleared port, the *Mt. Blanc* was on her way with a war cargo of TNT when a fire broke out in her hold. With all speed, she returned to Halifax and when abreast of Dartmouth, the crew took to the yawl boats and went to Dartmouth.

Tugs rushed to quench the fire if possible, and all hands were lost except — curiously enough — the sailors from the *Mt. Blanc.* There were probably 150 ships at anchor in the harbor — convoys waiting to depart for Europe.

The impact of the explosion shattered the area for miles around. Steamers and tugs lay on the shore, parts of them back in the fields, in streets, on rooftops — the stern frame of one in a field twelve miles away. Ships in drydock were blown to pieces and submerged by the tidal wave with complete loss of life. A schoolhouse within a picket fence was destroyed with its 240 pupils, but the fence remained undamaged. The roof of a train shed was snatched off while the shed was spared. A candy store clerk, only a few feet from a customer, survived — while the man was killed. A chimney 156 feet high turned on its base, and not a brick was dislodged. A woman driving a team of horses was blown to pieces. Horses, too, perished. The harness was unscarred.

The Canadian Minister of Marine contacted Tom Reid from Ottawa and he left at once for the scene with Louis Meyers. The train could approach only within three miles of the city of Halifax. Arriving in a howling blizzard, the men had to make their way on foot through scenes of horror. Canadian Coast Guard officials helped them find lodgings in a private home — one among a few undamaged. Thirty ships were allocated to them for salvage by the insurance Company.

Tom formed a Company there — The Maritime Wrecking Company. He brought the tug *Sarnia City* east; also the steam barge *Maggie Marshall* which he had converted into a wrecker equipped with a clamming rig. Pumps, hydraulic jacks, pontoons and other equipment were sent from the base at Sarnia, and the work was begun.

Among the ships salvaged were the following:

The ship *Caracas* — built at a cost of $500,000. Tom's Company bid $75,000 to salvage — made $25,000 on the job. . . . The ship *Bethlehem,* at the same figure. . . . *The Siberian Prince*. Bid $175,000. Worked on a commission taking cargo off. Forced to hire several schooners to use in unloading. Paid out $50,000. . . . The *Imperial Oil,* a barge. They took her off near the ocean. The underwriters paid $250,000 for salvaging her and another smaller ship. They never used her again. The Reid Company made a profit of $12,000 on this.

In salvaging the *Caracas,* when they went in, they found forty bodies. And when clamming out her grain cargo, they encountered dismembered bodies throughout. It was rumored that the grain was dried and taken to Quebec to be sold. . .

Twenty four hours a day the work of salvaging went on despite blizzards, sub-zero weather and the most adverse conditions; the work of restoring the supply line to needy allies overseas. Out beyond prowled submarines, awaiting their prey.

Tom spent much time during the next three years in the Maritimes. It was in that interval that another important ship met disaster. In July 1918, the Cunard passenger liner *Ascania* — worth $3,000,000 in peace time and $5,000,000 in time of war—–converted into a troopship and with troops aboard, went ashore on a tiny rocky island off the coast of Newfoundland, 42 miles off her course. . . . It was her seventh round trip without incident up to that time, and there was no loss of life.

The Canadian Minister of Marine and the insurance underwriters summoned Tom to Montreal to consider the matter of salvaging. Tom brought Louis Meyers over from Halifax to Sydney, Nova Scotia, and they left by ship for Port aux Basques, Newfoundland. There, securing a sailboat, they went on to examine the *Ascania* on the rocks near a little fishing hamlet called Petites. Going full speed ahead when she struck, the *Ascania's* bow stood high in the air above the rock on which she had foundered, her stern undamaged.

This salvaging project was a million dollar gamble. The contract was signed on a 'no cure, no pay' basis — except that the insurance underwriters agreed to pay a percentage of the expense incurred in rounding up proper equipment. A wrong guess could place the Reid Company in a serious financial position. Louis Meyers was confident the *Ascania* could be salvaged, as was Tom. There was only one catch — the weather. North Atlantic seas and gales had to be taken into consideration. Tom realized they would not be able to assemble proper equipment before September — if then. Man power was limited because of war demands. And with September, the storms would strike. However, the contract was signed, and a bonus promised for every man if the ship was saved.

In part payment on a deal for his wrecking company, Tom Reid had taken the little steamer *Mary Battle*— probably 100 feet long and 250 tons capacity — now in Montreal. Placing her in drydock, he ordered her hold cleared out for equipment and for the great wooden box to be built as a reservoir for fresh water. A circulating pump was found; boilers, purchase blocks, air compressors, gear for the derrick which was built on the stern, and other wrecking gear.

Time passed while they piped air compressors properly

to the air tanks and tested them, checked materials as they arrived from different distant points and started loading wrecking gear aboard. But the quest for labor was discouraging. There were bits of luck along the way, however. An old salt pausing at the dock one day to watch gear brought aboard, remarked to Louis Meyers—"Wouldn't need an extra man, would you? Any rigging to be done?" Meyers almost yanked the man aboard in his delight.

At last they were ready for coaling, for the stop at the munitions plant to put dynamite aboard, and the *Mary Battle* was on her way. By September first she arrived at Sydney, ready to go to sea. But the sea was not ready for her, and passage to Newfoundland was difficult and treacherous. From the daily report of Louis Meyers were such notations—

Sep. 5—At North Sydney. *Battle* ready to go to sea at 4 PM. Weather reports unfavorable.
Sep. 7—Weather still unfavorable for *Battle* to proceed to Port aux Basques.
Sep. 8—6 AM. Wind moderating. *Battle* left North Sydney at 1 PM. Weather good.
Sep. 9—Cold and raining. Had telegram *Battle* had arrived at Port aux Basques. Left North Sydney at 9 PM. with wrecking crew aboard local ship *Stanley* for Port aux Basques.
Sep. 10—Arrived Port aux Basques.

Tom Reid and Louis Meyers and wrecking crew of 46 men, with all equipment, had finally reached the shores of Newfoundland. At once they boarded the *Mary Battle* and left on the two hour run to the little fishing village of Petites where they unloaded supplies, put up tents and had their first meal ashore.

Men from Mars descending on a Kentucky mountain setlement would probably have caused less stir than these hardy salvagers caused at Petites. Natives came to gasp at the great iron range at which two camp cooks presided — and to marvel at cooking utensils, the dishes and food.

Children prowled about, gleeful at finding a discarded can, a bit of string or paper bag. They were delirious with excitement — all 56 of them, trained in a rude little school by a teacher from Sydney, whose stipend of $17.00 a month had to find its way back to and be distributed through the populace. This required her boarding with a different family every few weeks.

Tents proved inadequate against the violence of that wild sub-Arctic wind. And Louis Meyers' reports went on —

Sep. 11—Sleeping tents blown down and torn. Making arrangements to rent houses for men to sleep and eat in. Men taking supplies from *Battle,* putting same ashore. Found it impossible to hold big tent securely down. Went over to Harbor-Le-Cou to see about renting two houses for cooking and sleeping purposes.

Sep. 12—Moving range and supplies into houses, getting everything arranged for men's comfort. Also had motor engineer come from Rose Blanche to look at motor pumps.

Sep. 13—Got out alongside of *Ascania* with *Battle* at 8 AM. Connecting up steam lines to deck winches, started hoisting motor pumps and suction pipes on board *Ascania. Battle* had to leave at 5 PM, sea making from the SE. Getting for'd booms ready on *Ascania* to lift boilers and air-compressors on board. Left wreck with men 6:45.

Sep. 14—Raining and wind blowing hard from SE. Too much sea for *Battle* to lay alongside. Got balance of stores on shore. *Battle* went after fresh water.

Fresh water was scarce. But soon, fortunately, they were able to secure plenty when they discovered a little lake on a hill above Dublin Cove not far away, and piped it down to the shore.

Sep 15—Wind blowing hard from the east. Too much sea for *Battle* to lay alongside *Ascania.*

Sep. 16—Went out alongside *Ascania* in small boat, found there was too much sea to get aboard.

By the eighteenth, with a heavy dead sea rolling in from the southeast, they went out in a small boat and managed to get aboard the *Ascania.* But an hour later had to leave the wreck because of wild winds. And so it went, day after day. Too much sea to get aboard. Winds shifting. Big sea running.

Sep. 24—*Mary Battle* alongside *Ascania* at 8 AM. Too much sea for her to lay forward. Men working on wreck. At 1 PM shifted *Battle* forward and started hoisting off plates. Two small air-compressors, two boilers. At 4:45 PM half tide Captain reported *Battle* striking on bottom, ordered him to let go at once and in backing away from wreck *Battle* again hit bottom causing her to spring a leak. Left wreck with men at 6:20 PM.

Day after day, too stormy to work — and expenses mounting, mounting.

Sep. 27—Landed alongside *Ascania* with men in small boat at 7:30 AM. *Battle* arrived at 9AM, too much sea for her to lay forward to take off large air-compressor. Men working on wreck building founda-

> tions for boilers and air-compressors, also piping up steam line between decks. Sea making up from SE. *Battle* had to leave at 11:30 AM. Left wreck with men at 12:10 noon.

The men were familiar with the severe equinoctial storms on the Great Lakes, but not with the persistence of this brutal weather. Tom and Louis Meyers felt the restlessness of the men, and tried to provide for their comfort. Some found diversion among the scanty female population at Petites — one later marrying a Newfoundland girl.

There were amusing and pathetic incidents. The natives and their families, accustomed only to the barest necessities of life, were suddently faced with evidences of plenty from the world beyond the sea. Noticing the agitation of a worker one day, Louis Meyers questioned him. It seemed that each payday, his precious earnings had been carefully put away in an old trunk — when he would count the pile before adding to it. Last night he had gone to add his latest earnings and found the trunk empty. It developed that his little daughter, in a household bare of bright scraps for doll clothes, had appropriated the pretty colored pieces.

Another native approached Meyers one day and asked if he might have some of the excelsior in the mattresses aboard that had been used by the troops. And, too, his wife could use the ticking for the children's clothes. Since nothing of that nature was to be saved, Meyers gave him permission to take as much as he chose. And after that, each time he left the ship he took as much as he could carry. It occurred to Meyers that for excelsior, the bags seemed to 'weigh heavy.' Suspicious, he stopped the man one day to question him. And as the fellow dropped the bags to deck, there was a sharp thud.

Not excelsior entirely, but rivets filled the bags. Fishing nets required weights, and when this job was done, fishing was the only work to be had. Weights cost money and were hard to come by . . .

One setback after another bedeviled the salvagers. On October first, Meyers recorded in his daily report —

> *Battle* furnishing steam, setting up two boilers on foundation, filling tank with fresh water. At 4:45 shifted *Battle* forward and started hoisting out large air-compressor. Then hoisting engine let go and air-compressor went into the sea. *Battle* departed, went to anchor in Dublin Cove. Left wreck with men at 6:15.

And with weather growing worse day by day —

> Oct. 4—*Battle* arrived alongside *Ascania* at 12 o'clock noon. Furnished steam for hoisting air-compressor aboard. Put same in between decks. At 5 PM shifted *Battle* forward, hoisted up small air-compressor, channel-irons and diving outfit. Wind shifted. *Battle* let go. Left wreck with men at 6:30 PM.

Because of the war, it had been difficult to secure required materials. Tom and Meyers had noticed a Russian ice-breaker moored at the dock in Sydney. Inquiry revealed that it had been lying there several years. She was intended for salvage purposes also, it was evident, and, as they hoped, there were pumps aboard. The agent was contacted, and the gas pumps secured.

Louis Meyers started a helper on these, but they were of foreign make and difficult to manage. An engineer almost lost his life through a faulty exhaust. There were many such trying and dangerous incidents before the whole routine was working efficiently, and each day brought an encouraging lower water level aboard ship to compensate.

Again Meyers reported —

> Oct. 18—Landed men on board *Ascania* at 7:35 AM. Air-compressors running, iron-workers drilling holes in plates for No. 1 hatch, shore men shoveling coal, carpenter tearing out ceiling in No. 1 hold to discover air-pipes. Divers made examination of No. 4 hold, reported tank top torn up on port side of midship for about 26 feet for'd and aft and open 10 to 11 inches in center. Also found one hole in bilge plate. Divers tearing down temporary bulkhead. *Battle* came alongside at 1:30 PM with fresh water, took off gasoline, oils and foot valves. *Battle* let go at 5:30 PM. McGrath and his men taking down boat davits. Left wreck with men at 6:10 PM.

For days reports repeated themselves. Iron workers drilling and riveting. Divers working in holds, tearing out wooden bulkhead; carpenters making templets for divers, building oil room, making patches, cementing. Engineer from fog station working on motor pumps. Landing men aboard *Ascania*. Unable to land men. Too much sea. Rain . . . .

November came. But with good luck, it would soon be over, and the *Ascania* afloat again. The weather grew steadily worse, and the wind carried a core of threat that could make men glance up with unease. Excitement prevailed at the imminence of departure. The men would be going home with their good pay and a bonus for successful operation.

A dance was planned in the mess hall, and exceeded their expectations in pleasure. There was music, or what passed for music. But what was a sour note here and there? They were joyously celebrating a good job almost done! Everybody was happy — until the moon came up. And then the natives grew sober and thoughtful. For there was a circle around it — and three stars in the circle. That meant, three days from then, they could expect the terrible storm that came each year about this time.

The salvagers shrugged it off. Why the ship was almost ready! They could beat any storm. Hadn't they already met practically the worst the Atlantic had to offer?

On the third day, the wind began to freshen up from the south east. The storm came. Louis Meyers report read —

Nov. 14—Landed men aboard *Ascania* at 7:25 AM. Had to stay aboard *Battle* all day and night. Too much sea to return in launch.

Nov. 15—Wind shifted around to NW. Left at 4 PM with launch for Petites. Found lifeboats broken up on rocks. Still too much sea to get aboard *Ascania*.

Nov. 16—Went out to *Ascania* with Capt. Stewart and Rogers and made examination of damage done by storm. Found steamer had settled down 7 feet aft. Also found steamer had 3 degrees more list to port, 18 degrees in all. Decks had opened up more and sides buckled up. Forward boilers stove up, and piping buckled. 18 inch wrecking pump broken and all gear scattered about. Purchase blocks overboard. Left steamer and went to Steamer *Stanley* standing by.

The heartbreaking discouragement at sight of such destruction. After long hard weeks of bitter exposure and almost superhuman effort, all progress wiped out in a few hours!

Following the routine reports of clearing up wreckage came along. Then on November 28, the incredible notation —

> Landed men aboard *Ascania* at 7:40 AM. *Battle* arrived 8 AM. Got cable for sea anchor on board and started heaving same when fire broke out on *Ascania* about 8:40 AM. Got cable and anchors aboard then went alongside *Ascania.* Found her all afire for'd in No. 1 and deep sea tank. Started getting fuel for *Battle* at once, also mooring lines, diving outfit and other gear. Returned with men to camp.
>
> Nov. 30—Too stormy for *Battle* to leave today for Port aux Basques.
>
> Dec. 1—Started getting camping outfit aboard *Battle.* Left Petites with men and *Battle* 12:30 noon. Arrived Port aux Basques 5:20 PM. Had baggage removed on dock. Everything arranged for to leave on steamer for North Sydney. Departed 9 AM.

It was over. They were on their way, with wind and snow from the northeast and a sea possessed of the devil. Far off, a speck against the rocking sky, stood the *Ascania,* once proud lady yielding at last to the waters that refused to surrender her. And a million dollar gamble had failed.

CHAPTER SIXTEEN

Home again, Tom found Anna deeply troubled. Helen had become seriously interested in a Detroit man, Gray Hamilton Creager, and contemplated marriage. And Helen was not too well.

Argument had proved futile. And after Anna had persuaded herself to accept the inevitable, she set about making wedding plans. There was a brief, decisive scene in which she reminded Tom that he had invariably failed her in moments of crisis. Nothing must prevent his attendance at the wedding. If he failed her *this* time —

But he promised, adding that no expense was to be spared. More than that, he would provide a surprise that would thrill them all and make up for the disappointments of the past.

Familiar with his generosity, fantastic possibilities suggested themselves. What could the surprise be? Diamonds? New cars? — But they never dreamed of such a thing as the *Ramona* . . . She was a small steel ship of 59 tons, built back in 1886 built at a cost of $20,000 by the Canadian Starch Company at Cardinal, Ontario, for commercial purposes. She was destined to become the Reid yacht in 1920. Now he set about making her not only completely seaworthy but as attractive as possible — according to his conception of beauty.

June came, and the wedding day. Early in the festivities at the Reid summer home on Lake Huron's shore, Tom quietly withdrew. Driving swiftly the few miles down to Port Huron's Black River, he went aboard the *Ramona,* where a small crew waited, cast off and started up the shore.

There was music in the Reid garden, dancing in the tent. It suddenly occurred to Anna that she had not seen Tom for quite a while, and someone was drawing attention to a small steamer not far off shore — great rolls of heavy black smoke pouring from her stack. And someone else was bewailing the shower of soot that fell on organdie and taffeta and flower-decked hats.

Now the little steamer slowed and stopped. Anchors were thrown out, and a dory set off toward shore, heading directly toward the Reid place. At the oars sat Tom, coatless, sleeves rolled up, long arms bending savagely to the task, the hot sun burning his drenched, blackened face. Reaching their beach, he stepped out — and into the water, of course — pulled the dory up on the sand and called to his wife, "There you are, Anna! There's your surprise. It's your yacht."

She managed to smile, to beckon to him. And Tom Reid — looking more like one of his deckhands than host at a fashionable wedding reception — went to her with an uneasy, little-boy smile. She drew him into the house. The day had been a strain, but she could not hurt him, any more than she could a child who had blunderingly tried to please her.

"The people are beginning to leave, Tom," she told him. "Freshen up a bit — and come down."

"You don't like it, do you, Anna?" he sighed. "You don't like the yacht."

"Why, I haven't had a chance to look at it, Tom. There's time for that later. Helen is changing to leave on her trip."

After all had gone, she watched him as he climbed into the skiff and rowed back to the *Ramona.* Down in her heart, she would have loved to board that crazy boat and go with him — that reckless, loving red-head who never knew what it was to care what the other fellow thought. He was free . . .

Later that summer, the *Ramona* lay at a dock in Sarnia. It was a temporary arrangement, and Tom had plans for shifting her to a more desirable spot when, as usual, he was called away on business. Though not unaware of the dock owner's unsavory reputation, he had never encountered any particular evidence of wrong-doing — until the incident of the *Ramona.*

Though summoned just before the bride's return, which was to be observed by an evening affair, he promised solemnly to be on hand for it. In the meantime, it happened that some boys, swimming along the Canadian shore, and syping numerous cases of liquor piled high in the cabins, passed the word along the Sarnia docks. And word reached the police.

It was a matter of unfortunate timing. Only a few hours after the boys' discovery, the cargo would have been quietly transferred by its nefarious owner from a ship above suspicion to a well-disguised rum-runner.

Unaware of what had happened to his ship, Tom was back home enjoying the festivities when a maid announced the arrival of the police. There was a violent scene, but they carried off the profanely protesting Tom.

It was proven that his yacht had been used without his knowledge as a temporary storage space for bootleggers. A miscarriage of plans, due to boyish curiosity, had been the cause of it all. Through this incident, however, certain Chicago gangsters were apprehended, though Anna failed to find it amusing that her husband was accused of rum-running when liquor was seldom seen in their home. The post-bridal affair was not mentioned again.

But Tom was to redeem himself before the summer was over. Each year he sent his family and a few of their friends for a trip around the Lakes on the *Sharpless,* though he was seldom able to accompany them. This year, it was to be a family affair aboard the ship by way of celebration — the result of a little windfall that had to do with the Steamer *Fred Pabst.*

Some time before, this four-masted barge, (each mast wearing a beer keg as finial) built at a cost of $250,000 by the Pabst Brewing Company, and carrying 8,000 tons of coal, had sunk in the Rapids off Sarnia. Her bow was on the bank, stern in the St. Clair River. She was the only ship on the Lakes with a wooden tank-top, and not a likely subject for salvage where she lay, since her cabin had gone off in a storm on Lake Huron. A wooden box, improvised to close the stern, had been smashed away by the ice.

After working on her for a long period, The Reid Company declared she was impossible to salvage, and Tom Reid was given the entire wreck with cargo as compensation for removal from navigable waters. Tom knew he could profit substantially when left to his own resources as to disposition of ship and cargo, and he entered into the pleasures of that trip aboard the *Sharpless* to make it a happy time for all.

As a remembrance, he gave Anna a diamond lavaliere. And availing herself of his mood, she exacted a promise that he would take her to New York the following week to meet her sister and family who were returning from Europe. Tom claimed there was some business in Montreal that would take a day or two, but then they'd be off, and do the big town!

But in Montreal the manager of The Canada Steamship Company rushed him to the assistance of the distressed St. Lawrence passenger ship, the $100,000 *Rapids Prince*. 1,354 feet in length, she was built to accommodate those intrepid tourists who sought the thrills of a trip up the St. Lawrence River from Prescott to Montreal. Now with 500 passengers aboard, she had run on a rocky ledge, hung at an angle and, teetering there, received the full force of the Lachine Rapids.

There had been a similar instance some years before at Sault Sainte Marie Rapids when Tom had been called to help. Immediately now he located a diver, hunted up an Indian with a sturdy canoe and went out to examine the ship.

Afterward, bracing himself on the swaying deck, he gave the hysterical crowd an acceptable picture of the trouble and assured them there was sufficient time to carry out his plan if they would cooperate. Rounding up several Indians with their canoes, he began the long hazardous routine — far more anxious than his manner betrayed. A few at a time, the passengers were taken ashore, and the company paid Tom Reid $5,000 for that rescue.

The Donnelly Wrecking Company made the lowest bid for salvage — $25,000, and The *Rapids Prince* was salvaged and resumed her run the following year, with certain alterations in policy and course.

Instead of the New York trip, another newspaper accolade to Tom went into Anna's scrapbook. She had been married twenty-six years. She was used to such substitutes for reality.

Her sister caustically remarked, when stopping over from New York on her way home, "Well, if Tom decides to spend Christmas out on the Lakes again, at least try to make some kind of time for your family and yourself in Chicago with us. You're a fool, Anna."

"Maybe," smiled Anna, "but a lucky one."

Her loyalty was bitterly tried in December, with Christmas not far off and all of the family at home. Tom was called to Lake Superior once more to fight for the life of the $300,000 Steamer *J. H. Sheadle,* an 8,000 ton bulk freighter of the Cleveland Cliffs fleet. She had loaded iron ore at Marquette. Leaving the dock, bound for Lake Erie, she had run on a rock outside the breakwall, losing her rudder and damaging number one tank port side, causing her to leak in the cargo hold.

The rock formations along Lake Superior's shore provide a spectacular sight for the tourist, and immeasureable hazards for the navigator. Here are the famous Pictured Rocks including Miner's Castle, which served as the holy-water font used by Father Marquette when he blessed the Indians in their canoes. The boom of the surf echoes in the Cave of the Bloody Chiefs — where Indians once placed their prisoners of war, with escape impossible. From Virgin's Rock, Indian maids leaped to death when their lovers were killed in battle. And here the colorful strata wander on to beautify a majestic shoreline, and to crop up and menace such brave ships as the *Sheadle*.

Sending the Reid wrecker *Manistique* north ahead of them, Tom and Louis Meyers went by train to Marquette. Followed a conference with insurance agents who were anxious to have the crippled ship brought to the lower Lakes where she could be permanently repaired in dry-dock during the winter, and ready for the opening of navigation in the Spring.

Under frigid water, Louis Meyers drilled holes in the *Sheadle*'s bottom for a patch; made templets for form to fit outside of patch, and began fastening planks to outside of form. Then came the building and fastening in frames to support planking and covering the lower side of patch with canvas.

There was further examination of break amidships — steam raised on deck-winches, mooring cables brought out; an eighteen inch pump started in cargo hold and a ten inch pump in engine room. Later a ballast pump was started on water-bottom and side tanks, pumping all night. As soon as possible, the ballast pump was shifted over to the *Sheadle*'s own steam and took care of all water, and she was towed in to the dock.

Owners and underwriters now debated on whether to leave the *Sheadle* where she was for the winter — with no rudder and the break temporarily stopped, or to send her down to the Cleveland shipyard for repair. Her tank top had suffered a bad break in one compartment. She was a definite risk. But Tom was told by the owners to condition the ship as well as possible for the trip to Lake Erie.

Louis Meyers concreted the break, but the amount of concrete in the required area was of such quantity that only a substantial lapse of time could make it reasonably sound for the venture. And time was running out. Winter was closing in and the Soo authorities were impatient to close the Locks for the season. Days would have been needed to insure safety with that patch, and only hours were allowed.

Against the stern advice of Tom and Louis Meyers, the owners decided to send the rudderless *Sheadle* to Cleveland. Preparations were made for departure, with the ship *Secord* towing her, the wrecker *Manistique* guiding. At the outer breakwall, a leak developed in the boiler. The *Manistique* returned with her to the harbor and let go anchor. After the delay, with starboard boiler repaired and port boiler fitted out and steam raised, they hove up anchor and prepared to start again.

By now a towering sea was running. They shifted the *Manistique* around to the port side — the ship *Secord* in the lead — wind south, rain heavy, visibility bad. And they lay at anchor all day and night, for it was 'thick' by now.

But on the morning of Christmas Eve day the office and underwriters gave orders to cast off regardless, and final preparations were made to start down the Lake.

At the Reid home on Military Street in Port Huron, the family waited for the Christmas festivities — and Tom. And aboard the *Sheadle* and *Manistique,* holiday food had been prepared at Company's orders. Christmas Eve — — —

Having steam pumps aboard that might require extra

attention, the steamship authorities urged Tom to have Louis Meyers go aboard the *Sheadle* as an extra engineer. This he refused to do as he did not consider the ship in safe condition for the journey, and boarded the wrecker *Manistique* instead. It had taken fifteen days to affix a temporary patch, and hardly twenty four hours after the concrete was mixed and set, they were sending off the *Sheadle* in winter seas for the long run to Lake Erie; an idea of business men, not sailors or engineers.

The ship was hardly under way when Louis Meyers saw the temporary patch floating away. Outside the harbor, the sea was wild. In less than half an hour, the *Manistique* was forced to release herself. The *Sheadle* then started to shear, having no control. A few minutes later, the cable between the *Sheadle* and *Secord* parted. But by good seamanship and expert handling of his wrecker *Manistique,* Captain Richard Knapp and his crew managed to secure the tow line again on the *Sheadle,* and after several hours turned the steamer back to the harbor where she laid up for the winter.

There followed an interlude at The Breakers in Palm Beach for the Reids, by way of compensation to Anna and his family — though briefly for Tom, as usual.

In the early Spring, work on the *Sheadle* continued. Louis Meyers affixed a permanent patch in five days, and the *Sheadle* was readied for her trip to Lake Erie and the shipyard. And that permanent patch was displayed in the Cleveland Cliffs Steamship Company's offices so all could see the work that a skilled man could perform under the wild, icy waters of Lake Superior.

Tom's bid had been $25,000. The Reid Company made a profit of $15,000.

Once more, Tom Reid and his men had saved a ship. There were public accolades. There was another clipping for Anna's scrapbook. And as a gift for her patience and understanding, there was the deed to a twenty acre parcel of land in Detroit at Woodard Avenue and Seven Mile Road — then a wilderness, today a crowded metropolitan area . . . .

"Why did you waste your money like that?" she sighed. "Why, that's nothing but a stretch of country fields. It will never amount to anything."

"Time will tell," shrugged Tom, the man of vision.

Post-war readjustments were taking place, both economic and political. America's participation in the war had been attended at home by widespread and dazzling prosperity, in fitting climax to the great industrial revival of the period of neutrality. In order to stimulate production, the banks freely loaned money to borrowers, and the Government added the inducement of exceptionally high prices.

As a result of the abnormal trade relations with Europe, our sales abroad vastly exceeded our purchases. The position of the United States changed from a debtor to a creditor nation, and the passing days saw an increasing flow of gold into America available for investment.

The Reid Company felt the warm glow of this prosperity, and Tom Reid had struck a tempo that suited his restless, tireless nature. At the fine home on Military Street, a special room had been constructed overlooking the river; one wall of glass, handsome carved paneling; rugs, lamps, luxuriously comfortable chairs. All this for Tom's leisure hours. *Leisure* —

Tom and his brother Will had bought the Family Theater in Port Huron — a sound investment. Tom's big Packard never went under a roof, always ready for the take-off — a familiar sight as it flashed in and out of town, up and down the river road. He had established

Thom as manager of a local coal dock in which he had controlling interest. But industry still beckoned the son, and Tom knew that the boy would eventually take over the management of his own life. There was a girl in Chicago whose father had plans for him, too. It was hard to accept, but Tom was learning to meet the inevitable.

Anna carefully avoided the subject. She missed the early days when the family had belonged to her, and his work had not completely occupied Tom. Now Helen was married, the other girls away at school, young Thom seldom around, and Tom over in Sarnia at the office when not called farther afield.

There was the March day when loneliness and self-pity overcame her. Soon navigation would open. Then she would practically never see Tom. Well, let him go! She would be rid of those big black cigars — of coats flung on chairs, slippers kicked here and there, newspapers all over the floor. He was too busy with his own interests to care what happened to her. The house was simply another stop along the way where he could rush in and pick up a clean shirt and fresh suit — and a bag always half-packed and waiting for him. Her spell of self-pity continued to build.

Fighting tears, she dressed for the street and stormed out of the house into the crisp, March air. Flouncing along, nursing her grievances, she felt the core of Spring in the wind — saw the hint of yellow where forsythia bushes burgeoned, caught sight of swelling buds, the lilac and the pussy willow. And by the time she reached the bridge, Spring had exercised its magic.

In Knill's drugstore window, was displayed — among others — a box of Hoya de Monterey cigars, Tom's favorite. Spring sent her in; sent her, too, into Ballentine's store for some new shirts for Tom's drawer. The neglected wife told the spring-tipsy spouse that she was a fool. But Anna Reid went laughing secretly down Military Street toward home, pausing at Ullenbruch's for a bunch of violets that nodded to her from the window.

"Where have you been?" shouted Tom as she opened the door. He came thundering down the stairs. "And where the hell is my bag? If you'd just leave things alone and not try to be so damned neat — hey, what are you laughing at? What's so funny? And — where'd you get the violets?"

"Go and finish shaving. You look like Ichabod Crane."

He cleared the remaining stairs in a leap. "What's got into you? Where have you been? Who've you been with?"

"I can have a few secrets of my own, too." She tossed him the box of cigars.

He ripped off the wrapping. "Just what I need. Well — I'm off again, Steel Trust boat — the *Widlar.*"

"I thought the Great Lakes Wrecking people had been working on her."

"They've given up."

"Do you think you can do the impossible?"

"For $75,000 I can — that or 75% of the ship and cargo."

"Will it take long?"

"Plenty."

"Good. Now I'll have a little peace."

"What's got into you?" He laughed, but he was uneasy — annoyed at the twinge of jealousy and the disturbing stab of guilt; remembering certain indiscretions of his own that he would hate to have Anna suspect. She could strike terror to his heart with a laugh. Suppose, some time — just suppose Anna — After all, he was away much of the year, and she was attractive —

She was a poor actress. She looked up at him with

the clear-eyed smile of the sinless. "Do you think you're the only man in the world, Tom Reid?"

"I'd better be — for you!" He was rough, possessive. She loved it as she laughed against his heart . . . .

CHAPTER SEVENTEEN

The *Widlar,* $200,000 freighter of the Becker Line, had 'gone on' at Pancake Shoals along the Ontario shore of Lake Superior the last trip down the year previous.

Names on the land in that region have evolved from fabulous yarns. And Pancake Bay is identified with a misty character known as Pancake Charlie, a native of the little fishing village of Mamainse some miles north of the Canadian Soo near Batchewana. There he made his living with the nets.

There came a time, it is said, when the fishing was

poor and he took advantage of other opportunities at hand and 'put up' a considerable amount of maple syrup. That fall, a package freighter with a cargo of flour came down the Lake and ran on a shoal outside Batchewana, and foundered. Bags and barrels broke up and the whole Bay turned to batter. So Charlie loaded his maple syrup on dog sleds and drove down there, built bonfires and stayed to utilize the batter and make pancakes at a nice profit until he ran out of syrup. And that accounted for the name of Pancake Bay, Pancake Shoals — and Pancake Charlie.

Here the beaches gleam with quartz, amethyst, agate, lapis and carnelian. Here the colorful Indian Reservation at Batchewana skirts the bush. The little fishing villages dream in sheltered coves, the forest ranger keeps watch in his stern paradise at Echo Bay, and the highway winds along the Lake in a pattern of indescribable beauty. Here is the frequent gentleness of the warm Spring wind, the glory of dazzling white cumulus clouds bolting up from the horizon like great swift birds scudding against clean blue. Here, too, rage brutal storms.

Now, with the opening of navigation, the wrecker *Manistique* with Tom Reid and Louis Meyers aboard, left for the scene — an hour's run from Batchewana Bay. A fortune was tied up in the *Widlar*. They found the 8,000 tonner covered with ice, and it was necessary to round up some natives with axes to assist the not too cooperative winds of nature, so that salvage work might begin.

In that area are the French, French-Canadian, the Swede, Welsh and Britisher. There are the Scotch. There are the serious workers and the dawdlers. There are beverage rooms in the occasional bush-country hotel, where liquor cannot be procured. But liquor finds its way in quantity to the bush country, nevertheless.

It is lonely along that shore. Strange and dramatic things happen to men far removed from the pulse of the city. Life has no set pattern there to the north. Men live by chance; drink, wander into the bush and are never seen again. Explore, and stumble past another rock someday to yield millions. Drink, lope lazily along the shore, and slip into a sea which it is said never gives up its dead.

The *Widlar* still hung on a rock of Pancake Shoals. Tom Reid and Louis Meyers examined the ship. They set up an eighteen inch pump in the after hatch and a ten inch pump on cylinder heads in the engine room, and proceeded with diving investigations. A volume air-compressor was installed in the forepeak, also a ballast pump. With sounding pipes and vent pipes plugged, the main stem-line was repaired. Stopping the leaks in the forepeak, they installed a four inch siphon, cut holes in the deck and bulkheaded with acetylene and brought gravel and cement into the chain locker. Now installing a five inch siphon in the forepeak, they checked the leaks and began to pour the concrete. Next came the business of building forms and concreting the forepeak, with the four inch siphon taking care of all water; also setting a six inch pump in the dark hole. Fighting leaks all along the way, they built forms for concrete in the dark hole. Ore was clammed out of number two cargo hold and the area readied for the patch. Templets placed and holes drilled in the tank top for patch, and timbers fastened down.

By now a heavy sea was making up fast and it was imperative to leave for Batchewana Bay.

Next day timbers were bolted to the tank top and inside of the patch canvassed. There were supplies to bring, errands to the Canadian Soo for pumps and miscellany. Each day brought its own problems. Deadlights to close in engine room with pumps to set up. More leaks to check. A suction pipe was changed on a pump, pipes located to ballast pump — and with ballast pump now taking care of all water while a fire was built under the boilers.

At this point the pumps could be shifted onto the *Widlar*'s own steam, but the wind began to freshen up. Fires were pulled from under the boilers and the wreck deserted temporarily. A big sea running . . . Another day, but the sea was too heavy to permit landing alongside of wreck so they worked on the eighteen inch pump ashore. Days of overhauling pumps, clamming ore out of cargo hold and preparing steamer for drydock. Sessions of electric welding, fighting leaks in tank top, drilling holes in sides and deck for plates over the break. Riveting.

Finally they were able to fuel the *Widlar* with the wreck pumped out. Shifting the *Manistique* around to port side, they got underway shortly after midnight on August fourth with weather fine and an eighteen inch pump running and taking care of all leaks.

At Portage Lake Canal, the *Wildar* was fueled again and lay in Lily Pond awaiting weather. On August eighth they left Lily Pond early in the morning and arrived at Port Arthur that night. Now they proceeded to remove pumps and other wrecking equipment from the *Widlar* when Long Tom — the ten inch pump — broke down. They shifted the *Manistique* alongside the *Widlar* and hoisted pump on board and replaced it with Big Ben — another eighteen inch pump, and also put a siphon in the forepeak.

Another day of clamming ore from the *Widlar* hold where she was moored at the coal dock, and a volume air-compressor put aboard. Then by acetylene torch, a hole was burned in the side of the tank for air. At midnight on August thirteenth, the air-compressor was removed from the *Widlar* once more and next day all wrecking equipment was taken off. The *Manistique* was released, and left for Sarnia to tie up and await further orders. The *Widlar* was on her way.

Originally, the Great Lakes Wrecking Company had attempted to salvage the *Widlar,* but abandoned the task without success. After she was given up by the *Favorite,* Tom Reid's bid to the insurance underwriters for $35,000 was accepted. The Reid Company did not make over $15,000. She was sold later to the Colonial Steamship Company of Toronto. Tom Reid managed the sale and was given a check of $5,000.

Tom' satisfaction at the success of the undertaking sent him home happy, his bag bulging with gifts. But he was to meet the first great sorrow of his married life. Helen had died in her sleep only an hour before.

CHAPTER EIGHTEEN

Unwilling to leave Anna alone with her sorrow so soon after their loss, he insisted that she accompany him when he was called to Port Colborne, Ontario, a couple of weeks later. He was to salvage the little wooden steamer *India.* And that concern may have been the means of saving her life. It was shortly afterward that one of Port Huron's greatest tragedies occurred — the explosion of the ferry boat *Omar D. Conger* in Black River, a stream which bisects the heart of the town.

On a Sunday afternoon at The Falk Funeral Home,

services for a close family friend were in progress. Anna most certainly would have been in attendance. A roar shook the town, and almost at once a radiator came crashing through a window of the building. Several mourners were badly hurt, one blinded. The room was practically demolished.

The *Conger*'s boiler, it developed, had been blown from the ship; the largest section crushed a house less than a block away. Four people were killed. Later Tom Reid was to salvage the Conger, but now his immediate concern was for the $50,000 wooden ship *India* — sunk in Lock 15 of the Welland Canal, and delaying navigation east to the St. Lawrence River and the sea.

The Reid wrecker *Manistique* began clamming out grain from the cargo hold at once. Louis Meyers made an examination of the steamer's damage and secured a patch under water. A ten inch pump was set up in the after hatch, but shortly orders were given to stop as they were pumping too much grain. Then a six inch pump was set up in the engine room to clear it, and clamming was resumed until a few hours later when the port boiler gave out and there was no alternative but to let the steamer fill with water. With a ten inch pump working in number one hatch, Meyers made further examination under water, installed a five inch siphon in the forepeak and clammed out grain from the after hatch.

With the tug *Manistique* loaded, they left for Port Dalhousie where the barge took on grain. After cruising out into Lake Ontario to 'shoot ashes' and fill tanks with fresh water, they returned to the *India* to resume clamming. The swinging engine broke down and there was delay for repairs, more clamming.

Ten days after arriving at the wreck, Tom had freed the *India* from the Lock and she was afloat again. Navigation could be resumed. Tom had bid $10,000, had made a profit of probably five. Then he bought the wreck from the insurance underwriters for $3,000, repaired her at Port Dalhousie, gave her to a man in Montreal to handle. She ran a lot of bills, and he lost everything he had put in her . . . .

Now he tried to persuade Anna to go on with him to Montreal where he hoped she could be diverted by the shops and theaters in a city she loved.

"The girls will be leaving for school before long," she reminded him. They had often discussed Clara, now blossoming into young womanhood, and recently receiving ardent attention at home — as well as from a young New Yorker she had met at Palm Beach. If Anna could only discourage marriage for a while — She had decided that the convent of The Sacred Heart at Albany would prove a wise choice for Clara's school that fall, with Virginia returning to National Park Seminary.

Soon Anna was alone again except for young Thom whose ambitions toward industry were crystallizing; and more than ever since he had fallen in love with the beautiful Chicago debutante whose father was an industrialist. Marriage for Thom, it was evident, was not far off.

That was a busy year for Tom Reid. The Interlake Steamship Company's steel freighter *Adriatic* met with trouble that took weeks to straighten out. Hardly had Tom and his diver returned to Sarnia with the *Manistique* when they were called to the Interlake Company's 8,000 ton freighter *Arcturus,* sunk in the Detroit River. Again the routine examination; patch, pumps, air-compressors, the steamer afloat again, and Tom and his men and equipment were off to Sarnia.

In less than twenty four hours they were called to

Cove Island in Georgian Bay where the steamer *Matthews* was ashore. Aboard the *Manistique,* they ran into heavy seas above Harbor Beach and were forced to turn back to the river for the night. The *Matthews* was released after some hours of lightering and tow-line action. Next day a staging was built to facilitate examination of damage, and when determined, the *Matthews* was allowed to go on and the *Manistique* returned to Sarnia where further orders awaited Tom and his diver. The Pittsburg Steamship Company's 8,000 ton freighter *George G. Crawford* was aground near Algonac.

At the scene, they hauled out the tow-line and started pulling. The tow-line parted. They tried a wire tow-line; pulled out the tow-post and parted the wire cable, then started clamming ore. The steamer was released after some hours, the ore clammed back on the *Crawford.* She was towed to the head of Lake St. Clair and lines dropped there. This was hour work, and the job was finished in a little over a day at a figure of $1,000.00.

At Sarnia again, they found that a cable had become entangled in the wheel of the passenger steamer *Hamonic,* one of the Canadian Steamship Company's finest passenger ships. This was a minor trouble to befall the luxury liner which in the mid-forties was to burn at the pier . . . From the *Hamonic,* Tom and Louis Meyers, aboard the *Manistique,* went to the help of the Steamer *Earling* whose propellor had been damaged in the fog.

Now the Steamer *Agawa,* owned at the time by Canada's Algoma Central Railroad, went ashore at South Bay near Manitoulin Island. Originally a barge, built at a cost of $100,000, she had been converted into a steamboat and was carrying a cargo of grain to Georgian Bay when the accident happened. Contracted by her owners, Tom and his crew released the ship, towed her to Collingwood, put her on the bottom and left her there. Since she was considered a total loss, the underwriters gave her to The Reid Company in compensation for removing her from navigable waters. She was then placed in dry-dock, reconditioned, and in the winter of 1927 the Company sold her to The Toronto Elevator Company for $25,000. They had spent a lot of money on her up to that time, so there was no profit. She ran for a while under the name *Herring Bay,* and later was called *The Chicago Tribune.*

The *Midland King* incident followed the *Agawa* salvaging. This 400 foot self-unloader of the Canada Steamship Company, built in Collingwood,Ontario in 1903 at a cost of approximately $600,000, went on an uncharted rock in Georgian Bay between the Bustards and the mainland — her bow away out of water.

Tom went to her with the *Sharpless,* her captain calling out — "Don't hit us. We're liable to go off the rock!"

Tom boarded her and went down in the forepeak where the self-unloader boom machinery was located. Water was running through three broken plates like a falls, down through the belt tunnel. All braces on boom-mast were bent, and the Captain feared if the machine were started, great danger might follow. Men could not go down the tunnel.

There was a discussion between Tom, the Captain and insurance agent. It had to be the latter's decision. Tom said it would take three or four days to unload the *King.* By that time they might get a 'blow' and she'd go to pieces. She was on a rock.

At Tom's insistence, it was agreed to try the machine without a load. The move was successful. Then Tom went down with a couple of men — fortified with high rubber boots — and opened the hoppers, ran about 1,900 tons of cargo out onto the *Maplecourt*. The wrecker was loaded close to capacity when the *King* came off. Wind breezed up and they went on to a small port which was nothing but a Canadian Pacific Railroad Station between the Bustards and Perry Bay. It took three days to unload the *King* with only one clam shell on the *Maplecourt*. The chance Tom Reid took was a long one. Had he been less enterprising, the *King* would have gone to pieces. This was a job by the hour. He was there three days — a day going up, a day coming back. Five days in all, at $50.00 an hour.

Tom was able to lose himself in his work, but Anna had no such demanding diversion. And he found it more and more difficult to persuade her to accompany him to ports where business called him. Always deeply spiritual, now Anna seemed to find her only comfort in church and her Bible. Clara had left school. She was in love, determined to marry the charming John Sullivan, an older man who lived in New York. But Clara was young — too young, pleaded Anna. That was natural for a Mother, Tom realized, but he was remembering their own youth, their own love . . . .

Their lives daily seemed to grow more complicated. When in mid-December, Tom left on the tug *Sarnia* for Goderich, Ontario, where a steamer was in distress, he started out in a storm few would brave but welcoming the danger as a distraction from his personal problems. Testimony of conditions is this fragment of the ship's log—

Dec. 15—11:05 PM — Depart Sarnia.
11:35 — Huron lightship. Wind SW. Fresh.
Dec. 16—2:30 AM — Wind hauled to west. Still fresh. Tug rolling hard.
4:30 AM — Smokestack went by the board, taking

main whistle with it and breaking all steam pipes to deck machinery. Got steam stopped, and proceeded at 5 AM.

5:30 AM — Goderich Pier.

6:00 AM — Tied up in Goderich Harbor. Looked over the damage after daylight. Found about fifteen feet of pipe railing gone on starboard side, starboard ventilator damaged beyond repair. Port ventilator pulled from deck, telegraph wires and signal whistle wires pulled out. Main whistle-pull gone with whistle overboard. Breaking two windows and breaking wall between wheelhouse and Master's room.

Dec. 17—4:00 PM — Got part of jury stack aboard.

7:45 PM — Departed dock to help Stmr. *Mapledown* aground outside of harbor piers.

8:00 PM — Took *Mapledown*'s tow-line 7 in. from bow but could not move her. While backing to give slack to let go, backed tug into steamer's stem cutting out fender streak and bulwarks and top rails. We went after and took his heavy line, breaking his Bollard's. Shifted line to other side, and taking a pull we broke it. Captain of steamer called us alongside. He thought it better to lay till daylight, on account of the short jury stack it was hard to see with the smoke blowing over our bows. Departed steamer at 11:00 PM. Back at dock at 11:30 PM.

Dec. 18—7:00 AM — Departed dock.

7:15 AM — At *Mapledown*. Gave her our 7 in. line. Parted it about 10 in. from eye.

8:25 AM — Stopped pulling.

9:00 AM — Left *Mapledown* with captain of steamer aboard.

10:45 AM — Departed dock with Captain of steamer aboard.

11:15 AM — Alongside steamer. Lay alongside waiting for change of wind.

Dec. 19—7:45 AM — Started pulling with her line. Parted it and gave her our 9 in. line. Parted it, breaking about 70 ft. off. Stopped pulling about 10:45 AM. Went alongside and took captain.

9:30 PM — Back at steamer. Passed our lines and lay waiting.

Dec. 20—12:30 AM — Started pulling. Steamer freed. Took her into harbor, let go and took our lines aboard. Tied up at 2:00 AM. All through with Steamer *Mapledown.*

Home in time for Chirstmas, an event Tom dreaded this year. The first Christmas without Helen. Returning to Sarnia from Goderich, he was considering some special gift and diversion for Anna when he found on reaching the office that a wrecked barge in the channel near Amherstburg demanded immediate attention. The vigil of Christmas Eve — this, of all years! And the one time of the year that meant so much to Anna. Rehearsing an explanation, he telephoned home. It would be difficult to face her disappointment, with her heart still heavy at the loss of Helen. She had never needed him more. The number did not answer. Mystified, he called again.

An office clerk overhearing said, "Oh, there's a message here for you from your wife. She's gone to Chicago with your family to be with her sister for Chirstmas.

"Chicago?" For Christmas! He was outraged. What about him? What about his Christmas? She hadn't known of the emergency that would keep him away at Christmas time — or had she?

It appeared she had. Anxious about the time of his

return, she had called and been informed of the blocked channel at Amherstburg, and the inevitable sequence.

Guiltily then he considered his quick resentment. Now he knew how she must feel repeatedly when disappointed. Ashamed and remorseful, he ordered roses sent to her and enclosed a bounteous check in a special delivery letter in which his contrite heart overflowed.

The next day a messenger finally located Tom on the job. He had been sloshing around the submerged deck of the wreck, and had gone ashore in the tug. He opened the telegram indifferently, assuming the office was contacting him again. The telegram read,

> "Ten misspelled words in the letter and verbs terrible. Last sentence only one worth reading. I echo that sentiment."

The last sentence had read, "I love you . . . "

For three days and nights, Tom was without sleep, but definite progress was being made when he was summoned to Buffalo by his brother Will. He left the planned work with helpers.

The Reid Company had been dickering for the purchase of the Steamer *Windsor* from the Canadian Steamship Company. She was a wooden vessel of 1,769 tons, 242 feet in length, originally built for the Montreal Transit Company at the Lester Shipyard in Marine City, Michigan.

The *Windsor* deal was important. If successfully consummated, she was to be rebuilt at Port Dalhousie, Ontario. There had been considerable telephoning and correspondence by Tom and his brother during the past months with the possibility of negotiating a deal. Now Will was there awaiting Tom for the conference. They had hoped to make a goodly sum on the *Windsor* eventually.

They left their cars in Buffalo and went on by rail. The deal was — you had to get the *Windsor* away from the dock at Port Dalhousie. Feelng there would be a profit, they had agreed to pay $1,000.00 for the wreck — and had paid it. But once on the scene, they saw what had to be done and knew the plan would not work out. They gave her to the firm of John E. Russell Company in order to get her away, and lost the thousand.

Between Tom and his brother Will existed a warm relationship, though the nature of the Company's work did not permit prolonged association. And there had been a growing conviction in Tom's mind that Will was not well. A persistent cough had troubled him recently, and he was careless in his habits, indifferent to his health.

The business finished, the men returned to Buffalo to pick up their cars, and Tom suggested that they spend the night there as Will's condition troubled him. But Will, restless and feverish, stubbornly insisted on going on. Each drove his own car.

Shortly after passing through Hamilton, Ontario, the snow began. Before long, a blizzard was in progress. Will, ahead, drove on — the car slewing, wind howling, the scene a nightmare. Then at a point between Woodstock and London, they came to a detour. The alternate road was a narrow, desolate stretch. Snow was deep, visibility poor. Before long, Will's Peerless slewed off into a deep ditch.

In the distance the lights of a farmhouse twinkled, and the two men set off for help. They found a square dance in progress in the large old rambling place. They appealed for help. But not a man would consider leaving the party until it was over. The Reids would have to wait.

Tickets were now being passed to the men — a method of arranging partners for a special dance. And Will, despite fever, wet shoes and trouser legs — and the little wheeze — accepted a ticket, called out the name of the girl he had won and joined the dancers.

Exhausted, Tom stood on the sidelines, soaked clothes clinging to his chilled body. He was worried about his brother, for Will's eyes were a little strange, and there were bright red spots in his cheeks.

Toward three o'clock, a departing farmer drove his team out to the stalled cars and rescued the Peerless from the ditch. And Will brushed aside Tom's urgings to seek shelter until daylight at a farmhouse along the way. He wanted to get home, and fast. He wanted to do everything at top speed. In this instance, perhaps he sensed that only a little time was left to him. Now he pushed on ahead, Tom taking up the brisk pace in his Packard—the Peerless breaking a road, fighting snowdrifts; snow deepening, chains clattering as links broke.

About five miles out of London, Will's car ran into trouble again, slewed and stalled. He worked stubbornly to get it free, despite Tom's protests, and soon started on ahead and disappeared as Tom's car suffered a puncture. Somehow Tom managed to change tires in the blizzard and before too long to reach London. He found Will's car parked outside the hotel where they always stayed; went in and saw his brother asleep in a lobby chair — drenched, exhausted and feverish.

"Let's get on to Sarnia," Will muttered, eyes glassy.

"You're going to bed." Tom was firm. "The cars go into storage here. We'll take the train to Sarnia when you're fit to travel." Within the week they reached Sarnia where Tom was badly needed. The storms that had bedeviled Ontario had not spared Michigan and the Lakes. And at the little coastal town of Frankfort on Lake Michigan, the $300,000 Ann Arbor Carferry No. 4 had met with serious trouble. One of a fleet of railroad ferries, she plied across Lake Michigan to Wisconsin ports. Despite occasional ill luck, in October 1919, when nineteen ships went down in a terrific storm, she fought through. This time, too, she had put up a gallant fight in a blinding blizzard, punished by mountainous waves and hurricane winds in a temperature of twenty-two below zero.

Below decks bedlam reigned. Loaded railroad cars had broken loose from their fastenings. A box-car carrying new automobiles crashed through the wooden sea gate at the stern and went overboard. The waves rushed in carrying boulders of ice. None of her crew believed she would make port, but somehow she managed to clear the Frankfort Breakwall and sank just inside, her hull against the south pier — permitting the sailors to jump ashore. This news greeted Tom when he reached the tug office at Sarnia. The ferry was under water except for the top deck.

Ordering the *Manistique* sent over, Tom went by train with Louis Meyers who investigated below and found it impossible to get between ship and pier. He gave his findings, and it was decided to pull the freight cars from the stern of the vessel into the water in order to release her; secure a bulkhead across the back to reinforce her, and salvage the cars later. Tom's $50,000 salvage bid was accepted by the insurance underwriters. There were no other bids.

At this time word came for Tom from the hospital in Port Huron. Will was very low, suffering from double pneumonia. Not since leaving him had Tom been without a prodding, stubborn fear for his brother. But he concentrated on the business at hand with a wild, unfounded hope that things would turn out all right, and Will would recover. Will, the indestructible, had weathered many serious crises. Yet as Tom left the distressed carferry in the hands of Louis Meyers and caught the train for home, he realized that he faced the imminent loss of the brother closest to his heart — a contemporary who had shared the years. Childhood memories surged back, memories of boyhood, comradeship — the happiness and unhappiness they had known together; the rivalries, loyalties, the triumphs and defeats. There was a hot, fierce pain at the pit of his being as he though of saying the final farewell.

In one of his few lucid moments, Will recognized him and whispered — with a foggy twinkle in his eyes — "You old son of a gun. Why don't you get a good car?—"

His passing dealt Tom a hard blow. If there could be solace, it lay in the arms of the woman he loved. There was always Anna . . . . But his work recognized no personal considerations, and less than a week later, he was back in Frankfort at the scene of the wrecked ship.

In the meantime, Louis Meyers had followed through faithfully, and while placing a canvas over the bulkhead on the carferry almost lost his life. The weather was bitter cold. A scum of ice kept forming on the water's surface, movable according to currents. His one fear was the possible carelessness of his tender. He constantly warned the fellow of the danger involved. One bad move could have resulted in disaster.

The tender was scrupulously careful, but nature was ruthless. At one point when Meyers submerged, in his full view great blocks of ice approached each other and came within a few inches of going together — about to pinch the lifeline. Powerless to reach them, or to move fast enough in his heavy outfit to surface or communicate with his tender — for in those days they did not have the diver's telephone — he braced himself for what seemed the inevitable. Then, mercifully, the wind shifted.

The freight cars were run off into the water in order to release the carferry. These could be salvaged later. Yet despite these and other drastic steps, they found it impossible to pump out the ship and were forced to leave the salvaging until spring when ice no longer menaced their attempts. Successful then, they made a profit of $20,000.

Home again for Tom — home and Anna. The moment release came, the urge to go to her was like flame; the urge to be near her, with her — confident of her understanding, while she sublimated her sorrow to make his homecoming pleasant.

"It's been a lonely life," she said once, "but a good one, Tom. I wait in the shadows and watch you work miracles."

"Never in the shadows, Anna," he had denied. "You're the reason for it. You're why I do what I do."

"No, Tom, if you'd never seen me, you'd be a giant still. You've helped establish steamship Companies. You've saved fortunes for some people, and made fortunes for others. And you've made history on the Lakes."

Though mostly they spoke with an air of idle nonsense to each other, there were the serious moments, the inescapably significant ones. And her words occurred to him often. They were the sea beneath him, the stars by which he sailed. They constituted reward in a thankless world.

You've helped establish steamship Companies —

Yes — there had been the $30,000 ship *Overland,* laid up in disrepair in Buffalo one time, and for sale. Hearing of it he had investigated, examined her, bought her for $4,000, repaired and fitted her out and sent the tug *Fisher* to pick her up. With her flag changed to

Canadian, she was taken to the Port Huron drydock and sold to Captain Scott Misenar for $20,000 — the first ship of the fleet which is today The Colonial Steamships Limited.

And there was the Steamer *E. M. Peck* — worth $90,000 at the time of launching — that blew up at the dock at Racine, Wisconsin, on Lake Michigan. He had bought her for $4,200 as she stood; supervised her rebuilding, christened her the *Malton* and sold her to the then organizing Canada Steamship Lines Limited. Their first ship. She was a big carrier during World War I and had repaid her owners handsomely.

And again — there was the *Sarnian* which he had sold to a Toronto financier, and which became the first ship of the St. Lawrence Steamship Lines.

Yes, and he had sold the *Howard M. Hanna* to James Playfair — to be the first of the Toronto Elevator Company's fleet. The *Hanna* was sold for $100,000. Playfair paid the Reid Wrecking Company $20,000, and they were to deliver the ship to Collingwood, Ontario. They took her there, put her in drydock and notified Playfair he would have to pay by the month for repairs until they were finished. The money was not available, it seemed, and it was necessary to take the *Hanna* out of the drydock because she was in the Reid Company's name. Playfair soon managed the money and rebuilt her there. He bonded her after the rebuilding, and sent the Reid Company the tardy check. The Reid Company bought the *Hanna* for $13,000 — and with her came a rich cargo of coal. They made $50,000 on that job.

Not long after this, The Reid Company sold a second ship — the *Georgian* — to Playfair, under equally as happy circumstances . . . .

Anna had a way of bringing things into focus. What

would any of it have mattered without her? What could he do to give her a little happiness? Necessity had forced him to neglect her. The flowers he sent, the gifts, the infrequent letters he wrote with such unease — aware of his lack and her perfection — all were gestures from his blundering heart. He suffered over his inarticulateness, and recognized the jealous insistence of his work. She deserved the best, the most.

Then a matter long needing attention and one that could serve his purpose came to mind — some unfinished business concerning a repudiated contract. A score might be settled with a gentleman abroad, and a holiday managed for Anna at the same time. This concerned the ship *United States* — originally a yacht owned by Colonel Henry Green, son of the famous Hetty Green. Sold to Ernie Matthews of Toronto, she was converted into a passenger boat. Originally worth about $500,000 and 320 feet in length, she was easily adaptable for Matthews' purpose which was the run between Muskegon, Michigan, and Chicago.

But she failed to make money, and he brought her to Sarnia and laid her up at the waterworks dock. There was an insurance of $300,000 on her. She caught fire one night and burned off her cabins and superstructure, sank and rolled over as the Normandie was to do one day.

The Reid Wrecking Company took the contract for $35,000 and the boat. Tom raised her, pumped her out, and she laid at the dock for some time. They traded her for the Steamer *Sarnian* — a steam barge. She was originally a Canadian boat that was once the *Globe*.

When Tom Reid made his bid, he knew that the underwriters were not responsible for anything above the ship's value; knew, too, that 'if you take the boat, you take the risk.' The salvage operation had succeeded —

but when Lloyd's had paid Matthews the insurance, The Reid Wrecking Company had not received their fee, and Tom had warned Lloyd's to collect his salvage fee from the owners. This they had failed to do. And the owners ignored his claim.

During the intervening time Tom had vainly appealed to Lloyd's Cleveland representative. But at the London office presided Sir Joshua Lowry — an old nobleman whom Tom and his father had met one time in New York. There had been a brief, pleasant interlude together. Now Tom decided to go directly to Lowry and state his claim. Jealous of time, he felt the excuse would justify the jaunt with Anna.

Reaching London, he called at Lloyd's and was told that Sir Joshua was away and would not return for a week. Paris had been planned. Why not now? He set off with Anna for the Continent.

Under the spell of that beautiful city, they danced as in the old days. They strolled along the Bois, dined at enchanting haunts and savored a magic world. They laughed and loved and were young again. Loneliness and heartaches were forgotten. The long and frequent separations had given this holiday a long lost glamour.

By the time they returned to London, Tom had forgotten there was such a word as defeat. And once more, he stalked into Lloyd's. Again an attendant attempted to put him off with the excuse that Sir Joshua was away, when Tom happened to see the gentleman at his desk as a door opened just beyond. Brushing the clerk aside, he strode in and closed the door firmly behind him . . .

When the *Mauretania* sailed for New York with the Reids aboard, there was a check for $35,000 in Tom's pocket, and in their hearts were memories to see them through some lonely days to come. They began, characteristically, the moment of his arrival at home.

The sand-sucker *Hustler,* of the Kelly Island fleet, sank at Cleveland, Ohio, alongside the Railroad dock outside the Cuyahoga River. Her cargo shifted, with the boat poorly trimmed, and water poured in. Lloyd's Perry Jones asked for salvage bids, and Tom's offer of $35,000 was accepted. The Reid Wrecking Company raised her in a month, and encountering little difficulty, made $15,000 on the contract.

Things were going well. Tom was never happier than when business boomed and jobs succeeded. He was working hard, and welcomed the brief respite during the summer of 1925 when he celebrated the Fourth of July with Anna at their summer home near Windemere on Lake Huron's shore.

Anna had only begun to adjust herself to the loss of Helen and to Thom's marriage and departure to Chicago, when Clara eloped. Now only Virginia was left and, popular socially, she was seldom around.

It seemed strange with only themselves in a house once used to children. Tom missed the old days, but there was Anna, constant and devoted. He watched her idly one day as she worked on a piece of needlepoint, yarns fluffed against sprigged muslin, her brown head graying a little, arched above it.

Stretched out in the chaise lounge on the flower-edged terrace, his gaze wandered to the glittering Lake along which a freighter made its way toward the river beyond. The day was intensely hot, and there was scarcely a ripple on the water. This was completion. This was peace. He closed his eyes and dozed.

"We have a caller, Dad." Anna touched his shoulder.

Reverend Munday, rector of Grace Episcopal Church, was parking his bicycle just beyond.

"You mean to say he wheeled all the way up here from town in this heat?" demanded Tom.

"He hasn't got a car. He can't afford one."

There were greetings and a pleasant half hour visit. As Reverend Munday left, Tom reached for the telephone. "That you, John?" he asked a local business man. "Look here! Our minister just left. Came all the way up here this scorching day, trying to give folks like my Anna a little comfort. And what are we doing for him, I'd like to know? Now, listen. The man needs a car. Are you willing to go along if I can get a few others to chip in?"

John agreed. The plan was settled. Tom relaxed. "Why do you look at me like that?" he asked Anna. "Anything wrong with me?"

"Oh, nothing much." She paused beside him. "Except you're so selfish and — stingy, and — and mean —"

"Well, you don't need to cry about it," he grinned, and tossed her his handkerchief. "Maybe I'll reform."

As she dropped down beside him, the telephone rang.

The office. A wreck at Point Pelee in Lake Erie. In a bad spot, and a menace to navigation. Time was important.

CHAPTER NINETEEN

The wreck proved to be the sand-sucker and gravel boat, *Kelly Island* — worth $100,000 when built, and owned by the Kelly Island Transportation Company. Pumping sand to be delivered to Cleveland, she foundered and rolled over when a violent squall came up.

Tom's bid of $35,000 was accepted. Expectant of bringing her soon into Leamington, the nearest Canadian Port, Tom and his crew went to work.

Sand boats differ from lake boats. The main hold is left vacant for compressed air, and to avoid trouble in elevating the bow if necessary. To counterbalance the ship at this point, the Reid workers built a compartment on the exposed bottom with heavy material. They filled this with clamshells, took what earth was below, and put enough of this on the bow so her stern came out of water. Established on an even keel, they towed her the twenty six miles in that upside-down condition to Leamington, and left her over a mile from shore in twenty two feet of water.

Now the problem was to right the boat. In order to accomplish this, they utilized *The Pawnee,* a wooden steamer which, stripped, was lying in Sarnia Bay at the home port of The Reid Company. She was pumped out, taken down to Leamington, filled with sand and gravel and placed 600 feet away from the *Kelly Island* to be used as an anchorage. Then came the operation of installing machinery, winches and boilers and cranes that operate to roll the sand-sucker over. The operation took six weeks.

It was during this work that Louis Meyers almost lost his life. While submerged, he was moving slowly along when he felt a sudden intense pain in his left hand. Checking, he discovered that the healthy thumb nail was completely gone. He did not recall having bumped into any object or seen one that might have inflicted such a blow. Intrigued, he reversed his steps and soon came to what seemed an explanation of the accident. A small, circular iron cover on a hinge overhead had suddenly dropped down and out of his line of vision, but in range with his hand which pushed in a protective gesture against the water. Had the cover happened to strike his helmet instead, his career would have come to an abrupt end.

The Reid Company was successful in salvaging the *Kelly Island* and made a profit of $5,000 on that contract.

With late fall, the usual disasters began to happen. The 350 foot, 4,000 ton Anchor Line boat *Wissahickon* ran ashore in a blizzard on Duck Island in Georgian Bay. Perry Jones of Lloyd's contacted Tom. Would he go up and inspect and offer a salvage bid? The Great Lakes Towing Company was sending the *Favorite* to the scene.

Taking Louis Meyers along, Tom went to investigate and made a bid but The Great Lakes Company underbid him and got the job. As he was leaving, word came of the plight of the ship *Henry Steinbrenner* in Mud Lake near Round Island. She had been hit amidships by another freighter and suffered a hole about 25 feet long and clear down to her bottom. She was loaded with coal. The *Steinbrenner* was a 500 foot, 5,000 ton freighter built in 1901 for the Kinsman Transportation Company of Cleveland.

After examining the distressed ship, Tom returned to Sarnia and gave Perry Jones a bid of $35,000 to raise her. He had a particular understanding with the insurance underwriters relative to the turbid water of Mud Lake. He advised Perry Jones it was impossible to begin operations at that point, that divers could not attempt patching the vessel due to the roily water. With freezing weather, and ice, the water clears up, but in navigation season, the Lake traffic keeps the water stirred up.

There were about five feet of water on the decks. The pilot house of the *Steinbrenner* was out of water and her cabin about half submerged.

They took the tugs *Protector* and *J. M. Diver* — two divers, and two crews to work; fifteen men and two tenders. It was impossible to make headway until the ice got to be about twelve inches thick, at which time they cut the ice around the break and set the pump up on the ice. The ship was in the mud almost up to her deck.

Now it was necessary to build a trough from the pump on the tug to a hole in the ice 100 feet away. The diver then took the end of a ten inch rubber hose and achieving suction, worked to clear the mud away from the break. He would pump mud and water into the hold and back into the Lake again, so it would be clear in the area of the break. Then the divers put on the patch and had everything in readiness to coffer-dam her all around. But now they faced the tedious two months waiting period until the ice would melt and she could be pumped out.

While there, wearing snowshoes, Tom and some of his men would walk to a little town called Rabar — between St. Ignace and the Soo — about five miles ashore. They slept in a so-called hotel in bunks and with one big stove in the center of the room. The first fellow up had to build the fire, and a twenty-degree below zero temperature was not unusual.

The divers, Louis Meyers and Frank McDonald, met many difficult hours, for the temperature could be treacherous, and tenders had to hand air pumps to the divers in a warm place so the air wouldn't freeze.

For this job which was successfully executed, The Reid Company was paid $35,000, with a profit of $10,-000. With bids on a 'no-cure, no-pay' basis, Tom Reid was the only one among rival wreckers who would always take the chance.

Perry Jones, Lloyd's representative in Cleveland, being notified of a wreck, immediately summoned such men as Charles Lincoln, Captain St. Clair, Captain Morrison and William Pilkey — their local agents. Then he would send one of them to the scene with Tom Reid who would make a statement of the cost of repairing a boat.

When the estimate of cost of repairing a ship had been made, Perry Jones' decision was final. If he thought it would cost more than three fourths of the insurance, he would advise the underwriters to abandon ship. Then the whole amount of insurance was paid in ninety days.

There were different forms of insurance. Some companies carried total loss. Some carried full policy. Some carried part of the insurance themselves. If the repairs cost more than three fourths of the value and the loss was not total, then the owners had to foot the repair bill. With a total loss policy, if the cost of salvage and repair exceeded the value of the boat, then she was a total loss and the insurance Company paid.

In the case of the *Steinbrenner,* The Reid Company was fortunate. There were instances, however, in which they were not so lucky. Typical was the case of the barge *Eleanor*. On the night of April 8, 1927, the Steamer *Peter Koenig* laden with sand, sank at her dock at the foot of Chene Street in Detroit. And the contract for raising her was given to The Reid Company.

Within a few days, the Company's tug *Smith* brought their wrecking barge *Eleanor* alongside the *Koenig* to begin wrecking operations, and the *Eleanor* made fast along her starboard side heading upstream with the tug *Smith* outboard of her.

Tom Reid went aboard the *Eleanor* to organize the work, and finding that more hands were needed, asked the Captain if there were any men around for hire. As a result, George Gray, cook aboard the sunken *Koenig,* and another member of her crew named Greiber, hired out to The Reid Company.

In raising the *Koenig* it was necessary first to lighter her cargo of sand, which was to be done by use of the *Eleanor's* boom and clam shell. The *Koenig*'s boom was down, lying across the sand box, and had to be moved out of the way before lightering operations could begin.

With her engine submerged, there was no power aboard the *Koenig,* so it was decided to raise her boom by means of the *Eleanor*'s boom and then swing the *Koenig*'s boom to port, away from the sand box.

A discussion followed between Tom Reid and Fred Smith, cranesman aboard the *Eleanor,* in reference to this. Tom suggested that a block and tackle be made fast to the topping lift of the *Koenig*'s boom, and that as the boom was lifted up by the *Eleanor,* the slack in the topping lift be taken up and held by use of the block and tackle. Smith, however, thought it would be easier to handle the boom if several men took hold of the topping lift, and as the boom was raised, the slack taken up without the aid of a block and tackle. It was finally decided to follow Smith's suggestions.

Two chains belonging to the *Eleanor* were secured to the end of the *Eleanor*'s boom and then made fast around the *Koenig*'s boom about a third of its length from the outboard end. Smith, Gray and three other men undertook the handling of the topping lift and taking up the slack as the boom was raised. The *Koenig's* boom swung on a mast just aft' of the pilot house (which was on the forecastle deck) and the men in handling the topping lift stood between the mast and the after end of the pilot house. The *Koenig*'s boom was lifted about three feet and then Tom Reid, who was operating the boom, stopped machinery on the *Eleanor* and waited for the men to take up the slack in the topping lift.

When this was done, the *Koenig*'s boom was raised about four feet further and the machinery on the *Eleanor* again stopped, Tom Reid leaving the operating house on the *Eleanor* to go aboard the *Koenig* to see that the topping lift was properly secured before the boom was swung around.

Before he arrived aboard the *Koenig* and before the topping lift had been secured, the chain suspending the *Koenig's* boom broke and the boom fell to the deck, the topping lift as it was straightened out acting like the string on a bow.

Smith, who had hold of the topping lift was thrown into the water against the forward starboard deck winch of the *Koenig,* which was partly submerged. And Gray, whom it was thought must have had all his weight against the topping lift was thrown head first through the rear window of the *Koenig's* pilot house, his head striking against the iron and brass steering wheel.

Smith was rescued by members of the *Koenig's* crew and, with Gray, taken ashore and then to the hospital in a police ambulance. Gray, who never regained consciousness, died on the way.

Smith, it was found, had suffered a double compound fracture of the right arm. The arm improved as much as could be expected in view of the serious nature of the fracture, but months would be required to restore even a measure of its function. And there was a question as to whether there would be any permanent loss of use of the arm.

Smith worked the year round for the owner of the *Koenig*. Gray, at the time of the accident, was working for The Reid Company, having entered its employ for the period of the wrecking job, but his regular employment was as cook aboard the *Koenig*. In the winter he was generally employed in the engineer's gang, assisting in repair work on the *Koenig,* or in the owner's Yard. A man of about forty, he left a widow and two small children.

Probate proceedings were perfected in the Gray estate, and a suit instituted by the administratrix in the United States Court at Detroit under Section 33 of the Jones Act, which affords to mariners the benefit and protection of The United States Railway Employees Liability Act.

Since this suit arose out of the relation of employer and employee existing between The Reid Company and Gray, the defense was taken over by the underwriter carrying the Company's workers' compensation and employers liability insurance.

The Smith claim was one on account of which, in the lawyers' opinion, the owner of the *Eleanor* would undoubtedly be held liable in damages. The work was being carried on under the supervision of the wrecking company's head, the chain which broke belonged to the *Eleanor* and was rigged by her crew, and the operating of the *Eleanor*'s boom, which was used to lift up the *Koenig*'s boom, was in charge of a member of the *Eleanor*'s crew.

Smith, as a member of the *Koenig*'s crew was rightfully aboard the vessel and as such was one to whom The Reid Company owed a duty to exercise due care; nor did the fact that he gratuitously offered his services in the raising of the boom alter his status or lessen the obligation of The Reid Company to use the proper degree of care for his safety, as well as that of others aboard ship.

It was argued that Smith, having been the one who suggested the topping lift be handled by hand rather than by block and tackle could be charged with contributory negligence. But such contention, in the lawyer's opinion, would only be a question of fact for a jury, particularly as the method finally adopted was approved by Captain Reid.

Furthermore, the indirect cause of the accident was the breaking of the chain. There was no evidence that it was faulty or inadequate or improperly rigged, or that the boom on the *Eleanor* was improperly handled. The fault, it seemed, was chargeable to the owner of the

Eleanor. And in the lawyer's opinion, in event of trial the case would go to the jury and a jury would return the verdict in favor of Smith and against The Reid Company.

The amount of damages which the jury would award Smith was problematical, at least from the standpoint of allowance for pain and suffering. The time that he would lose on account of the accident and the amount of wages that he would have earned during such time was however fixed fairly and definitely.

It would undoubtedly be six months before his arm had regained sufficient strength for him to return to work. The period of disability would be at least five months. If it developed that Smith would have a permanent diminution in the use of the arm, such loss, together with pain and suffering, would materially increase the amount of any award of damages.

Following Smith's return from the hospital, the Company lawyers had a number of conferences with him relative to the question of settlement. The only manner in which the suit instituted by the Gray estate affected the matter in so far as the claim of Smith was concerned, was from the standpoint of proceedings for limitation of liability. In event the suit instituted by the Gray estate was tried, the lawyers felt it would result in a substantial verdict for the plaintiff, and it was not improbable that the verdict in that case, together with the amount that would be awarded Smith, if his case also should go to trial, would exceed the value of the barge *Eleanor*.

And now came the additional complication. It was not certain, however, that the owner's liability was limited to the value of the *Eleanor,* inasmuch as she was accompanied by a tug and there was some authority for the proposition that the barge and tug should, when operating in that case, be held as a unit; and that the value of the two vessels and not the barge alone was the owner's limit of liability.

In addition there was no means of telling in advance of the two cases being tried and verdicts returned, whether the combined verdicts would exceed limitation value of the wrecking outfit.

In the claim of Smith and that of Gray, the facts were such that in the lawyers' opinion the claims did not come in the same category; Gray, and Greiber — the other member of the *Koenig's* crew hired out by The Reid Company for that job.

The legal opinion was that the defense in the Gray case had been taken over by the underwriters carrying The Reid Company's Workers Compensation and Employees Liability Insurance, since Gray at the time of the accident was in the employ of The Reid Company.

It seemed the underwriters had assumed that the other member of the *Koenig's* crew employed by The Reid Company must have been Smith and had based their conclusion that the two cases were alike on that assumption. Such, however, was not the situation.

When the *Eleanor* arrived alongside the *Koenig,* they maintained, Captain Reid, who was on the dock, went aboard the *Eleanor* and shortly afterward inquired of Captain McCowan of the *Koenig* whether there were any men about whom he could employ.

Gray, cook aboard the *Koenig,* was on the deck of his ship at that time and Captain McCowan asked him if he wanted to go to work for The Reid Company, which he said he did. Gray then went aboard the barge and hired out to The Reid Company for that particular job.

A little later, Greiber, also a member of the *Koenig's* crew, hired out to The Reid Company. Only two of the

Koenig's crew were employed by Captain Reid — Gray and Greiber. Smith, who was employed year round by the owner of the *Koenig,* at no time hired out to The Reid Company, and at the time of receiving his injuries he was still in the employ of the *Koenig.* The assistance which Smith offered and rendered in the moving of the *Koenig's* boom was voluntary on his part and was offered as a member of the *Koenig's* crew and not as an employee of The Reid Company.

The facts accordingly were that Smith, at the time of the accident, was not in the employ of the *Eleanor* but was a member of the *Koenig's* crew, and had become a member of the *Eleanor's* crew for the period of the wrecking job.

The suit eventually brought by the Gray estate was founded on Section 33 of The Jones Act and arose out of the relation of employer and employee existing between The Reid Company and Gray.

The Reid Company had a policy of insurance covering Workers Compensation and Employers Liability and the Company carrying such insurance had recognized the Gray claim as coming within the scope of its policy, and accordingly had undertaken the defense of that suit. In Smith's case, however, the liability did not arise out of the relationship of employer and employee as that relationship did not exist, but instead out of the duty owed to third parties.

There was the question of whether the *Eleanor* and her tug could be considered as a unit for the purpose of limitation of liability. Cases were quoted, and the Court left open for further consideration the question of whether both vessels should be surrendered.

Cases were cited where, in the Court's opinion, it was held that the derrick scow and tug were component parts of a wrecking outfit, and that in order to limit liability it was necessary for the petitioner to surrender the entire outfit.

Finally the Court ruled that the liability was held to the *Eleanor* as the 'offending thing' — inasmuch as the chain which broke belonged to her.

Previous Court decisions also held that the contract price of the salvage job — on a 'no-cure, no pay' basis — if 'freight pending,' within the meaning of the limitation statute, must be surrendered along with the ship. This did not mean that the entire contract price was to be treated 'freight pending,' the decision as to this resting on whether the tug and barge were a unit for purposes of limitation of liability or were separable.

If the tug and barge were a unit, then the entire contract price would go into the fund, whereas if the tug and barge were separable, it would be necessary for the Commissioner to then determine what portion of the contract price should be attributed to the efforts of the *Eleanor,* and only such portion would become part of the fund.

Checking on back decisions, it was held that the words 'freight pending' in the statute relation to limitation of liability of ship owners, did not include salvage earned during voyage. There were cases however involving salvage services by ships engaged in carrying cargo or passengers, and the services were merely incidental to the voyage and not the real business of the ship as was the case where the *Eleanor* and the tug were engaged in purely salvage work.

In a previous case, the Court held that the raising of the sunken ship was the essential and only purpose for which the enterprise was undertaken, and that on such account the contract price of salvage should be treated as 'freight pending' and go into the limitation fund. There was manifestly a difference between ships engaged in salvage work and those rendering salvage services as a mere incident in a voyage on which cargo or passengers were being carried. The distinction, they pointed out, was proper and necessary.

The question of the value of the *Eleanor* came up. Tom Reid expressed the view that she was not worth, for limitation purposes, over $20,000 and that her value might be fixed as low as $10,000 despite the fact that she had considerable equipment and machinery aboard, which formed part of the ship for limitation purposes.

A surveyor who was familiar with the vessel, stated that in his opinion the *Eleanor* and the equipment aboard at the time of the accident would be of the value from fifty to sixty thousand dollars.

As the question of value was one of the facts for the Court to determine, there was no way of telling definitely in advance what amount the Court would fix, but from the difference between Tom Reid's evaluation and that of the surveyor, it was apparent there was some possibility of the claimants being able to establish a valuation of at least $20,000, and possibly in excess of that amount in limitation proceedings.

The owner would also have to surrender part at least of the moneys received from the salvage contract so that such amount would have to be added to the value of the *Eleanor* in determining the owner's limit of liability.

What the result of limitation proceedings would be was necessarily speculative, but certainly not to the advantage of The Reid Company. The lawyers urged immediate settlement rather than chance limitation proceedings, and this was done.

The case of the *Eleanor* was typical of numerous such incidents throughout Tom Reid's career — periods nerve-wracking and suspenseful, responsible for Tom's abruptness and unreasonable impatience and the burning remorse he suffered at inflicting his moods on his family.

CHAPTER TWENTY

1927 was a memorable year for the Reid family. Clara's son was born. Now Anna found an outlet for her emotions. She prevailed on Clara to spend the holidays at home, and ordered a handsome layette since little Johnnie Sullivan's christening was to take place in mid-December. There was to be a dinner for a few close friends, following the ceremony. Tom ordered gifts and flowers. That was one day they could count him out at the office! And then—

The Reiss Steamship Company's big $300,000 steel

freighter *A. M. Byers,* loaded with grain, was racing down Lake Huron bound for Buffalo to make unloading deadline, for she was not carrying storage grain. She was booked for drydock for winter repairs. A Captain's record and a fat bonus were at stake, and the Steamship Company stood to lose by any delay. They were making good time when, after passing Harbor Beach along Michigan's eastern shore, a vibration began and became so violent that the Captain was forced to reduce speed. Something was wrong with the *Byers.* By ship's telephone, he called Point Edward and asked The Reid Company to have a representative and diver meet him at Miller's Coal dock in Port Huron.

Tom and Louis Meyers boarded a tug and brought along a steel scow and diving equipment. They were waiting when the *Byers* was sighted on Lake Huron. An examination of the ship revealed that a propellor blade was missing. The opposite blade could be removed, which meant the ship could travel but speed must be reduced. As an alternative, all new blades could be affixed, but complete replacement meant greater delay. And time was vital.

The Captain's record was without incident, and now he was within a few hours of success at the end of a good year — last trip down.

"How much time have we got?" asked Tom.

The Captain reckoned. "Seven hours at the most. If I can run her at normal speed after repairs, I can make Buffalo just ahead of deadline."

The Reiss manager in Sheboygan, Wisconsin, okayed the service at $1,500, and the men decided that new propellor blades could be put on within the time limit if no further complications developed.

Working against a sharp current under icy water,

Meyers finished the job in approximately six hours. The *Byers* steamed off to Buffalo, while Louis Meyers proudly pocketed a check for $250.00, bearing a grateful Captain's signature.

Tom returned home toward midnight.

Anna had lived too long with disappointment to feel its edge now. "He never even cried," she said sleepily, as Tom opened the bedroom door. "He just smiled — like a little angel . . . They think he looks something like you."

"What do you think, Anna?"

"Well, his features are better, and his hair won't be so red. But — his smile! well, I'd say there's a resemblance. And, oh yes, Tom — there was a message from some Sarnia city official. Can you meet with their city commission tomorrow night?"

"Tomorrow night?"

"He said it was vital, Tom. He said they need you badly."

"He was just kidding you," grinned Tom. He had not told her that with agitation for a new Blue Water Bridge to span the St. Clair River from Port Huron to Sarnia, the Sarnia City Commission had asked him to present his appraisal of the national and international need for such a structure before the Ontario Parliament. His opinion, they had maintained, was vital toward the accomplishment of the project.

There were such proud moments, and there were the troubled ones. Such as in 1929, when The Foundation Company of Port Huron failed, and The Reid Company was forced to take the drydock back.

A little later, after his mother's death, there was a heavy turnover in Reid affairs. Tom sold the property to a real estate firm and paid off his brothers, sisters and Will's widow for their shares.

At this time he was being urged to join a powerful Canadian merger. The Sin-Mac Lines were being formed. It was a consolidation of the Sincennes-McNaughton Tug Company of Montreal, the Port Arthur Tug Company, the Russell Tug Company of Toronto and the Donnelly Wrecking Company of Kingston — and they were hoping to include The Reid Wrecking and Towing Company of Sarnia.

The Reid family met, considered the proposition, and voted to merge. And the new Sin-Mac Lines — of which they were now a part — were bonded for $1,500,-000. A Mr. R. A. Campbell of Montreal was appointed manager. The Reid Company took a substantial block in the new Company, and Tom's sizeable salary for managing the salvaging generously augmented his income. John E. Russell of Toronto held an important post in the new Company, but the three Simard brothers were the basic power. The latter had built a great industrial empire in Sorel, Quebec, and their interests covered utilities, resources and manufacturing — and now transportation and salvaging.

It was shortly after this that the beautiful Reid home on Military Street was sold, and Tom moved his family to Toronto where a new home was bought — the move made necessary because of increased contracts in Canada. Though Tom was still active on the Lakes, his territory was enlarging.

This was a blow from which Anna never recovered. She had loved her home and treasured it for the memories it held of family life. Though she did not complain, and tried to appoint the new Canadian home on Rosedale Heights Drive in a manner that would please her husband.

She had managed to accustom herself to his long and frequent absences. In Michigan where she had lived for so long, friends were near, sights familiar. But now, Toronto was a strange city in a strange country which, though friendly and attractive, lacked the virtue of being her homeland. No longer young, adjustment was not easy. She found excuses to return to Port Huron when business called Tom to the Lakes.

Toronto offered an impressive shopping district — Eaton's, Simpson's, Birk's, the finest in china and silver and linens and woolens. But she hungered for the old scene and the friendly greetings and service in the haunts she loved; the leisurely pleasure of browsing in MacTaggart's book shop—selecting gifts in Patterson's jewelry store, responding to a call from Ballentine's where her tastes were known, her wants anticipated — considering a choice of hats at the PARRA where they had pleased her for so long.

And when the Steamer *Ralph Budd* met with trouble on Lake Superior, she hurriedly packed and went along with Tom as he left for Sarnia. She kept the house in readiness for such emergencies.

Tom said, "There's fireman blood in you somewhere! All I have to do is say the word and in five minutes you're ready."

Occupied as he was, Tom was never to know the loneliness she endured without complaint, her longing for her children and friends and familiar scenes; Michigan Spring, the beautiful St. Clair River—

As the train sped along, they sat in silence — her heart glowing with happy anticipation, his mind anxious as to the conditions he would find at Eagle Harbor on the Keweenaw Peninsula where the Steamer *Ralph Budd* had gone on the rocks. . . .

He found her hanging on a ledge at a precarious angle, a prize package-freighter of the Anchor Line, a twin-decker worth $200,000.

It seemed that the pound of the sea could have sent her to the bottom any moment. Standing beside her, Tom pushed a boulder into the water. He said it must have gone down to hell for he never heard it land.

Constructed with between-decks, the *Budd* carried a full load. With engine room and boiler room flooded, it was doubly dangerous to attempt to take her off. With the *Manistique* standing by, and employing hydraulic jacks, they managed to manoeuvre her into position where the main hold could be pumped out. Meyers then patched the ship's bottom temporarily, and she was taken to Sarnia for repair. The underwriters gave her to the Sin-Mac Company for their bill, which was $50,000. Sin-Mac sold her to Playfair of Toronto, and profited $40,000 on the transaction.

But when his part in the project was over, he found he could not return to Sarnia as planned, and telephoned Anna. "I know this won't break your heart, but I'm going up to Parisienne Island. The *Lambton* wreck."

"I thought she went on the rocks last year."

"Right. The Matthews people want us to bid now on salvage and make a start. I've got to look her over. See you in probably a week — so make the most of your time."

"Take care, Tom—"

The *Lambton* — $150,000 caller owned by the Matthews Steamship Company of Toronto — had gone ashore on Parisienne Island up along the eastern shore of Lake Superior in a snowstorm the winter before, and laid there ever since. It was a particularly tragic affair, as some of the crew panicked, fearing the ship would go to pieces. Against the urgings of the Captain, they got into some new patent suits which had not been tested, but which were supposed to contain everything necessary for a man's survival in case of shipwreck. The seas were high and wild. The men missed the island and later were found frozen to death on the rocks, while those who stayed aboard were rescued.

The seas fought for the *Lambton*. When Tom and his men went to salvage her, they found they could not pump out her midship hold, but managed to get up steam aboard her. The *Manistique* started to tow her to Port Arthur. On the way, a violent storm came up and the boat rolled so hard that she almost turned over. Water swept into the hold. She would veer away over, hesitate as if deliberating on ending it all, then slowly come back. Each time it seemed would be the last.

They managed to get her to Marquette harbor where Tom, knowing he shouldn't do such a thing, but forced to make immediate decision, ordered her grain cargo pumped out into the harbor. Meyers then went down and patched her and they were able to pump out the hold. Again she started off for Port Arthur, in the wake of the *Manistique,* and this time she made it. Tom had bid $25,000 for the job. The profit was $10,000.

When he stopped off at Port Huron for Anna, "It didn't take you too long," she observed. "Probably just light jobs."

"That's right. All in a day's work . . . "

Her reference had a double meaning. The great depression lay like a smothering blanket over their world.

CHAPTER TWENTY-ONE

Tom's next project was of such major proportions that no one was deceived. Early in May of 1930, The Canadian Department of Marine Dredge *DM5* struck a rock opposite the mouth of the St. Maurice River at Three Rivers, Quebec. Puncturing her hull, she sank within twenty five minutes — though without loss of life — presenting a major menace to navigation.

Three Rivers, an important city and port of Quebec, lies at the confluence of the St. Maurice and St. Lawrence Rivers. Flowing in from the north, the St. Maurice is divided at its mouth by two islands, and the channels account for the town's name. One of the oldest in Quebec, it is one of the most picturesque as well as one of the most prosperous, due to the large lumber trade and the manufacture of wood pulp, and its great shipping activities.

Dredge *DM5* was one of the largest ever to be operated in inland waters on the North American Continent, with an overall waterline dimension of 168 feet, and a crew of thirty. She was built in 1926 at a cost of $500,000 for the Dominion Government, at the Government shipyards at Quebec. She was of the elevator bucket or endless chain design with fifty two cast steel buckets of five-ton capacity revolving over an underwater mechanism, which made the dredge effective to a depth of nearly fifty feet.

In submerging, the dredge had turned upside down and edged itself into the bottom of the river with smokestack and spars pointing downward. The wreck had occurred too far off shore to make a solid point on land available as a base for the heavy pull necessary to right the craft. It was evident that tugs were not the answer but a firm, immovable base to accommodate the great strain required — and that, less than 300 feet toward shore.

Contract bid of $100,000 for salvaging having been awarded the Sin-Mac Lines, operations were now begun under Tom Reid's direct supervision. He conceived measures here that were unique and proved to be successful.

He grounded the 1,900 ton former ocean-going ship *Turret Court*. And digging in the St. Lawrence mud bank, he created a 250 foot channel as a bed for the scuttled ship. Under twenty five feet of water, he placed four huge turbine pumps for purposes of removing water from the submerged wreck. But river currents now offered a challenge. Twice a day at extreme low tide, the current passed over the wreck at five miles an hour. This was a bad hazard to overcome, and would retard salvaging.

Divers dynamited the heavy chain of buckets to pieces so as to make their removal possible, and lashed in the center of the vessel's hull the sixty five ton submarine structure over which the buckets normally revolve. They were required to handle all stoppage and patchwork necessary on the hull before pumps could be applied for emptying it.

Months passed, and the restoring of the dredge to normal position was now considered an impossibility by all but Tom Reid. He had learned to be patient with the sea. The seven to eight hundred ton strain on heavy steel cables strung from the scuttled *Turret Court* to the submerged wreck he knew would eventually have their effect. Yet, time after time, when victory seemed almost at hand, the suction in the blue clay and mud bottom on which the dredge lay prevented the wreck from moving more than six or seven inches in a night after the maximum strain had been applied on the cables before nightfall.

Three times the pumping and pulling efforts of the salvagers were frustrated just when success seemed imminent. In each instance, the dredge was brought out of the water, only to slip back and turn over on its port side once more.

Then Tom Reid decided to secure, if possible, from the Montreal Harbor Commission their huge floating crane. Through the kindness of the Federal Minister of Marine, Honorable Alfred Duranleau, he succeeded. With this piece of equipment, which is capable of lifting obstacles to a maximum weight of some 275 tons, he was able to remove the 'ladder' from its place in the 'well' of the wreck.

Cold weather had now set in, and for hours — never considering his health — Tom worked day and night, chilled and half-sick from lack of sleep and anxiety. At one point, he was taken ashore and worked over for hours to reestablish normal circulation, warned not to return for a matter of days, and returned in a few hours to take up vigil, study, order and try to bring to a successful conclusion the toughest job he had ever tackled.

Another year came. By now Virginia had married and gone west to live. Clara had established her own home, and Thom — successful in business in Chicago, was seldom with the family. Anna was alone. And when Tom wrote, urging her to come and join him, admitting his need of her at the time of a very trying ordeal, she closed the house and went to join him.

She wrote to Clara from the Hotel Saint-Maurice Limitée, Les Trois Rivieres, Quebec –

> ". . . I miss you and little Johnnie and cannot say definitely when I will see you. All depends on Dad. The men have everything in readiness to make a lift Thursday at 5 AM at high tide. Can only work under water and lift then. Men are working like beavers to get through. All French people here. Seems strange . . . "

And again —

> " . . . I hope it won't be long now. It is so lonely here. Raining hard again today. The French pilot on the tug that runs Dad back and forth says if it rains August 3 (and it did), it will rain all month of August. His predictions are right. It has rained every day . . . "

Another message —

" . . . Dad is up at dawn — never back before six. If he is through this week, he is planning on leaving as soon as that *animal* comes to the surface. They made an attempt Saturday. Something went wrong. Discouraging — but Dad goes at it the following day again. Two months now I've been here this time — and Dad in his second year . . . . "

More —

" . . . This is later. Yesterday Dad made a lift. The boat came to the surface, then dropped out of sight. Today the divers stopped the leak, and at high tide in the morning will begin to pump that *animal* up. I do hope Dad has good luck. He has lost considerable weight. A terrific responsibility. I wonder how he endures it all. I will go home soon, but return, since I don't believe he takes care of himself at all when I'm not here.

Today the diver is going down in a bad place. It is hazardous, but he has to patch the *animal.* Dad has two more to do before fall, but I wonder if he can make it. This one looks bad . . .

Again —

" . . . A church near by — I can see the steeple bells. They toll all day, from early morning. You can imagine how it would make you feel.

Dad is discouraged over the labor situation here. It can't be helped. He will be tied up here a while longer, I'm afraid. The tide is something only God can control. Toward fall now, it comes in at later hours. The French pilot it familiar with the hours. Some days the divers can only work two hours out of the twenty four. It's beyond me how they get anything done in a day . . . .

The labor situation was indeed discouraging for Tom Reid. And the moods of the tides. There was, as well, difficulty in following through as his ideas dictated, for he was surrounded with opinionated people close to the Government. When at last he insisted on pumping out the dredge, Joseph Simard sent a representative of the Merritt-Chapman marine experts to inspect the situation and confer with him. Chapman's man stormily forbade Tom to follow along the lines of his own reasoning. "Don't do it, Reid," he insisted. "The decks will collapse."

Other salvaging Companies were asked for consultations, and all agreed with the Chapman representative. "Don't pump her out!" was the general verdict.

"But she's all ready to pump out!" declared Tom, desperate with frustration.

Simard, himself, gave the final edict. "I forbid it!"

"It would work," argued Tom, "if I could get enough lifting power to take her stern out."

Simard at first was adamant to this suggestion, but finally agreed to furnish four pontoons of one hundred tons each, and a great derrick, each costing $100 an hour. But Tom was still denied permission to pump her out.

When all was ready, they began trying to force the water out of the pontoons. The weather was foul — rain and wind, with a hint of sleet. The derrick was doing its best, but its best wasn't good enough.

Tom knew he faced final failure unless he could follow his own judgment. He was confident of success otherwise. There was no time to hesitate. It was one or the other, and it had to be now. He dispatched his first assistant to shore on an errand. The moment the fellow left by tug, Tom went to his diver. "Jeff, go down and start that eighteen inch pump in the engine and boiler room."

"Don't do it, Captain!" begged Jeff.

"Who's running this thing?" thundered Tom. "I said — *go down!*"

Jeff reluctantly obeyed and started the pumps. Soon, up came the dredge, leaking, of course, but not too badly. Once pumped out, decks still safe, they made ready to tow her in to land.

Hours later, when he could, Tom telephoned Manager Campbell. "The dredge is raised." The work of three years was over! Tom Reid himself says it was a miracle. A job next to impossible had been accomplished. More than pontoons and derricks, he declares, were responsible. Anna's prayers . . . Experts said it was the greatest single piece of marine salvaging in the history of the Dominion.

The bid had been $100,000. The Sin-Mac Lines had made no money, but had achieved a magnificent feat, and gained invaluable publicity.

A ceremony followed and in the presence of Government officials from Ottawa, and other departmental dignitaries, the Department of Marine Dredge *DM5* was refloated in the St. Lawrence River about two miles east of Three Rivers. These people made a great occasion of Tom's achievement, but to him the look in Anna's eyes was the praise he most relished.

The operation had cost the Government hundreds of thousands of dollars for salvage work and for commandeered equipment. The Sin-Mac Lines were awarded the amount of the contract bid and the wrecked barge itself, which seemed useless for any further work. In reality, it was a dock hazard. A wrecking barge was made out of the hull and Dredge *DM5* still had some years of usefulness left, but a few years later, she ran on a rock in a fog near Rimouski. This time the sea claimed her permanently.

Dredge *DM No. 5* had served her purpose in many ways, not the least of which was the occasion to prove the skill and ingenuity of one of America's great salvagers. And that skill and ingenuity — and the shippers' need for salvaging, despite the national economic slump, was sought after by needy if skeleton Companies in order to retain such marine assets as they had.

Banks were failing as frenzied depositors withdrew funds. Mortgage-holders were ejecting families. Installment houses were repossessing diamonds, cars and household furniture. Dark rumors abounded. The world waited for the big break, and some felt it came with the inauguration of Franklin D. Roosevelt. Many were not so sure. But there was action, and in action — hope.

CHAPTER TWENTY-TWO

Tom Reid never consciously permitted Anna to suspect his secret apprehensions. Despite the darkness of the circumstances, he always put up a good front.

Due to his affectionate insistence in one instance, she had accompanied him to Montreal for a few days. He had been called there to confer with Company officials relative to the salvaging of Canadian Dredge *DM14,* which had suffered a fate similar to that of *DM5,* and which bitter challenge he eventually met successfully, this man who refused to accept defeat . . . .

One evening during their stay in Montreal, he suggested a popular night-club for an after-theater supper. A featured singer in the floor show seemed peculiarly familiar. The girl was striking in a cheap, pretty way. She held his attention.

"Someone you know?" Anna finally asked.

"You might put it that way," he smiled. "Remember the job I took up at Newfoundland last year?"

"I should," she sighed. "We were out of touch for two weeks during one of the worst storms of the year. But — why change the subject?"

He told her the story . . . In the late fall, a Canadian package freighter, loaded with flour, had run afoul a rocky island off the southern coast of Newfoundland. Summoned to accompany the inspector and insurance representative to the scene, Tom secured the services of a fisherman who claimed to be familiar with the spot in question, and they started out in his fishing launch.

It was blowing a gale, with a heavy sea. The craft itself, was not too substantial — filthy, besides, and reeking of dead fish. Though used to rough weather and the roll of the sea, Tom became genuinely concerned for their safety. Watching the fisherman, he realized that the fellow was not too familiar with the course.

They stopped the first night out at a Hudson's Bay Post on the Gulf of the St. Lawrence. With morning, they resumed the journey through a day more stormy and difficult than the previous one. The second night they drew in at an island and sought food and shelter in the house of a French-Canadian family. All others, it seemed, were Esquimaux.

The family consisted of a man and wife and adolescent daughter named Jean. The girl did not join them at first, and the parents kept glancing uneasily toward the bedroom door. She was singing, her voice untrained but appealing. At last she appeared when they were seated at the table, about to partake of the slim meal their hostess had been able to provide. She introduced herself and took her place.

Jean had striking features and a positive personality. She was hung with cheap jewelry. Her hair was ridiculously dressed, and somewhere she had found cosmetics to achieve the flamboyant mask she had made of her nice face. She asked pointed questions about life in Montreal, in particular about the theaters, hotels and night clubs. Her forcefulness dominated the scene. Learning the nature of the strangers' business in the area, she glanced at her father with a mysterious smile.

"You will never salvage that ship," she told Tom.

"But, why?" asked the insurance agent.

"You will see," she said airily. "You will see."

She made the arrangements for the night, deciding where the men would sleep — and how; deciding on price. It would cost the strangers five dollars apiece for a not-too-clean quilt and a soggy pillow on the kitchen floor. Food was extra. And the reeking fisherman brought to the ill-aired place all that was necessary to make the night practically intolerable.

The daughter of the house would get to Montreal, Tom was sure, if these rocky islands continued to serve as a menace to navigation.

With morning, the fishermen took them out to the island on which the disabled ship had foundered — lurching through wild seas. The launch had not been cleaned in the meantime. The floor was slippery and nauseating with dead fish, filthy cans, cloths and tarpaulins.

The place was inhabited almost entirely by Esquimaux. Natives moved out from their huts, curious and resentful when they saw the men approaching the wrecked ship — its bow out of water amidship, its stern submerged. The sea pounded it mercilessly.

The natives muttered ominously among themselves. Then their leader approached Captain Tom. Soon he began to make sense of their angry protests. They were hungry! Their people sometimes starved. Here was flour for bread. Barrels and bags of flour — a whole cargo of it. The Lord had sent it to them, and no one was going to touch it! Determined, they began to surround the strangers.

There were eleven tiny rocky islands in the group. A glance revealed increasing numbers of natives alerted . .

The conference between Tom and his companions was brief, and the decision inevitable. The package freighter would remain on that rock until the sea eventually claimed her. Jean had been right. She understood these people.

Once more the men climbed into the putrid launch and started the long haul back through deadly waves. The discomfort and danger had all been for nothing. They would stay at the Hudson's Bay Post until the next passenger ship came out in probably a week's time. And they would have baths, good hot coffee and decent food. With relief, they watched the launch nose into the little cove at Hudson's Bay Post.

Tom took out his bill fold. It was a disappointing end to a disgusting experience, and he was privately deploring the loss of many thousands of dollars that would have come his way through the salvage job. He said to their pilot, "I don't know how you pick up any passengers in a dirty trap like this. Much as a fellow's life is worth to trust himself aboard it." He tossed the bills into the filthy, outstretched hands.

The fellow shrugged. "Passengers? You're the first I ever took. Never been out to that place before."

"You — *you* — " roared Tom. "You mean to say —"

"Why did you take the chance — even with your own life?" snapped the insurance agent.

"Need the money."

"Our time hadn't come, that's all," decided the inspector. "Let's get the hell out of this."

Tom and Anna smiled at each other as Jean, sweet and demure, sang tenderly of love . . . .

But Tom had little time to devote to diversion, with trouble constantly dogging him. He returned home to be notified to leave at once for Goderich, Ontario, where the Canadian freighter *Saskadoc* had met disaster. Built in 1900, the 500 foot, 5,000 tonner *Saskadoc* (née *Uranus)* owned by the Paterson Steamship Company of Fort William, missed the piers at Goderich in a south west 'blow.' The final syllable in the names of this fleet, including the *Novadoc* and *Saskadoc,* identifies them with the Dominion of Canada.

Meyers of the United States Salvage Company contacted Tom ashore and asked him to be on hand in Goderich when the wind went down. Boarding the wrecker *Manistique,* Tom went up at night.

On her bow, the *Saskadoc* carried a five ton anchor with 1,000 feet of two inch cable for pulling. She also had some equipment aft' for pulling with 2,000 feet of cable.

The picture had changed by the time Tom reached the scene, and he lay at anchor waiting for daylight when a wind sprang up from the north west. He 'blew' for a tug to come out and run a line out to the *Saskadoc.* It was a hard gale from the north west with a big sea running. The tug took the 1,000 foot running line, pulled on the two inch cable and then ran a line out to the bow of the *Saskadoc.*

With three anchors out to hold him, and pulling the cable, Tom got the running line through the bow of the boat. They heaved on the line with windlass, made fast, and started pulling. It took about three hours to get her off, and she went into the harbor under her own steam with her cargo of 160,000 bushels of wheat. If she had not been released at that time, she would have broken in two on the sand and been a total loss.

For this the insurance underwriters awarded the Sin-Mac Company $3,500, a job done in one day from the time of leaving Sarnia until returning.

CHAPTER TWENTY-THREE

Since the Lindbergh kidnapping, Anna had been restless and apprehensive about little Johnnie Sullivan. Clara would reply to the urgently concerned letters with affectionate patience, when adjured to watch carefully over her son. But, reasoned the mother, Clara must realize that anything could happen these days, and Clara lived a social life and had someone in often to care for her child.

So when Tom was called to the Sarnia office at the time of the *City of Bangor* wreck, she packed in record time and declared her intention to accompany him. He smiled at her gravely announced plan to bring little Johnnie back home with her on their return.

"Of course, his mother doesn't care what happens to him," he said with amusement.

"Oh, you know I don't mean that," she defended. "But, Tom, if anything happened to that child—"

"You'd better not let Clara hear you say that. What you mean is — it's just a good excuse to kidnap him, yourself." And while his manner suggested tender understanding, his thoughts were rather with the grim problem that lay ahead.

Built at a cost of $200,000 by the Lake Transit Company of Bay City, Michigan, the *Bangor,* with a capacity of 4,200 tons and carrying 250 Chrysler cars, went ashore at Keweenaw Point, the tip of Michigan's Keweenaw Peninsula, that tapering portion of land that juts out into Lake Superior and resembles a weary traveler leaning against the wind. Driven by a wild northwest blizzard, and seeking to negotiate passage between Manitou Island and the mainland and find shelter at Béte Gris, *The City of Bangor* 'went on' near Copper Harbor high across the beach. Her crew had been forced to abandon ship, and making their way to Copper Harbor in the blizzard, suffered frozen arms and legs as they stumbled about in the savage Arctic wilderness.

Some days after the accident, commissioned by the insurance underwriters to investigate the situation and offer a salvaging bid, Tom left for Hancock, the last town accessible by rail in that region. Beyond there, facing seven foot snow, travel by snowmobile was necessary. The underwriters informed Tom they had sent their adjustor to the scene two weeks before and there had been no word.

The trip from Hancock took Tom through wild, snow-smothered country. Reaching Eagle Harbor late one afternoon, Tom was told by the driver that further travel toward Keweenaw Point was impossible under the conditions. Copper Harbor and the *Bangor* was still fourteen miles away.

Tom found the insurance adjustor lounging in the hotel parlor, claiming he was sick. But his breath told the story. When questioned, he merely gestured toward windows sash-high with snow.

It seemed hopeless to find some way to reach the disabled ship, but at last Tom contacted the Coast Guard Station at Bête Gris, eighteen miles across the Peninsula. In a few hours the Coast Guard crew were fighting their way through high seas toward Eagle Harbor in a thirty five foot launch with only a canvas top.

Storm signals were up. The men conferred on a course of action after arrival. Tom was restless and impatient. "Do you think we can take a chance, and go over and examine the wreck before the blow?" he asked the Coast Guard Captain.

The plan was decided upon, and though the barometer kept dropping, they left in the Coast Guard boat for the scene of the disaster, though without the insurance inspector. After a hard pounding, the ice-covered launch finally reached the *Bangor* and, boarding the steamer from the stern, Tom went through the lower hold to the bow. He found that an enormous rock had pierced the ship's bottom. Only a few of the cars were undamaged.

On deck again, he braved the raging blizzard that further mantled the exposed cars which had already become shrouded in ice. He crawled along the icy surface to the stern of the ship for further examination, then in view of the weather, decided to seek shelter as the storm came from the northwest and they were openly exposed to the blasts.

Back on the launch again, with each wave it seemed the craft must capsize — water roaring over them and freezing as it struck. Nearing Copper Harbor, they decided to make for shore. They threw the sea anchor overboard and dragged it. Entering the mouth of the little harbor, they found an inch of ice. The wind was high and they were forced to roll the boat in order to break the frozen surface and make the way passable. Here, communication with the outside world was impossible since all lines were down. It was useless to attempt to return to Bête Gris at the moment, and Tom now realized the futility of considering immediate salvage. The *Bangor* would have to wait until spring and take her chances on being battered to pieces in the meantime. He figured on the job, and planned a bid of $40,000 for removing the cars and delivering them to Houghton. He would use sleighs, load one car on each. He would string a cable across to shore, hoist the cars from hold to deck with a tackle, or cut a hole in the *Bangor*'s side.

Conditions held him there a week. When the weather cleared sufficiently, Tom found a team and drove the nine miles to Mandan. Then he hired a fresh team and went on to make connections the remaining distance to Hancock. At Hancock, the insurance underwriters were contacted by phone and he made his bid. Tom was underbid by another Company and settled for $50.00 a day for his time and services while traveling and investigating.

The other Company damaged the cars in removing them, drove them through ice and snow, not on sleighs. The operation cost heavily according to local rumor.

The *Bangor* went to pieces where she lay, dissolved with time, and today her pilot house stands on the shore at Copper Harbor, mute testimony to one of the tragedies of the sea. . . .

At Hancock, after he lost the deal with the insurance underwriters, Tom telephoned the office at Sarnia and was informed that they had not heard from the Reid tug, *Sarnia City,* which had been sent up to assist *The Langell Boys* — a little lumber steamer — and her two barges on Saginaw Bay. The situation looked serious.

The *Langell Boys* and barges had taken a load of lumber from Garden River in Canada, bound for Bay City. In below zero weather she tried to break the ice in Saginaw Bay while towing barges at the same time. She finally had to stop and they had sent the *Sarnia City* to help her. The *Langell Boys* had frozen in, the *Sarnia City* had damaged her hull in the ice, and one barge was leaking.

Tom left at once for Bay City where he found that the tug *Sarnia City* had drifted out twenty miles. A crew-man had chanced the walk ashore to get food. Ice was twenty inches thick. They were forced to burn wood, all available stock, to keep warm and to keep steam up aboard ship.

Tom ordered his car brought at once to Bay City. He drove out on the ice and found the boats all lying together, and he made plans for rescue.

Coal was ordered to be hauled out in trucks from Bay City — seventy five tons at five tons a trip. Tom Reid's Packard flew back and forth from the distressed ships to shore. The Company lawyer from Cleveland, there to take depositions, rode with Tom several times. Gray with apprehension, he viewed the car doors — tied back with twine, so that in case of a crack in the ice, or of unexpectedly encountering an air-hole, the men could jump free.

At last Tom devised a way to bring in the little fleet. With thirty six inch motor ice-saws loaded on a sleigh, they cut through the ice so that the floes would break more easily. They laid a course with the compass, and in this way achieved two miles a day toward shore.

When the *Sarnia City* was about half way to shore, her stem broke in the heavy ice. Under incredible difficulties, they tipped her up and installed a new stem out in the open, with visibility practically nil. Soon the *Sarnia City* reached port with the barges and was laid up for the winter, and Tom returned to Sarnia aboard *The Langell Boys*. The job had netted the company $10,000.

Tom telephoned Anna in Port Huron.

"Was it bad, Tom?" she wondered. "The papers say the weather up there was terrible. Have you had a hard time?" Anna continued to get her news of her husband from the newspapers.

"Oh, I've seen worse." He winked at the telephone.

Swing-Bridge at Duluth

The *Turret Cape* in Lock along St. Lawrence River.

Wrecker *Manistique* at scene of *Hustler* wreck, Cleveland, Ohio.

Wrecker *Manistique* and Lighter *Eleanor* working on sand-sucker *Hustler* at Cleveland.

Wrecked sand-sucker *Hustler* at Cleveland, Ohio.

Reid Lighter *Redfern* ashore in Rapids in St. Lawrence River. Tugs *Donnelly* & *Frontenac*.

Sand boat *Kelly Island,* sunk off Leamington, Ontario.

The *William Brewster* after being raised.

Turret Cape cables at work on Dredge DM No. 5.

Wrecker *Manistique* and Lighter *Eleanor*.

Petites, Newfoundland

Dredge DM No. 14

Ayecliff Hall

Ayecliff Hall

Bow of *Ayecliff Hall*

Louis Meyers preparing to submerge at sand-dredge wreck in Toledo.

Raising the *William Brewster*.

Tug *Ralph* ashore near Montreal. Salvaged by Reid.

Lachine in drydock at Great Lakes Engineering Co., Detroit.

Reid dismantling a John E. Russell Lighter ashore below Port Colborne. She defied salvaging.

Reid wrecker *Lachine*.

Anchor with fluke buried ashore being used as power source in releasing grounded tug in St. Lawrence River.

Reid tug *Rival, Turret Cape* and wrecking lighter *Brighton* with Dredge DM No. 5.

Dredge No. 24 — turned over at dock at Port Welland, Ontario.

Louis Meyers submerging on wrecked *Saxona.*

Reid pulling on passenger ship *Manitoulin* aground at Owen Sound Bay.

Sydney, Nova Scotia, 1918

Frontier

View of the crippled *Ascania*.

Reid workers examining a sunken scow at Grimsby Harbor between Port Dalhousie and Toronto on Lake Ontario.

Five ton clam-shell on Reid wrecking barge *Eleanor*.

Steamer *Vulcan* sunk at dock at Houghton, Michigan.

Ramona

Passenger Steamer *Hamonic*—picture taken after fire—being towed by Reid to Windsor and scrap heap.

Steamer *Noronic*. A passenger and freight vessel built for Canadian trade. Strictly up to date in all parts. Fitted with cargo handling apparatus, wireless telegraph and other equipment necessary to the comfort and convenience of modern travel.

Working on Dredge DM No. 5.

Manistique and Tug *Smith* at *Kelly Island* scene after she was raised.

Louis Meyers submerging.

Tug *Bon Voyage* towing a gate-lifter built at Collingwood, Ontario, to be placed along Welland Canal lock.

Montreal tug sunk in Gulf of St. Lawrence with all hands aboard.

Lighter *Londonderry* raising dump scow for Government in St. Lawrence River.

Reid wrecker *Lachine*.

Lighter *Brighton* lightering Norwegian ship.

Reid wrecking Steamer *Julius H. Barnes* ashore at Point Edward, part in current.

The *Red Cloud* — first of Welland Canal Diesels, owned by North American Transport Company and built to carry 60,000 bushels of grain.

One of Reid Company's pontoons.

Sand dredge wreck in Toledo,

Oil Barge sunk in Lake Ontario towed by Reid to Toronto.

Dredge No. 10 at Walpole Island Reid wrecking her.

Reid wrecker-tug *Maplecourt* towing two steamers to scrap heap at Sturgeon Bay, Wisconsin.

Novadoc — sunk in Lake Michigan.

18 inch pump in action on Steamer *Widlar*.

Wrecker *Manistique* at scene after raising *Kelly Island*.

Reid working to free foreign ship *Trajan* — aground near Iroquois on St. Lawrence River just below Lock.

Turret Cape pulling on Dredge DM No. 5.

Derrick on Dredge DM No. 14

Square pontoons being lowered on *Ayecliff Hall*.

Working on 18 inch pump on barge *Brighton*.

Canal and Lock at Iroquois, Ontario — the town that is no more, recently inundated by Seaway.

Tug *Sarnia City* breaking ice for *Langell Boys* and her barges going into Bay City.

Novadoc — sunk in Lake Michigan.

Tug *Ralph* ‘on’ near Montreal.

The *Maplecourt* — Wrecker.

Reid salvaging *Turret Cape* ashore on Michipocoton Point.

Captain Tom Reid on scene at Government Dredge DM No. 5.

Reid tug *Whalen* breaking ice at Port Arthur.

Pittsburg SS Co's Supply ship *Frontier* sunk after collision at Soo.

Government Lightship *The Golden Rule* sunk near Buffalo.

Norwegian package freighter ashore near Cardinal on St. Lawrence River.

Canal at Iroquois on St. Lawrence River.

Norwegian package freighter ashore at Iroquois on St. Lawrence River.

Tug *Guardian* of Pringle Barge Line, St. Clair, Michigan, towing Govt. boats near Iroquois on St. Lawrence River.

Wrecker *Manistique* and Barge *Eleanor,* the lighter.

Dredge No. 10 at Walpole Island. Reid wrecking her.

Two foreign ships collide in St. Lawrence River — shown here with Reid Lighter and tug.

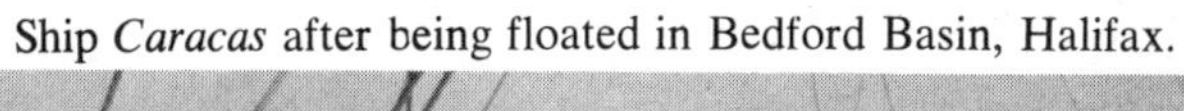

Ship *Caracas* after being floated in Bedford Basin, Halifax.

Turret Cape wrecking Dredge DM No. 14

Steamer *Ralph Budd* — ashore at Eagle Harbor. Picture shows where storm had smashed her Texas and elevator.

Pittsburg SS Co.'s Gut Wagon at Soo after raising. *Frontier*.

Hutchinson ship *Thompson* after collision above Rapids near Port Huron, Michigan.

Lumber steamer *Langell Boys* frozen in Saginaw Bay required circular saw to cut channel and release her and two barges.

Dredge DM No. 5.

Dredge DM No. 5 — rolling her up.

Dredge DM No. 5 — lying on side.

Wrecker *Londonderry* at scene of Dredge DM No. 5.

Wrecking on Dredge DM No. 5.

Turret Cape pulling on Dredge DM No. 5 — with Lighter *Londonderry*.

Reid pumping out scow sunk in Soulanges Canal, Canada.

Ramona

Salvaging gravel boat sunk at Toledo.

A Self-unloader owned by Smith of Green Bay — on the bottom at entrance to Green Bay.

Chicago Tribune

Frontier — with *Maplecourt*

Black River, Port Huron, Michigan.

Scene from wrecker *Manistique* along Soo River.

Lumber carriers heading north into Lake Huron.

Scene at Port Huron, Michigan.

White Star liner Steamer *Tashmoo* in her prime—circa. 1905.

Steamer *Charles S. Price*.

Tugs *Reid* and *Ottawa* w
Duluth Harbor.

ken Steamer *Mataafa* in

Wrecking tug *Mary Battle* and Lighter *Brighton* lying at anchor in the St. Lawrence River.

Stern end of Steamer *William Brewster*.

Barge *International* standing by during salvaging of *Hibou*.

Steamer *Henry Steinbrenner*.

Reid Company coffer-damming Canadian tug *Pearson* owned by paper mill in Calumet, Ottawa River, Canada.

Reid Wrecker *Cobourg* preparing to coffer-dam a flat scow laid on bottom. Derrick is handling timber.

The *Langell Boys* in Saginaw Bay with barges.

Reid Tugs (circa. 1903)
J. M. Diver *Sarnia City* *Smith* *Whalen* *James T. Reid*

Last picture of the once beautiful White Star Liner *Tashmoo* before she was dismantled for scrap. Reid was underbid at time of her sinking.

Reid tugs laying anchor fluke for salvaging in St. Lawrence at Kingston — to pull boats in current.

Putting cables down in raising of *Hibou*.

Reid Tug *Sarnia City* locked in ice on Saginaw Bay.

Steamer *Manitou* — passenger boat on Owen Sound. Reid brought her down at time of *Hibou*.

Raising the *Hibou*.

Steamer *Brewster after raising.*

The *William Brewster* sunk at Walpole Island in the St. Clair River.

One of beams going from *International Ferry* to *Londonderry*—while salvaging the *Hibou.*

Barge *Redfern*—one of 6 built by Reid. Now owned by Beacon Steamship Co. of Canada.

Tug *Donnelly* in St. Clair River releasing Barge *Redfern.*

Lighter *International* (nee ferry at Port Huron - Sarnia) in river at Owen Sound during salvaging of the *Hibou.*

Lighter *Brighton* with tug as Dredge DM No. 14 comes to the surface.

Scene aboard *International,* carferry from Port Huron converted into wrecking scow, and wrecker *Londonderry* at *Hibou* salvaging.

Lighter scow — Diver going down working on Dredge DM No. 5. *Turret Cape* in distance.

Frontier — Pittsburg S.S. Co., supply boat sunk in collision at Soo. Looking down inside coffer dam.

Working on Dredge DM No. 14.

Working on Dredge DM No. 14 — Lighter *Londonderry*.

Turret Cape wrecking Dredge DM No. 14.

Dredge DM No. 14, afire after being raised.

Raising the *Ralph Budd* at Houghton, Michigan.

CHAPTER TWENTY-FOUR

These were troubled days, the country slowly emerging from the depression with readjustment in order. The great dust storms plagued the middle west in retaliation for infamous practices with the sod, and played havoc with the nation's convalescing economy. Political storms were rampant between those for and against Roosevelt. There were rumors of unrest in Europe — the growing danger of dictators rising to power, and Louisiana's Huey Long reminding one of what dictators can accomplish.

But life went on, and the national picture improved.

The northern mines produced, freighters carried their yield down the Lakes, and the railroads again hummed busily across the nation.

In the Spring of 1935, a New York Central passenger train approached the town of Welland, Ontario, about to cross the Canal bridge. Through a confusion of signals, and unaware that the bridge ahead was open, the train proceeded briskly. Locomotive and tender dropped into the Canal. With air brakes, a severed pipe automatically halts the train. Fortunately the coaches caught and were derailed, an accident with minor loss of life.

Tom Reid was called to the scene. He considered the salvage problem, computed the cost and offered a bid of $25,000, and was given the contract to deliver the locomotive on the tracks — a condition being that the salvaging would not necessitate opening the bridge and interrupting railroad schedule.

This was a formidable complication. The locomotive weighed ninety tons and was in a bad spot. Again the magic of air-power was employed by the man who had been dedicated to it from the beginning. Whatever his private apprehensions were, Tom optimistically went ahead. Summoning his wrecking crew, he brought into use four steel pontoons, each with a lifting power of 100 tons. These were sunk and filled with air. In less than three weeks he had raised the locomotive, after which it had been taken down to Port Colborne between pontoons and placed on the bottom. At the dock it was restored to the tracks by three cranes using cables. On this job, he made a profit of $15,000.

The conclusion of the *Ayecliff Hall* incident was not so happy. This $150,000 Canadian canaller sank after a collision with the Steamer *Westland* off Long Point, a dangerous spit of land that juts out into Lake Erie from the southern shore of Ontario. Badly cut abreast of the boilers, the *Hall*'s spar was half out of water, and she was a menace to navigation along the channel.

Tom's bid of $30,000 to remove the wreck was accepted. With his wrecker *Maplecourt* standing by, he put an air-compressor to work and floated her bow up so the for'd end was out of water. He then concluded that he could raise her, but there was no way he could patch the break in her side which had occurred at the time of the collision. The damage had happened in the boiler room, and had run onto Number Two hold.

Tom strengthened the mid-ship bulkhead and placed four pontoons under the ship's stern. He then passed chains under her, and fastened them to the pontoons. They were ready to blow out the water, but when the divers went down to hook the air-hose on the pontoons and empty her, the pontoons had disappeared. Somehow, they had broken loose.

Tom figured he would drag her into shallow water and try new measures, but a storm came up and rolled her over. They never found her afterward. He conjectured that she had probably slid into a deep hole on the Lake's floor. His one satisfaction was that he had cleared the channel of an obstruction, and lived up to the terms of the contract. The bid had been $30,000, but the expense of attempted salvage had been great, and he considered his company lucky to break even on this deal.

CHAPTER TWENTY-FIVE

By 1940, the Reids had returned to Port Huron, taking a house on Military Street not far from their former home — but too close. For Anna, the old mansion was still home, with the boulder of *Matoa* history there in the front garden where it could be seen in passing.

Now her grandchildren filled the lonely days. Clara's Johnnie, whom she saw daily, and whose father had died long since; and Clara's new baby, Jimmy Pengra, child of Clara's second marriage. Virginia's Tim and Linda —

children of her marriage to Harold Reiman. And Thom's children who came on occasionally from Chicago only a few hours away. Thom was a busy industrialist now, enjoying substantial success.

More than emotion had weakened Anna's heart; an organic condition was making headway with the advancing years, and now all realized the significance of her slowly ebbing strength. These days she was unable to travel with Tom, or join him in the ports where his work called him. He censored the reports he gave of his projects, the chances he took of necessity and the sometimes precarious condition of his health. And it was well she was unaware of his narrow escape that next Spring.

It happened that he was directing the raising of a sunken ship at Three Rivers, Quebec, when he received a telephone call from Manager Campbell in Montreal. Government Steamboat No. 22 was in trouble down the Saguenay River near Chicoutami. Insurance officials were flying down the 600 miles, and Campbell urged Tom to go along. They would pick him up enroute.

At the time, Tom had been without sleep for forty eight hours, as the problem at Three Rivers was one in which a speedy salvaging was imperative if it was to succeed at all. He had been exposed physically to the most severe and gruelling weather, and was fighting a bad chest cold. He felt he could not honestly abandon the work he was doing. Privately, too, he was considering Anna's objections to his flights in those small bush planes.

The Government insisted. There were men, weren't there, who could carry out Tom's plan for salvaging at Three Rivers? This job was vital to Government needs. His arguments over-ruled, Tom agreed to be ready when Campbell and his associates reached Three Rivers.

At Chicoutami they found other wreckers already on hand. But after investigation, these people refused to bid as the situation looked hopeless. The 10,000 ton freighter, on her maiden voyage down the Saguenay River two miles from Chicoutami, had gone on the rocks at high tide. In her hold was a cargo of coal. The machinery was amidship with two holds for'd and one aft'. When the tide ebbed, she had broken in two on a rock.

Tom realized it would be one of the most difficult jobs he ever attempted, but he felt confident it could be done. He made a bid of $215,000 to raise ship and cargo.

It was necessary to wait for a certain high Government official to arrive before the final signing of contract. The other officials present maintained that all insurance was for salvage, and that she would cost more to repair than she was worth.

Irritated, Tom declared his intention to return to Three Rivers. Then — the fact that the Government had received no other bids interested him. And he decided to wait until that special official should arrive for the decisive conference. At which time they bluntly asked, "Will you take $200,000 to raise her?"

"You've got the contract," he told them.

Work was begun. Tom delegated his assistants on the job at Three Rivers to take over in full while he proceeded to get action at Chicoutami. They clammed the coal out of the ship, working at top speed with a heavy crew. On the seventh day, they brought the ship to dock. They had raised her, lightered her, and she came together as Tom had figured. They plated her sides, strengthened her deck and towed her to Sorel where she was rebuilt. The Sin-Mac Company made $50,000 on a contract that no other company would touch!

But the success of that job almost cost Tom Reid his life, for during the ordeal, he had had little sleep, and his chest cold had grown steadily worse. Hope and excitement had kept the giant physique functioning, but collapse came with relaxation. The day the Government ship sailed for Sorel, they took Tom Reid to the hospital at Chicoutami with pneumonia and a fever of 105 degrees. The inroads of the infection had been so long and steady that there was feeble response at first to care and treatment. On the third day, the doctors decided to advise the family.

Anna's heart condition would not permit even a knowledge of the crisis, and it was Thom who made the journey. Many hours elapsed before he could reach the remote town in Quebec.

Rounding a bend in the hospital corridor, he heard his father's voice, husky but belligerent and determined.

"By God, I'm not hanging around this place any longer. I've got work to do. Had to leave a job half done at Three Rivers. I tell you — I'm going to get out of here!"

When Thom stepped into view, he was leaning against the door-jamb, shaking his finger at the nurse. Then he saw his son. "Well, hello, Thom! What are you doing here? You know — this is a great country. Good fishing — wonderful country! — " He brushed off the nurse, weakly grasped Thom's hand. They got him back to bed against a barrage of protests. "I'll be out of here tomorrow, mark my words," he promised Thom, sinking back with a helpless sigh of relief. "By the way, have you got a cigar?"

He was game, tireless, shrugging off a twinge, a crick in the back, a numb hand now and then. There were seventy hard, exhaustive years behind him, but he refused to recognize the passage of time.

He was facing major surgery when the *Novadoc* got into trouble on Lake Michigan. Defying the doctor's warning at delay, he left at once for Ludington.. . . It was near here that this 253 foot Canadian pulpwood carrier, owned by the Paterson Steamship Company of Port Arthur, came to grief on Juniper Beach, when one of the worst storms ever to strike Lake Michigan took a toll of six ships and sixty five lives, in a white November hell!

Seventeen sailors who clung to the broken hulk of the *Novado*c for more than 24 hours on the beach were finally rescued. Two crew members were lost, but the other seventeen were removed by the fishing tug, *Three Brothers,* of Pentwater.

Tom Reid drove to Ludington and took a boat out to the scene of the wreck where she had settled deep in the sand, leaving all decks and part of the superstructure awash. After inspection, he made a $25,000 salvage bid. A Cleveland salvager bid $9,000 and was awarded the contract. He worked for months without results.

Paterson then contacted Tom and asked him to go to the scene again and check, and offer whatever suggestions he might have. Tom agreed, but once at the scene found that the method being used could never result in success. Seasonal bad weather lay just ahead. It was then too late, with the already shattered condition of the ship. He withdrew from the scene, advising the company that if the matter had been handled properly earlier, the *Novadoc* could have been saved.

Company business awaited him at the head office. A tug deal with Russia had come up. The Sin-Mac Lines had built two powerful steel tugs in England. Later they were sold to the Russian Government, which claimed they needed such vessels as ice breakers. (By a curious coincidence, the second World War broke out shortly after the transaction had been consummated). The Russians stipulated that the tugs were to be delivered to the port of Seattle on the Pacific coast, a detail that eliminated the possibility of confiscation. On their side, the Sin-Mac Lines stipulated that the Russian Government place the agreed amount on deposit in a bank in Seattle, as well as the expense of delivery.

Tom suggested to Manager Campbell that they drive out to Seattle to be on hand when the tugs arrived, since the crews had to be paid off and sent home. Campbell agreed. They brought along a Captain, and left after receiving word that the tugs had passed through the Panama Canal. This gave them time to reach Seattle by the time the tugs were due. They took turns driving Tom's new Packard, and leaving Port Huron late on a Sunday afternoon, arrived in Seattle Wednesday noon.

The tugs soon appeared, but there were no Russians on hand to greet the officials, and the bank handled the details. Two engineers were left to keep ship until the owners should arrive. The men then drove along the coast to Los Angeles, on to Tulsa and home. They had made over seven thousand miles in eleven days, and handled some gravely important business in which a sum of seven figures was involved. Age was not slowing up Tom Reid.

When Manager Ferbert of The Pittsburg Steamship Company called him late in the fall of 1940 to come to their aid once more, Tom hurried off with his diver as usual, eager to take on whatever problem lay ahead, even though his step was not quite as quick as usual nor his breath as even.

The $500,000 Steamer *Eugene J. Buffington,* a 13,500 ton freighter, 580 feet in length, had run on Ballard Reef at Beaver Island in northern Lake Michigan where she hung precariously over the Reef, back broken, bow and stern sections over forty feet of water. Their insurance representative had given her up because they felt she would slide off into deep water any moment.

With Louis Meyers, Tom drove to Charlevoix on the east shore of Lake Michigan. A gale was blowing, and the Coast Guard cutter had to fight all the way to bring them out to the stricken steamer. The Great Lakes Towing Company's tug *Favorite* had already arrived — a firm in which the Pittsburg Steamship Company had an interest, and had brought along their Company's shore Captain. When Tom and Meyers went aboard the *Buffington,* they found the surveyors there also. The *Buffington,* was drawing eighteen feet amidship, thirty three feet aft', six inches over Number One hatch with two feet of water on deck.

Tom discussed his finds with the shore Captain, and contacting Manager Ferbert gave a salvage estimate of $160,000. Ferbert demurred heatedly. There was a sharp argument. Then Tom offered him $100,000 for the *Buffington* where she stood.

Ferbert was furious. "I'll blow her up first!" he declared. "She's one of the finest ships of our fleet."

Company employees figuring the ship was doomed had stripped her of everything movable. Plumbing, compass, steering wheel, engine room telegraph; everything that could be pried off was taken, much of it smashed in the process, and valuable only as scrap.

In the meantime, the Great Lakes Towing Company's

tug, *Favorite,* working on the damaged ship with a lighter, was charging $2,500 a day.

"Why don't you take the contract?" Ferbert asked Tom. "No cure — no pay."

"Oh, no!" Tom was emphatic. He knew that if the ship failed to 'come up', he would get nothing, and she was in a dangerous spot.

In the midst of the discussion, Ferbert whirled abruptly and asked, "How long would it take to get her off?"

Tom calculated. "Fifteen days. That is, if you leave your men there and give us anything we need. And I know that's a lot. But that's the way it's got to be." The Steel Trust ships were passing the spot frequently on their way to and from South Chiacgo and Gary, Indiana. And Tom knew he could send out a tug and pick up extra equipment from time to time.

"Very well." Ferbert flung back his chair. "If you get her off in fifteen days, we'll give you a bonus of $5,000."

They welded plates to her hull at the break so they would lap over when the ship was straightened. Then they lightered her, discarding cargo. Bow and stern came up and the plates slid over the break. They welded the projecting plates to the other part of the hull and thus mended the break sufficiently to float her away for more permanent repairs. The entire job took only fourteen days.

Tom had more than kept his word. He now took her in to Harbor Springs, pumped out the hold in Number One and Three compartments. There was a temporary repair job of plates on her starboard side to make her secure for the cruise down Lake Michigan. The contract was fulfilled, the bonus paid, and Anna had a mink coat as a remembrance.

"Well, anyway," she laughed shakily, "I have the figure for it now if not the face."

"That was the idea." But his chuckle didn't quite come off."

"Tom Reid, you're a cad!"

"It ain't taken you close to fifty years to find out what I am, has it?" She looked so small and frail —

"It certainly *ain't,* sir!"

Oh, Anna, Anna — don't leave me —

CHAPTER TWENTY-SIX

The war was on. Tom Reid had listened to the grave radio announcement that fateful Sunday, December 7, 1941. He had heard the incredible account of the Japanese attack on Pearl Harbor. And he seemed to hear again his father's words of long ago, when America annexed the Philippines after the war with Spain —

" . . . You may live to see trouble over this thing . . . McKinley's a great man, but he's flung the American flag across the path of Japanese imperialism. Some day those little yellow men may sink their fangs into us . . . "

He smiled grimly, remembering. The old lion had always known the answers.

1942 was a bad year for Tom Reid. The first blow came in late February when his good friend and expert diver, Louis Meyers, engaged in salvaging aboard the barge, *Fueloil,* came to grief. This barge was an important link in a project on Maumee Bay off Monroe, Michigan, carrying fuel from Toledo to two dredges working to clear the channel. A south west storm came up, the tug's tow-line parted, and the *Fueloil* was driven ashore. She was a valuable property, particularly in this emergency. They tried to dredge in to where she lay, and the delay was grave.

Working on this salvaging job for the Sin-Mac Lines and Tom, Louis Meyers lost hold of a luff block, on which he had a strained hold, and fell backward over the ship's side. There were no railings and nothing to grasp and he fell fourteen feet to the floor of ice where he smashed both ankles and broke his left hip. This was to result in semi-invalidism for the rest of his life.

It seemed to Tom Reid that the whole framework of the familiar was crumbling about him. Anna's decline, once begun, had progressed steadily. Her courage and morale belied the significance of pallor and weakness.

"Now no more of this nonsense," she said one day, gesturing about the bedroom bright with flowers. "Tom Reid, it's sheer extravagance. *Every* day — fresh roses!

At first he had been able to fence with her, to laugh and joke a little. But as time went on, the best he could manage was a smile that creaked with effort. And while he felt the need to be near her in these waning days as much as possible, the sight of her slow withdrawal from life depressed him unbearably. He feared to betray the terror he felt — the panic at thought of losing her.

Within reach on her counterpane lay the latest letters from her children, and the scrapbooks with clippings recording his achievements. Carefully she had entered them, and when propped up, would pore through the pages.

When emotion overcame Tom, he would drop to his knees beside her and hold the wasting body close. And she would lie silent and acceptant, her feeble strength responding to his handclasp, between them memory and oneness.

She was keenly observant, and recognizing the old look of restlessness and indecision that clouded his face one day as he sat beside her, she questioned him. He finally told her of the message from the Government regarding the possible salvaging of the $100,000 passenger ship *Hibou*.

"What are you waiting for?" she demanded. Then characteristically, she brushed aside his arguments and concern for her. "Nonsense! You mean to say you would reject such a thing? Why, Tom Reid — they've tried and tried to raise that boat. It's a famous wreck. Are you afraid you can't manage it?"

"You know why I'm not going to bid, Anna," he fumed.

"I don't know any such thing. I won't have you using me as an excuse to dodge a hard job."

His gaze was intent, proud, and he laughed with her. "It means a long pull, Anna. Months — maybe more. A long time away from home."

"It's our way of life, Tom. I want you to go. I want you to carry on. The *Hibou* is a menace to navigation where she lies. This is your part of the war effort."

He had chafed at the restraint of circumstance — reluctant to leave her yet impatient to do his part. Anna always solved things. Anna made the way straight . . . .

Tom's bid for salvaging the *Hibou* at $40,000 was accepted, and the Government would give the ship to the Sin-Mac Lines if they raised her.

The little ship *Hibou* on Owen Sound off Georgian Bay had defeated several salvaging attempts by other wreckers. It represented what was considered a hopeless undertaking. But there was a war — waters must be cleared, and there was the possibility of reclaiming ships when ships were precious.

The *Hibou's* story began back in 1907 when a Toronto shipyard turned out a handsome little craft called the *Alice,* on Dominion Government order to be used as a quarantine ship. 122 feet in length and twenty six foot beam, she was equipped with complete apparatus for fumigation. Fitted as a steam tug, with headquarters in Quebec, she plied the Gulf of the St. Lawrence, and carried on this work until the Spring of 1926 when she was purchased by Mr. John Tackaberry and taken to Midland, Ontario, where her steam boilers were removed and she was equipped with twin Diesels. At the same time she was conditioned to carry passengers. Upper decks and cabins were installed, as well as the required appointments.

For a year and a half she operated between Owen Sound and Providence Bay, and was then sold to the Dominion Transportation Company in April 1928, when her name was changed to the *Hibou.* A trim little craft, she became a familiar sight at the city of Owen Sound where her headquarters were established and where she served natives and tourists.

During the 1935 season, the *Hibou* was operating on a route out of Kingston up the St. Lawrence, but in 1936 she returned to Georgian Bay, and with other ships was operated under a pool arrangement between the Dominion

Transportation Company and the Owen Sound Transportation Company.

With July of that year, she had been running as a ferry between Tobermory and South Bay Mouth, finishing that service November 16th. On Tuesday the 17th, she was put in temporary service, making some special freight trips between Meaford, Collingwood, the city of Owen Sound and Manitoulin Island. On Saturday, November 21st, which was to have marked her last trip of the season, the tragedy occurred.

The morning was dark and grim, typical of late November mornings in that northern country. Come Spring and Summer, no shore can rival that lovely stretch north from the city of Owen Sound through Leith and on to Balaclava and Cape Rich.

The waters of Owen Sound are a rich blue where willows brush feathery waves, and maples stir in breezes fragrant with pine and balsam. Across the Sound comes the lonesome whistle of a train, the echo of a boat's signal and the harsh beauty of a gull's cry. Come Spring and Summer — But with November, stark loneliness prevails. You hear it deep in the core of the wind, in the surge of waters and the shuddering trees. The rich blue of the water is gone, and in its place gleams a cold steel gray, like an armor against the bitter season at hand.

Here the beach recedes gradually. At that particular time it was sparsely settled — a few summer cottages and the year-round homes of sailors and farmers. North along the shore road and five miles out lies the tiny hamlet of Leith. Among the few mid-Victorian dwellings with gingerbread trim and weathered clapboards, was the home of sailor Bernie Gibbons, a name loved and revered by the people of the city from the morning of the wreck of the *Hibou.*

Bound for Manitowaning on Manitoulin Island, with a cargo of 150 tons of general merchandise — hay, sewing machines, pork slabs, canned goods and such — the *Hibou* left her dock at Owen Sound at four thirty in the morning in command of her long-time skipper Captain Norman McKay, and manned by a crew of seventeen. Less than an hour later, and about a mile and a half south of Squaw Point, on the east side of the Sound, the *Hibou* went down and only ten of her crew were saved.

There was no storm, no sea. Cold lay in deadly stillness over land and water. The *Hibou* had mysteriously listed and sunk, in a matter of minutes. According to a crew member who managed to get ashore — " — she took a list to starboard and then went down . . . "

"She never came back, once she started to list," the surviving second mate declared, as his chilled body shook under a pile of blankets, face gray from cold. "It was my watch. We had just come off the ranges when Captain McKay said 'Port a little'; then, 'Starboard some — ' I followed directions, but when I tried to bring her back, she never came back. We had a new compass — "

The first mate, Captain James Agnew, told his story — "There was no shifting of cargo, as someone said. That was impossible the way she was loaded. And no crew members were trapped. It was my duty to see that everyone was out as soon as the danger was realized. And I saw to it." Gray, half-frozen, he tried to flex stiffened fingers.

"We were trying out a new compass. The captain didn't like the old one. When the boat didn't come back after she started to list, McKay gave orders right away to get the men on deck, and loosen the rafts and lifeboats. And then he said, 'Let everyone look out for themselves.'

"He was sending up flares by now — you could hear the suction below. A kind of roar. The fellows were working at the rafts and lifeboats. The lifeboats stuck and got wedged, but we got the rafts off, and by then the water was almost to the top deck of the ship.

"There was one woman in the crew — Iona Johnson. The stewardess. She came on deck when the alarm rang. She'd just grabbed anything at hand to put around her. It wasn't much — like a scarf over her shoulders and she was in her nightgown. She didn't get excited. She just stood awful still. I think she was praying. The cold was brutal.

"Orville Parr, the Purser — he ran to get a warm coat for her, and he was only in pajamas. When he got back she was gone. She made a leap for it — and missed. It was pitch dark — " he shrugged. "She didn't have a chance.

"You couldn't see your hand before your face. A wind was coming up. We were about three quarters of a mile off shore, and three miles from the end of the breakwater — as it turned out. But we didn't have an idea about direction. The sky was thick and black that early, and no stars. It was around five o'clock in the morning. The Captain ran out flares. And then all of a sudden, a light showed up on shore. A single bright light. We started for it, praying it would hold. The Captain was still on the bridge when the rafts floated away.

"We kept shouting — for all the good it did. On our raft we had a paddle. The fellows on the other raft had to use their hands. It was like dipping into ice water. We tried to stick close together and make our way toward the light. A wind came up — and a wash began right away. That didn't help . . .

"We batted our way to shore and day broke as we

reached the reef — if you could call it daylight. Then we had to get the raft over the reef and into shore water. Some of the fellows collapsed and slipped off into the water. We had to haul them out — and we had no feeling in our hands. Hard to hang onto them. Parr — he's the Purser — he was only in pajamas. He had a pretty close shave. He was almost gone there once — I wonder yet if he'll pull through . . . That trip to shore was an icy hell none of us will ever forget. Some didn't make it. . . "

But that morning, those who did found a warm shelter awaiting them. It was in the window of the Bernie Gibbons home that the light had been placed by his wife when she saw the flares — and her Bernie at the time off on Lake Superior wheeling on another Canadian ship. She had made a kettle of strong coffee and built a roaring fire in the grate; stripped beds and storeroom of blankets, hauled out quilts and mattresses.

Along the beach waited the roused natives, eyes hard on the sea to catch a glimpse of bodies possibly washed ashore. And Captain McKay was one of them — a familiar and beloved figure in Owen Sound. Then another body, that of Jimmie Menard, a fireman, and a particular crew favorite. They laid a coat over the bruised face and brought him up on land.

Daylight now revealed the wreck-strewn sand with splintered boards and ship's furnishings scattered about. An upturned white lifeboat had been impaled on a shore rock. The sea grew rough. More wreckage came ashore — windows with panes broken, mattresses and such.

They carried young McIntosh into the house, almost dead from exposure and strain. Off watch, he had been about to drift into sleep when his toothbrush slipped off a ledge near by. Instantly he realized that something was wrong. With a bound, he and his room-mate were out of their bunks and on deck. Scantily clad, he managed to survive the bitter exposure that followed.

The bodies of five of the seven drowned sailors were recovered and buried with the highest honors in the city of Owen Sound. But no trace was ever found of the lost engineer and the stewardess, Iona Johnson.

Shortly afterward, the ten survivors presented Mrs. Bernie Gibbons with a large brass lamp in tribute to her service which undoubtedly saved their lives. On the base was engraved their names and the date of the disaster. And on the spot where the *Hibou* lay was placed a lighted buoy which is still there and can be seen from shore, and from the little gable window of the Gibbons house.

Every effort possible was made to recover the bodies. Divers repeatedly tried to search the wrecked ship, but the attempts were balked by the great depth of water at that spot, and bad weather.

Six years passed from the time of sinking until Tom Reid took hold — years in which other salvagers tried and failed. With expert divers and using barges and pontoons, he struggled through weeks of trial and defeat. Many had said he was foolish to attempt such a project. It couldn't be done. Others had tried and failed. What made a man his age think he could succeed against such odds? He shrugged them off. It was a job that needed doing.

Frequently he was approached by sincerely interested citizens and by members of the families of the missing stewardess and engineer. Was there any hope — any chance of their loved ones being trapped in the sunken ship? Such appeals were difficult for him to face. It was not easy to discourage hope.

There was great excitement in the city of Owen Sound when on October second, the *Hibou* was brought to the surface. Numerous boats circled about to watch the sight no one had ever expected to witness. Again, the value of air-power was demonstrated. After a long, precarious procedure, seemingly hopeless from the beginning, Tom Reid and his men had raised a ship out of ninety feet of water.

The steel pilot house was intact, though the windows were broken; steering wheel, signal telegraph, searchlight and other equipment were discernible. The upper deck was a mass of wreckage — a piano sagging in the midst of it, and the unmistakable evidence that the whole framework had collapsed under pressure of water.

The business of removing the debris from the decks began, and this was another challenge to the salvager. The staunch derrick on the barge *Londonderry* was brought into use, its capacity strained but holding. And Tom permitted no pumping until the debris should be gone. In the debris was found a shawl and slipper . . . .

The shore road from the city of Owen Sound to Leith and beyond was never quiet those days. The salvaging project held the general interest — a reminder of one of the worst tragedies ever to occur in the region or on the Lakes. Each day when Tom returned to his hotel, there were questioners waiting and wondering — what would be done with the *Hibou*, once she was salvaged? And what of the cargo?

A large percentage of the latter was completely destroyed by the long stay under water. Cases of oranges and dates were tossed overboard, and the vile stench permeated the district for days. Cases of canned goods — their labels like snow on the water, were sent to the bottom. Lard formed a substantial portion of the effects, and this went to the Government for use in the manufacture of explosives. Sewing machines were useless, and pork slabs went ashore to decompose and torment the citizenry.

But the *Hibou's* hull was in good condition, and her Diesel engines could be put into use again, since the water in which they had been immersed was fresh.

On that October day when the *Hibou,* supported between barges, was refloated and brought to the Elevator dock at the city of Owen Sound, Tom Reid stepped off to be greeted by a cheering, excited throng. He had completed more than half a century at the work he loved. To him — though now seventy two years old, the accolade rather than carrying a note of finality was one of timeless confidence.

The Owen Sound DAILY SUN-TIMES gave notable tribute to Captain Tom Reid —

" . . . So much public interest has been shown in raising the motorship *Hibou,* it seems timely that something should be said about the man at the helm during all the operations necessary to bring the craft back to service . . . " Whereupon they launched into an eulogy of Tom Reid that spilled through from front page to back, under wide headlines.

The Sin-Mac Lines made a profit of $30,000 on the job, and receiving the ship, sold her to an eastern steamship Company for $35,000, after an expensive reconditioning. There she finished out her life in the banana trade.

But Tom's true payment lay in his reception at home. No one had known that as he worked with his men to free the *Hibou,* he was meeting the bitterest crisis of his life with the imminent loss of his beloved Anna. When he returned, on the coverlet beside her lay the clippings from the Owen Sound daily. She raised a weak hand to greet him, smiled. "Not bad, Captain Reid. Not bad at all."

"It took me long enough — " Voice husky, he dropped to his knees beside her. Pretense between them was no longer possible. The heart's weariness and terror and suspense could not hide indefinitely behind the gallant smile, the idle word.

"I knew you'd do it, Tom," she told him. "I — waited . . . The sun is setting on the river. I'd like to see it once more. The doctor is so careful and strict. What does it matter — now? You're here . . . "

He carried the frail body to the window above the blue stream that she loved and along which for so long she had watched his boats pass — waiting for a sight of his tugs, the sound of his whistles. The bright gold and flame of the dying sun sketched glorious patterns on the water and against the burnished woodlands of Canada's shore beyond.

"You've given me beauty from the first, Tom. You've been a wonderful husband . . . "

"I ain't done half enough for you," he groaned. Oh, the things he had planned for them both with retirement! And now she was leaving him, and all of it sacrificed to the demands of his work, to the things he had to do.

"Who says you — ain't?" She smiled at him, and closed her tired eyes.

CHAPTER TWENTY-SEVEN

Within the week she was gone.

Soon Virginia and her family came on from the west to be with him. But the Port Huron home held too many memories of Anna, and a new one was sought. A house on Vidal Street in Sarnia was finally decided on, but loneliness pursued him. There, too, was the ghostly sound of the familiar step on the stairs, a voice humming softly through the halls, the illusion of her hand on the piano keys. There, too, he was haunted by the memory of the swift give and take, the quick impatient word —

the forgiving or repentant kiss to right it. There he imagined the sight of the graying head with its saucy hats poking through the door of the room where he sat sprawled in his big chair — Anna saying, "Is it too young for me, Tom? Am I silly to wear such a thing?"

Too young, Anna? What was ever too young for you? . . .

Infrequently in the past, he had gone to church with her. Now he moved down the aisle on Sunday, the ghost of her beside him, her hand on his arm, her voice repeating the lines from the Bible by which she lived — *"Be still and know that I am God . . . "* As he said the words, he found himself doubting their truth since Anna had been taken. And then with aching remorse, he would hear her gentle rebuke — her plea for patience and understanding and acceptance.

Friends would invite him to dinner — with another woman beside him at table. It yielded no diversion, merely intensified loneliness. And so it went. And though loving his children deeply, even with them he failed to find the answer to his heart's need. Thus consuming loneliness drove him to resume his work when pressed.

With February came the call from the office of the Secretary of the Navy. The *Normandie* had sunk at the pier in New York harbor. And Tom Reid's success in the field of salvage had not, apparently, escaped the attention of the nation. He was summoned to meet a Naval Commander at the Merritt-Chapman Company in New York where, with a Company executive, he would go over the sunken ship and state his views.

Conferences lasted several days. Already three million dollars had been spent on attempts to salvage the great liner. Tom disagreed with the methods that had been used and bluntly said so. He offered a plan he guaranteed would be successful, but his ideas were coolly received and the contact did not end too happily. However, he had the satisfaction of learning that when the ship was raised, his method had been employed . . . .

He was finding it difficult to reconcile himself to the gradual relinquishing of his life's work. But there were crises where his wisdom and judgment were so vitally needed that the Company was forced to turn to him.

He impatiently silenced his family's protests when Manager Campbell called him regarding the trouble in which the $300,000 self-unloader *Material Service* found herself. She had sunk just outside the South Chicago pier. Despite growing fatigue, he went to her.

Dave Seagrave, his diver at the time, went along, and at once began the search for bodies — three crewmen having been lost. The half-crazed widow of the engineer kept vigil on the dock.

The cabins were all below deck, and the diver had no success. At last he decided to surface. He was closing the port holes when he found one resistant. Since it would not close from outside, he went in to investigate when he felt an insistent nudging against his back. Reaching around, he caught hold of a dead body by the hand. Though accustomed to frequent grim experiences, the incident unnerved him.

He telephoned the tender, asked for Captain Reid and instructions. He was directed to tie the lines, which were being sent down, to secure the body, and the Coast Guard would be notified by wireless.

Orders soon were given for the body to be brought up, and a morning hour was mentioned when officials could be expected. The diver managed to ease the body through the scuttle hold, so bloated that when surfacing, it bounced out of the water. A plank was dropped and worked underneath the dead engineer, then taken ashore. Until the coroner was summoned, the diver could not attach a line around the corpse.

Tom Reid estimated the price of salvage and gave the Company a figure of $75,000 or 75% of the ship and cargo to 'take her up.' The bid was accepted and the contract signed.

Work was begun. While they were patching, Tom received a call from The Pittsburg Steamship Company agent at Sault Sainte Marie, urging him to come at once and see what could be done about salvaging their 'Gut Wagon' — a provision supply ship which serviced their fleet in passing, and which had been sunk in a collision. She was the *Frontier* — 121 feet long and 421 tons, built in 1910 by her owners.

Organizing the work in South Chicago, Tom left by car with his diver for the Soo. Examining the ship, he put in a salvage bid of $21,000. There was a delay, as the Pittsburg people were considering bids from other salvagers. Refusing to waste any more time, Tom declared his intention to withdraw, whereupon Manager Ferbert telephoned him from Cleveland. "Will you take $20,000 to raise the boat? If so, I won't consider any more bids."

Tom agreed. He hired a tug and lighter at the Soo, left the diver to build a coffer dam and manage the planned work with his men while Tom returned to Chicago.

In the meantime, the workers had tried to pump out the *Material Service,* according to instructions, but the decks went down and the ship filled. There were approximately ten feet of water on the decks when Tom returned. The *Manistique* had unloaded her cargo of gravel and taken it aboard.

Tom was baffled at such a disaster. He had carefully studied the blueprints of the *Material Service* and found her beams strong and heavy and knew they should stand the pressure of water at that depth. Re-examining the ship after consulting the blueprints, he found that substantial structural changes had been made that had not been disclosed. It seemed that the owners had cut her decks open a few years back and built a dunnage room below and installed lighter beams. Of course this completely changed the picture as to salvaging procedure.

They had pumped the ship down before she collapsed.

A lawsuit resulted. Underwriters refused to pay the claim. The owners sued the underwriters. But underwriters insure a ship against a Master's acts. Should an owner order a Master to overload a ship or otherwise menace its seaworthiness, the insurance Company is not liable.

The result in this case was defeat for the owners. And with the 'Gut Wagon' problem to be solved, Tom Reid was busy enough. He wanted no further contact with the *Material Service* since, due to prevailing circumstances, she was a total loss, and the underwriters would have made her his responsibility if he had raised her.

The *Material Service* was the only project Tom Reid ever gave up.

CHAPTER TWENTY-EIGHT

At seventy three, the inevitable effects of major surgery had slowed Tom Reid down to a tempo that infuriated him. He fought against time. He blustered through situations with false strength, bolstered by the hard determination of years.

"You can't mean that you intend to take on the *Brewster* job!" worried his daughter Virginia, the day word came of that disaster.

"Why, she's only down river," he scoffed. "What are you talking about?" There wasn't the old volume to his voice, but there was confidence and purpose. He jammed his hat on his head and went to the assistance of the $500,000 freighter.

The *Brewster* was an American ship, 250 feet in length, one of the five lend-lease vessels launched a month previously at Superior, Wisconsin, and christened by the Dionne quintuplets.

Built by the United States Government, she was leased to the Canadian Government. Carrying a lend-lease load of 90,000 bushels of wheat from Port Arthur, and bound for England on her maiden voyage, she collided with the ore freighter *W. D. Calverly* in the St. Clair River opposite the city of Algonac.

Her Captain, James MacLaren, 53, of Dundee, Scotland, was a typical 'old salt' of the ocean trade, with — until that time — a perfect record. And despite the fact that through his quick thinking was averted a tie-up in the Great Lakes transportation system in war time, the blow went deep. A salt water sailor from boyhood, MacLaren had been a shipmaster since the age of twenty four. He had retired in 1938 after thirty four years on the Atlantic, but only for one year. The war had brought him back on the seas.

A confusion of signals, it seemed, was the cause of the accident. A Montreal pilot was on duty. But Captain MacLaren swerved the ship out of the main channel and cleared the life-line of the steel industry. The thirty four officers and men aboard reached safety when the ship sank.

Rolling toward the shore of Walpole Island, a Canadian possession on which is located an Indian Reservation, the *Brewster* spilled some of her grain cargo which the natives hastened to salvage for themselves. The huge cargo became saturated, began to swell, and buckled the ship's plates where she lay in thirty feet of water, her keel visible and the top of her sixty foot spar above the surface.

While the accident occurred through the misunderstanding of signals, yet there had been grumblings from the crew since the *Brewster* had stopped at Port Huron on the way down, to correct troubles that had been happening since leaving port. The men were beginning to think the ship a jinx.

The *Brewster* was damaged below the water line on the port side just after midship. So quickly did she submerge that there was barely time to beach her.

While speed was vital in raising her, she proved a stubborn subject for Tom Reid. She lay over on her side — a dead-weight monster; no menace, however, to the Indians who joyously helped themselves to available grain.

The summer passed with the *Brewster* still resistant, but Tom Reid welcomed busy days and difficult problems in a world strange and lonely without Anna. The use of cables on the ship proved ineffectual due to her position. But because of it, there was no other method possible.

With September, Tom won his battle and she was finally straightened, patched, refloated and on her way to the shipyard at a time when every available ship was badly needed — much to the regret of the natives of Walpole Island.

After that, the Reid doctor bluntly forbade any further activity, and Tom was forced to accept the situation in view of certain painful and troublesome disabilities. But the brooding mind disregarded the ailing body, and when in November 1947 he was urged by an executive of the Canadian Steamship Company to come to the assistance of one of their ships, he defied the doctor and drove with the same reckless speed to Rogers City, Michigan, the scene of the wreck. The $150,000 full-size canaller, *William C. Warren,* carrying 80,000 bushels of grain, had gone on the rocks outside the Michigan seaport, while enroute from Fort William, Ontario. Tom made a bid of $40,000 which was accepted, and summoning his helpers began operations.

Sub-zero weather had settled early. The freeze had taken hold. There were violent gales and blizzards. His attempt to free the ship at that time failed, and the Steamship Company's insurance underwriters decided that to leave her through the winter might mean the loss not only of the ship but cargo as well, and offered the wheat cargo for sale.

Though Tom disapproved of the action, he made an offer which was accepted. He knew that without her cargo, when the sea struck again the *Warren's* hull would suffer more damage. But her fate was not his to decide. An especially rigged pipeline was set up, and the grain pumped ashore and into trucks, brought to Sarnia and stored in grain elevators there.

Controversy regarding the ship followed between owners and insurance underwriters, but the *Warren* was considered a total loss and insurance paid. Confident that he could refloat her when the worst of the winter was over, Tom made an offer of $5,000 for the *Warren* wreck. He was acting as agent for the Mohawk Steamship Company of Montreal, with which he was connected. His offer was accepted and on April eleventh, with the Reid wrecker *Lachine* and barge *Londonderry,* he arrived at the scene.

They found the *Warren* covered with ice. Tom notified the new owners that it was too early to begin salvaging. It would be necessary to thaw off the ice, a costly matter, and the delay of a few weeks would mean substantial assistance from the sun. But the Mohawk people had plans for the *Warren* that season, and a long delay in the shipyard could disrupt them.

Augmenting his crew overnight, on April twelfth Tom again approached the *Warren,* but was driven away by the wind. Again on the thirteenth he made a third try, and operations began in earnest. On April twenty seventh the *Warren* — shaky, leaking, limping along — was delivered to the drydock at Collingwood, Ontario, by the *Lachine.*

The Mohawk Company had made no mistake in taking Tom's advice. Into their hands had been placed a potentially valuable asset at the suggestion of an expert. The *William C. Warren* is worth half a million today — a sum she has already earned, herself.

CHAPTER TWENTY-NINE

Before dawn one late September morning in 1949, Tom was awakened by an urgent telephone call from the Toronto office of the Canadian Steamship Lines. The queen of their fleet had burned at the pier.

Making her last trip of the season with a full passenger list, the $2,000,000 Steamer *Noronic* was bound from Cleveland and Detroit to the Thousand Islands with a full passenger list. It was a merry crowd, saying farewell to summer. Many said farewell to life when, catching fire at the pier in Toronto, the *Noronic* burned to a heap of twisted steel.

Sketchily dressing, and ignoring arguments, Tom stormed out to his car and on his way. He knew the *Noronic* from stem to stern. When he reached the handsome ship and saw her condition, it was as if he viewed an old friend in her death agonies. To inspect the wreck was extremely hazardous for one whose feet were not quite steady, whose hands had begun to fumble, whose sight was no longer too keen. But the feebleness of eighty was brushed aside as he faced the problem before him. He grasped the ladder and climbed aboard to see what could be done.

On her maiden voyage years before, he had gone to her aid when, tied up at the Sarnia dock to load freight, she had started to list outboard. Worried, the officers had ordered freight trimmed to balance her. At that point, she slipped off the spiles and rolled down so that her cabin struck the top of the freight shed.

A protest went up from the public. The *Noronic,* they declared, was unseaworthy. Tom knew that she was safe, knew that the ship had been faultily loaded and faultily trimmed. But he knew as well that if some measure were not taken, the handsome steamer would be avoided in the future. So he suggested that the Company place her in drydock and 'bustle her out' to give her more buoyancy.

This satisfied the public, and from then on, the *Noronic* enjoyed great popularity. She was the pleasure ship of the fleet, and Tom had always taken a particular interest in her. Now as she lay gutted and broken, he made his way along a deck littered with twisted steel. Moved by emotion, he realized that the concern of his family and physician had not been groundless. He faltered at obstacles. His eyes struggled to focus. A great weakness came over him. He stood quite still; then braced himself, and went on.

Somehow he managed an adequate inspection, jerking away from steadying hands while he computed the price of coffer-damming, pumping and such, so that the blackened hulk could be taken to Hamilton and scrapped. And he arrived at a figure of $40,000 for the bid.

He realized now this was the end. Times and Tom Reid were meeting the change together. There would be fewer wrecks from now on because of radar and instrument navigation. His day was over, his life's work done. He groped to stabilize himself and ignoring anxious offers of help, he made his way to the ladder. Squaring his shoulders, he stepped on the top rung, grasped the rail with both hands and began the descent from a stricken ship for the last time.

With that same apparent stoicism, he met the loss a few years later of Virginia and Thom. He had learned through a long, hard lifetime to put up a front. He had learned how to 'take it.'

Captain Tom Reid died unexpectedly in his Florida home on Sunday afternoon, July 20, 1958.

CHAPTER THIRTY

There is a garden in Florida beside the sea where the old Viking sits in the sun — Anna's Bible beside him. Friends, likewise retired, come to visit with him now and then.

A jet thunders overhead.

"You know," he muses, gesturing skyward, "those fellows have got the right idea. We only live once. A man gets bogged down in the grind of routine. Adventure — that's the answer. Yes, sir," he sighs, "if I had it to do over again, I'd take adventure . . . . "

INDEX TO SHIPS

GENERAL INDEX